T0367676

GREAT
INVESTMENT
IDEAS

World Scientific Series in Finance
(ISSN: 2010-1082)

Series Editor: William T. Ziemba *(University of British Columbia (Emeritus),*
ICMA Centre, University of Reading and Visiting Professor of
University of Cyprus, Luiss Guido Carli University, Rome,
Sabanci University, Istanbul and
Korea Institute of Science and Technology)

Advisory Editors:
Greg Connor *(National University of Ireland, Maynooth, Ireland)*
George Constantinides *(University of Chicago, USA)*
Espen Eckbo *(Dartmouth College, USA)*
Hans Foellmer *(Humboldt University, Germany)*
Christian Gollier *(Toulouse School of Economics, France)*
Thorsten Hens *(University of Zurich, Switzerland)*
Robert Jarrow *(Cornell University, USA)*
Hayne Leland *(University of California, Berkeley, USA)*
Haim Levy *(The Hebrew University of Jerusalem, Israel)*
John Mulvey *(Princeton University, USA)*
Marti Subrahmanyam *(New York University, USA)*

Published*:

*To view the complete list of the published volumes in the series, please visit:
www.worldscientific.com/series/wssf

GREAT
INVESTMENT
IDEAS

William T Ziemba

University of British Columbia (Emeritus)
and
London School of Economics

World Scientific

W JERSEY · LONDON · SINGAPORE · BEIJING · SHANGHAI · HONG KONG · TAIPEI · CHENNAI · TOKYO

Published by

World Scientific Publishing Co. Pte. Ltd.

5 Toh Tuck Link, Singapore 596224

USA office: 27 Warren Street, Suite 401-402, Hackensack, NJ 07601

UK office: 57 Shelton Street, Covent Garden, London WC2H 9HE

British Library Cataloguing-in-Publication Data
A catalogue record for this book is available from the British Library.

World Scientific Series in Finance — Vol. 9
GREAT INVESTMENT IDEAS

Copyright © 2017 by World Scientific Publishing Co. Pte. Ltd.

All rights reserved. This book, or parts thereof, may not be reproduced in any form or by any means, electronic or mechanical, including photocopying, recording or any information storage and retrieval system now known or to be invented, without written permission from the publisher.

For photocopying of material in this volume, please pay a copying fee through the Copyright Clearance Center, Inc., 222 Rosewood Drive, Danvers, MA 01923, USA. In this case permission to photocopy is not required from the publisher.

ISBN 978-981-3144-36-1
ISBN 978-981-3144-37-8 (pbk)

Desk Editor: Alisha Nyugen

Typeset by Stallion Press
Email: enquiries@stallionpress.com

Printed in Singapore

Contents

Preface

This book contains twelve articles with great investment ideas. These papers were published in the *Journal of Portfolio Management* from 1993 to 2015.

In "The Effect of Errors in Mean, Variance and Co-Variance Estimates on Optimal Portfolio Choice" by Vijay Chopra and me, we investigate the effect of errors in means, variances and co-variances in portfolio selection problems. Earlier in 1981 and 1984 papers with my Ph.D. student Jerry Kallberg from University of British Columbia, I found that the impact of errors on expected utility were about 20:2:1 for means, variances and co-variances, respectively. So errors in means were much more important than variance or co-variance errors and variance errors were about twice as important as co-variance errors. In this paper done with Chopra while I was consulting at the Frank Russell Company from 1989–1998, until they sold the company, we redid the earlier studies on new data and investigated the impact of risk aversion on these relative errors. The main result is that the lower the Arrow-Pratt risk aversion is, the greater is the impact so with utility like log with essentially zero risk aversion, the relative errors are more like 100:3:1.

During 1988–1989, I was fortunate to be the first visiting Yamaichi Professor of Finance at the University of Tsukuba in Japan and consultant to the Yamaichi Research Institute in Tokyo. There I studied stock market crashes and stock market anomalies. That led to three books and a number of research papers. In "Comment on 'Why a Weekend Effect?'", I tested Miller's weekend hypothesis for the Japanese stock market. Miller argued that the weekend effect could be explained by a tendency for self-initiated sell orders to exceed self-initiated buy trades over the weekend, while broker-initiated buy trades result in a surplus of buying during the remainder of

viii Preface

the week. This causes security prices to fall over the weekend and during the day on Monday as market makers sell back stocks on the open. Prices then move higher during the week because of broker-induced buying. This, like most anomalies, is strongest for small cap stocks. Miller's idea is predicated on the fact that people are too busy to think about stocks during the week. If they do anything it is to buy based on brokers' recommendations. Miller did not test his theory with real data. I tested the theory using daily Japanese data from May 16, 1949 to September 28, 1988. Individual investors were not selling stocks in Japan as well as the US 1981–1989. At that time, there were one and two day weekends with Saturday trading two weeks each month. Saturday returns were high. What I found was that in two day weekends the Monday fell on average but on the one day weekend the fall was on Tuesday.

Studies in the US, Japan and other countries tend to rise at the turn of the month (TOM). The reasons seem to be institutional since pensions and other investments are made then, and employees receive their salaries then so the excess cash flows have a tendency to go to a large extent into the stock market. In the US, the TOM is trading days −1 to +4, where −1 is the last trading day of the previous month and +1 the first trading day of the current month. In Japan, the TOM has been −5 to +2 when the salaries are paid, see *Calendar Anomalies and Arbitrage*, published in 2012, by World Scientific. In "Investment Results from Exploiting Turn of the Month Effects", Chris Hensel and I discuss these results from 1928 to 1993. Three of the TOM days had significantly high returns on average while no other days in the month had excess returns. Overall, all days returned 0.0186% daily, the TOMs returned 0.1236 (with a $t = 5.94$), the first half namely trading days −1 to +9 returned 0.0703((4.13) and the rest of the month returned −0.0235(−3.71). The paper discusses the use of these results by institutional investors for buying and selling timing for the S&P500 and also for small cap stocks and other assets. A story about this paper is in the November 7, 1996 the *Wall Street Journal*.

One of the biggest Wall Street scandals was the rise and demise of ENRON. They were an energy trading company and rose from modest beginnings to become one of the most valuable US companies. There was fraud and eventually the stock value collapsed to essentially zero. In "Stock Ownership Decisions in Defined Contribution Pension Plans", Julian Douglass, Owen Wu and I studied the effects of this decline on the employees' pensions. Most of the employees had their pensions solely in ENRON stock. This was all lost. Also they lost their jobs. In the paper, we analyse with two models (a static mean variance and a stochastic programming) when it is optimal to have most of one's pension in a single stock where you work. To invest this way, one must have either very low risk aversion or very high expected mean return for that company stock relative to other investments and the market index. The effect is even stronger when job loss is considered. (This was also an issue in Japan where employees were strongly encouraged to invest their savings in the company stock.)

In the winter term of 2005, I was a visiting professor at the Sloan School of Management at MIT. I always wanted to teach at MIT ever since, as an undergraduate of UMass in chemical engineering, we went for a field trip to MIT and each door had the name of one of the books we were using. I taught an investment course in the Masters program and used my own materials, Professor Andy Lo's notes and the Bodie, Kane and Marcus investment book. Many of the students were Ph.D. students in engineering, robotics, and other related disciplines trying to retool into financial engineering and other Wall Street jobs. The students, while all were good, were mostly nervous about getting the top grades, something they had all received thought throughout their careers to obtain admission to MIT. The learning while important was secondary.

I was able to have a guest speaker, Lawrence Siegel, who was the lead researcher for the Ford Foundation Endowment. Their mandate, to maintain their tax-free status, was to earn 5% in real terms plus about 0.3% for expenses. They closely followed the Harvard and Yale endowments with lots of private equity, which had high returns. Their mean return was below the S&P500 and, most interesting for me, below Warren Buffett's Berkshire Hathaway with a higher Sharpe ratio then either of these because of their low standard deviation to returns. Part of the low variation was from the private equity which was not marked-to-market frequently. I wanted to devise an evaluation method to show, as I believed, that Buffett was the superior investor. Siegel kindly gave me a data set with monthly data from December 1985 to March 2000 for the Windsor Fund of George Neff, the Ford Foundation, the Tiger fund of Julian Robertson, the Quantum Fund of George Soros and Warren Buffett's Berkshire as well as the S&P500 total return index, US Treasuries and T-bills.

My idea, which I had used before in the 1991 *Invest Japan*, Probus book, was simple. The Sharpe ratio considers the losses and gains equally. So why not eliminate the gain and create fictitious gains that are equal, namely the mirror image of the losses. One just modifies the ordinary Sharpe ratio by replacing the standard deviation with a made up standard deviation based

only on the negative monthly outcomes. The idea of focusing on losses
has been used by others such as Sortino who has his own measure. His
papers were later than my 1991 discovery and my approach modifies the
Sharpe ratio rather than devising a new measure. This symmetric downside
Sharpe ratio (DSSR) improves only one of the investors in the data set,
namely Warren Buffett. His DSSR is comparable but not better than
the almost identical Ford Foundation and Harvard Endowments' DSSRs.
Berkshire from 1985 to 2004 had a geometric mean gain of 22.02% per
year about double the S&P 500. Why then did Berkshire's DSSR not beat
the Ford Foundation? The answer is that while Berkshire had many huge
monthly gains, it also has the largest monthly losses. So to show Berkshire
is dominant, another approach must be used. Buffett's monthly results are
similar to what one would expect as a full Kelly investor, namely high
monthly returns, very few asset positions, many market losses, and a violent
wealth pass, but the highest final wealth most of the time.

In the 2007 book of revised *Wilmott* magazine columns entitled
Scenarios for Risk for Management and Global Investment Strategies
published by Wiley by Rachel Ziemba (who works at Roubini Global
Economics, New York and London) and me, I found that the Renaissance
Medallion Hedge Fund organized by Jim Simons, a famous State University
of New York at Stony Brook maths professor, had a very high DSSR of
26.4 versus an ordinary Sharpe of 1.68. There were 17 monthly losses in
148 months from January 1, 1993 to April 2005 when my data set ended.
The DSSR is needed to show their true brilliance. My colleague Edward O.
Thorp in his Princeton Newport hedge fund had only three monthly losses
in twenty years from 1968 to 1988 resulting in a DSSR of 13.8

I wanted to investigate this more fully. Were there even better funds?
My colleague Tom Schneeweis, who runs the UMass hedge fund database,
gave me access to their some 4000 hedge and other funds. Olivier Gergaud
and I then studied this data set and we wrote the 2012 paper "Great
investors: Their methods, results and evaluation" published in the *JPM*.
This paper discusses the Renaissance Medallion and Princeton Newport
results plus other great investors such as the Yale Endowment and John
Maynard Keynes running the King's College Endowment at the University
of Cambridge. We found some funds that with even higher DSSRs than
Renaissance Medallion's, but they were funds that are now closed. We did
find one fraud with an infinite DSSR.

In "The Predictive Ability of the Bond Stock Earnings Yield Differential", Klaus Berge, Giorgio Consigli and I study the bond stock earnings

yield (BSEYD) model. I devised that model in Japan in 1988–1989 and it is based on the difference between the most liquid long bond relative to the earnings yield measured by the reciprocal of the trailing price earnings ratio. When the measure is too high there almost always is a stock market crash. I, with along with some co-authors, have applied this model to Japan, the US, Iceland, China and other countries in various papers and book chapters; see my website www.williamtziemba.com for references. In this paper, we investigate the long-term use of the model. The basic question is if an investor goes to cash when the BSEYD measure is in the danger zone, which is about 20% of the time over long periods, and invests in the market index otherwise, does this beat the market index? Using various entry and exit rules, concerning the length of time used in estimation, historical versus normally distributed data and fractile percents for exits and entries, the results indicate that the strategy provides about double the final wealth with less standard deviation risk for the five countries US, Japan, UK, Canada and Germany during 1975–2005 and 1980–2005.

In "Do Seasonal Anomalies still Work?", Constantine Dzbaharov and I investigate whether or not traditional seasonal anomalies such as the January and monthly effects, the January barometer, sell-in-May-and-go-away, holiday and turn-of-the-month effects still exist in the turbulent markets of the early part of the 21st century. The evidence using futures data from 1993–2009 and 2004–2009 for small cap stocks measured by the Russell2000 index and large cap stocks measured by the S&P500 is that there is still value in these anomalies. The effects tend to be stronger for the small cap stocks. The results are useful for investors to tilt portfolios and speculators to trade the effects. For more on this, see Chapter 1 in *Calendar Anomalies* (2012), World Scientific.

William Poundstone's book, *Fortune's Formula*, brought the Kelly capital growth criterion to the attention of investors. But how do full and fractional Kelly strategies preform in practice? In "How Does the Fortune's Formula-Kelly Capital Growth Model Perform?" Leonard MacLean, Yonggan Zhao, Edward O. Thorp and I study three simple investment situations and simulate the behavior of these strategies over medium term horizons using a large number of scenarios. The results show:

1. the great superiority of full Kelly and close to full Kelly strategies over longer horizons with very large gains a large fraction of the time;
2. that the short term performance of Kelly and high fractional Kelly strategies is very risky;

3. that there is a consistent tradeoff of growth versus security as a function of the bet size determined by the various strategies; and

4. that no matter how favorable the investment opportunities are or how long the infinite horizon is, a sequence of bad scenarios can lead to very poor final wealth outcomes, with a loss of most of the investor's initial capital.

Hence, in practice, financial engineering is important to deal with the short term volatility and long run situations with a sequence of bad scenarios. But properly used, the strategy has much to commend it, especially in trading with many repeated investments.

Pension funds typically suggest the 60-40 stock-bond rule to lower risk since during stock market declines bonds tend to rise. However, US investment returns have been presidential party dependent; and returns in the last two years of all administrations exceed those in the first two years. The strategies small cap stocks with Democrats and intermediate bonds or large cap stocks with Republicans yields final wealth about six times the large cap index, 50% more than small caps and more than twenty times the 60-40 mix since 1942. Chris Hensel and I studied this and this in a paper in the *Financial Analyst Journal* in 1995. I redid the study adding presidents Bill Clinton, George W. Bush and Barack Obama and the results remain the same as reported in "Is the 60-40 Stock-Bond Pension Fund Rule Wise?"

In "When to Sell Apple and the NASDAQ? Trading Bubbles with a Stochastic Disorder Model", Alexander Shiryaev, Mikahil Zhitlukhin and I apply a continuous time stochastic process model developed by Shiryaev and Zhutlukhin for optimal stopping of random price processes that appear to be bubbles. By a bubble we mean the rising price is largely based on the expectation of higher and higher future prices. Futures traders such as George Soros attempt to trade such markets. The idea is to exit near the peak from a starting long position. The model applies equally well on the short side, that is when to enter and exit a short position. In this paper, we test the model in two technology markets. These include the price of Apple computer stock AAPL from various times in 2009–2012 after the local low of March 6, 2009; plus a market where it is known that the generally very successful bubble trader George Soros lost money by shorting the NASDAQ-100 stock index too soon in 2000. The Shiryaev-Zhitlukhin model provides good exit points in both situations that would have been profitable to speculators following the model and who employed the model.

The Kelly Capital Growth Investment Strategy maximizes the expected utility of final wealth with a Bernoulli logarithmic utility function. In 1956, Kelly showed that static expected log maximization yields the maximum asymptotic long run growth. Good properties include minimizing the time to large asymptotic goals, maximizing the median, and being ahead on average after the first period. Bad properties include extremely large bets for short term favorable investment situations because the Arrow-Pratt risk aversion index is essentially zero. Paul Samuelson was a critic of this approach. His various points sent in letters to Ziemba are responded to in ""Response to Paul A Samuelson Letters and Papers on the Kelly Capital Growth Investment Strategy". Samuelson's criticism is partially responsible for the current situation that most finance academics and investment professionals, except superior investors, do not recommend Kelly strategies. Samuelson's points are theoretically correct and sharpen the theory. They caution users of this approach to be careful and understand the true characteristics of these investments including ways to lower the investment exposure. His objections help us understand the theory better, but they do not detract from numerous valuable applications, some of which are briefly surveyed in the paper. My approach is to describe the critiques and then respond to them one by one. This is done for his four basic points. A lot of this is over-betting risk of full Kelly strategies, so half Kelly, which Samuelson says "fits the data better" is often a useful strategy that balances growth and security. I explained all this in a five hour talk in August 2011 to Fidelity Investments in Boston. They knew Samuelson was skeptical of full Kelly strategies but not why. So I explained that to them.

Acknowledgements

This book contains twelve articles with great investment ideas that were published in the *Journal of Portfolio Management* from 1993 to 2015. Many thanks to Sandra Schwartz who produced this material and to Frank Fabozzi for accepting these papers in the *JPM*. Harry Katz has been very helpful in getting the articles submitted properly and with other aspects of the production of these papers. Four of the papers are single authored by me. The other eight had co-authors including Vijay Chopra and Chris Hensel of the Frank Russell Company, my UBC PhD students James Douglass and Owen Wu, Klaus Berge from the Dresden University of Technology, Giorgio Consigli of the University of Bergamo, Constantine Dzhabarov who works with me on futures and futures options trading and research in Vancouver, Leonard MacLean and Yonggan Zhao of Dalhousie University, Edward O Thorp of Newport Beach, California, Olivier Gergaud of the Kedge Bordeaux Business School, France and Alexander Shirayaev and Mikhail Zhitlukhin of the Steklov Institute in Moscow.

Chapter 1

Comment on "Why a Weekend Effect?"*

University of British Columbia,
Vancouver, BC V6T 1Y8, Canada
and
The Yamaichi Research Institute, Tokyo, Japan

The weekend effect in U.S. security markets has been documented by French (1980), Gibbons and Hess (1981), and others. Miller (1988) argues that the effect could be explained by a tendency for self-initiated sell orders to exceed self-initiated buy orders over the weekend, while broker-initiated buy trades result in a surplus of buying during the remainder of the week.

This causes security prices to fall over the weekend and during the day on Monday as market makers sell back stock on the open. Prices then move higher during the week because of broker-induced buying. Osborne (1962) presents a similar hypothesis, which also argues that institutional investors are less active on Mondays as effort is made that day to plan the week's trades.

The day-of-the-week variation is higher for small-capitalized than for large-capitalized firms because of the larger bid-ask spreads and the thin trading in these generally low-priced securities. Keim and Smirlock (1987) document this for U.S. markets, and Stoll and Whaley (1983) confirm the bid-ask spreads.

Miller's idea is predicated on the fact that people are simply too busy to think much about stocks during the week. If they do anything, it's more

*He thanks Asaji Komatsu of the Yamaichi Research Institute in Tokyo for research assistance and helpful discussions. Comments on an earlier draft by Edward Miller improved the comment. Thanks also to the Yamaichi Research Institute for financial and other assistance in conducting this study.

often than not to buy upon the recommendation of a broker. Brokers have a vested interest in purchases. First, they do not have to find people who own stock and suggest they sell it. Second, they reveive two commissions for the purchases (usually recommended by the broker) and the sale (usually initiated by the stock owner).

Groth *et al.* (1979) survey 6,000 broker recommendations. Eighty-seven percent represent purchase and only 13% sales recommendations. Dimson and Marsh (1986) report similar recommendations by U.K. financial analysts. As individual investors think about their holdings over the weekend, they tend more to sell than to buy. Individuals, on balance, are net sellers of stock.

Exhibit 1 from Ritter (1988) illustrates buy-sell ratios with data on individual orders at Merrill Lynch for January and the rest of the year between 1971 and 1985. There is also a strong turn-of-the-year effect for small stocks on trading days −1 to +4.

Although Miller's story is plausible, he did not test the theory with real data. Lakonishok and Maberly (1990) have provided such a test with New York Stock Exchange (NYSE) odd-lot sales and purchases, sales and purchases of cash-account customers of Merrill Lynch, and NYSE block transactions. They find that Monday has the lowest trading volume. Insititutional trading is the lowest on Monday of all trading days, but individual trading on Monday is the highest relative to other days of the week.

Individuals also sell more on Mondays. For example, odd-lot sales minus odd-lot purchases relative to NYSE volume were 29% higher during 1962–1986 on Monday than for the average of Tuesday to Friday.

Theoretical support for imbalances on different days in trading volume, mean returns, and volatility based on the interaction of various traders has been advanced by Admati and Pfleiderer (1988, 1989).

Day-of-the-Week Effects

Previous, studies of holiday effects in Japanese spot and futures markets reveal strong and significant positive preholiday effects and negative post-holiday effects over the 1949–1988 period (Ziemba 1989; 1991). Hence it is appropriate to separate out the day-of-the-week effects.

Additional research on day-of-the-week effects in Japan appears in Jaffe and Westerfield (1985), Kato (1990), Kato, Schwartz, and Ziemba (1990),

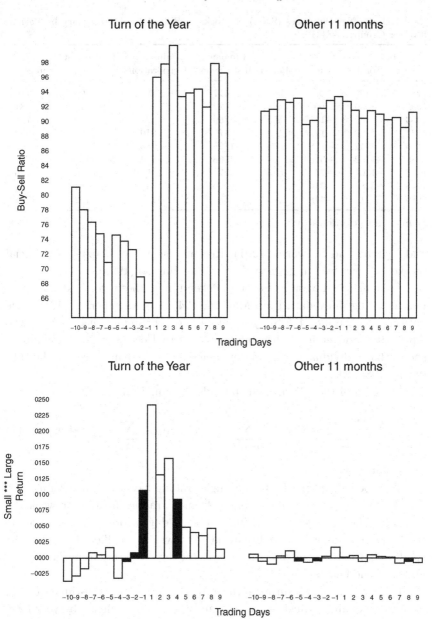

EXHIBIT 1:   Mean Buy/Sell Ratios and the Excess Return on Small Stocks by Trading Day in January and the Rest of the Year, 1971–1985.

Source: Ritter (1988).

4 *William T. Ziemba*

EXHIBIT 2: Net Purchases (Sales) of Stocks in Billions of Yen February by Various Investor Groups, 1981–1989.

	Individuals Total	Cash	Margin	Financial Institutions	Industrial Corporations	Investment Trusts	Foreigners
1981	−425	na	na	417	287	−95	110
1982	−330	na	na	422	82	17	181
1983	−862	−1417	555	769	27	−69	726
1984	−55	−1228	1173	1479	319	324	−1922
1985	−942	−1586	643	1825	283	468	−869
1986	−1762	−3109	1327	4568	754	1057	−3787
1987	−1307	−3350	2043	6274	1150	1811	−7196
1988	−3288	−5102	1814	4365	626	1730	77
1989	113	−4485	4599	4683	−1150	−2192	3348

Source: Yamaichi Research Institute.

and Ziemba and Schwartz (1991). Recent research on Japanese financial markets is surveyed in Ziemba, Bailey, and Hamao (1991).

This article investigates the weekend hypothesis for the Japanese market using daily data from May 16, 1949, to December 28, 1988. The data are broken into 475 ten-year subperiods beginning with May 1949 to April 1958 and ending with January 1979 to December 1988. Exhibit 2 shows that individual investors were net sellers in Japan as well as the U.S. during 1981–1989.

For each of the 475 ten-year periods the equation

$$R_t = \sum_{j=1}^{6} \hat{\gamma}_j \times \text{day}_j + \sum_{j=1236} \hat{b}_j \times \text{before}_j + \sum_{j=1236} \hat{a}_j \times \text{after}_j \quad (1)$$

is estimated.

The coefficients a_j refer to the single trading days that are after $aj = 1$, $j = 2$, $j = 3$, and j = 6-day break from a trading holiday or weekend. Similarly, the b_js refer to the single trading day before a 1, 2, 3, or 6-day break from trading. Hence Equation (1) gives as coefficients γ_j for the six days of the week the pure effects of these days separate from the holiday and weekend effects.

Exhibit 3 gives the mean returns by day of the week estimated from Equation (1) after adjusting for pre- and post-holiday effects by year from 1949 to 1988. Each ten-year period is plotted at its final month. For example, May 1949 to April 1958 is ploted as April 1958.

Hence there are 475 such points for Monday, Tuesday, to Saturday in the estimate of γ_1 to γ_6 in Equation (1) for that ten-year period.

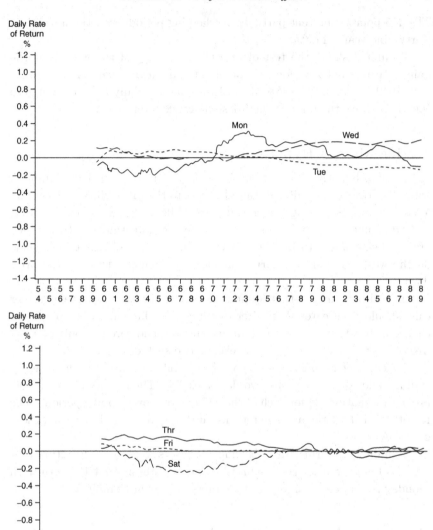

EXHIBIT 3: Day-of-the-Week Effects by Ten-year Period Ending in the Plotted Month for Periods Ending in April 1958 to December 1988 with Holiday and Weekend Effects Separated Out.

Source: Yamaichi Research Institute.

The 475 points represent partially overlapping periods over the more than thirty-nine years of data.

Exhibit 4 shows the test of hypotheses by day of the week that the daily return is not zero for each of the months in the years of the sample May 1949 to December 1988. Most of the time the daily return is not zero (i.e., it is above the line) at the 5% significance level.

Testing Miller's Hypothesis

A test of a hypothesis along the lines of Miller's is shown in Exhibit 5 with P-statistics in Exhibit 6. Here P refers to the probability of accepting a false hypothesis using a two-tail test. Miller's argument implies that individual investors reach net sell decisions on each weekend day (when they are not being urged to buy by brokers). These net decisions to sell made on the weekend come to market on Mondays, tending to force the price down.

This theory implies that Monday declines after two days free of broker calls should be greater than after one day. The Japanese data provide a chance to test this prediction because some weekends provide only one day free of broker's calls, and other weekends two such days.

Case A_1 refers to the one-day weekends following weeks with Saturday trading, and A_2 refers to the two-day weekends. The coefficients $â_1$ and $â_2$ are from Equation (1) for each of the 475 ten-year overlapping periods. The hypothesis is that the average returns on the A_2 days are lower than those on the A_1 days.

Exhibit 5 confirms this, showing Monday's average daily returns for the 475 ten-year periods. P-values for the hypothesis that the return on Monday is not zero using a two-tailed test appear in Exhibit 6.

One-Versus Two-Day Weekends

Sales efforts are intensified before holidays and weekends, which results in high returns on the preholiday Fridays and Saturdays. Exhibit 7 shows that the daily rise before two-day holidays and weekends is larger than far one-day breaks from trading using the $\hat{b}_1$ and $\hat{b}_2$ coefficients. Exhibit 8 gives the P-values for the sample period 1954–1989.

The results provide further evidence that Monday returns (based on the time between the close of the previous week's trading and the end of Monday's) do not relate to a time in the investment cycle that would

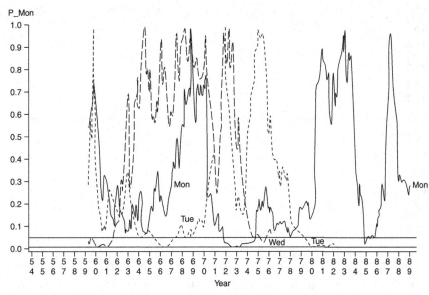

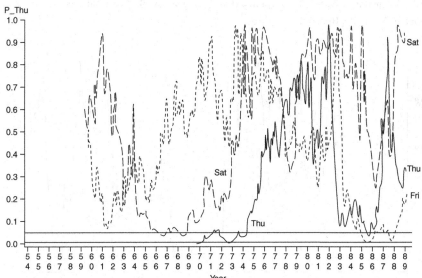

EXHIBIT 4:   P-Statistics for Hypothesis That Daily Return Is not Equal to Zero (Two-Tailed Test) for Exhibit 3.

Source: Yamaichi Research Institute.

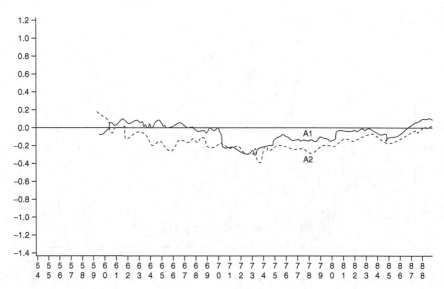

EXHIBIT 5:　Mean Daily Rates of Return on Mondays, Net of Holiday and Weekend Effects, on the NSA, for One-(A_1) and Two-(A_2) Day Weekends, 1960–1989.

Source: Yamaichi Research Institute.

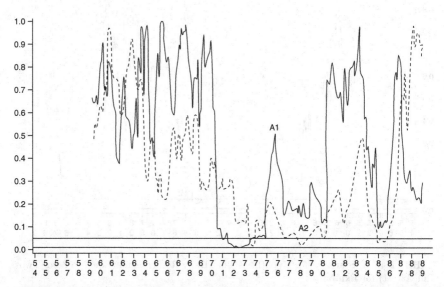

EXHIBIT 6:　P-values for the Hypothesis of Non-zero Returns on Monday Using a Two-tailed Test.

Source: Yamaichi Research Institute.

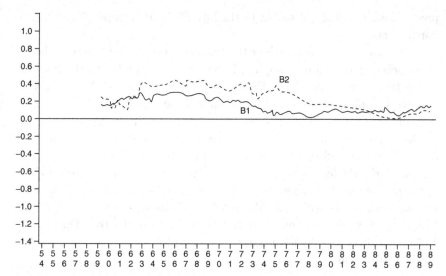

EXHIBIT 7: Mean Daily Rates of Return on Preholiday and Preweekend Trading Days for One-(B_1) and Two-(B_2) Day Trading Breaks on the NSA, for the 475 Ten-year Periods, 1949–1988.

Source: Yamaichi Research Institute.

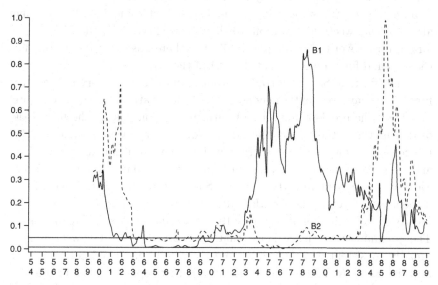

EXHIBIT 8: P-values for the Hypothesis that the Returns on the Preholiday and Preweekend are Not Zero With a Two-tail Test.

Source: Yamaichi Research Institute.

predict high returns, but rather to the buy-sell relationships of the market participants.

The results are averages over the ten-year periods, but the periods are overlapping. To avoid overlapping, Equation (1) is applied to the decades of the 1950s (including 1949), the 1960s, the 1970s, and the 1980s for four non-overlapping periods. Exhibit 9 describes the results.

The next-to-last column gives the coefficient $b_{A1}-b_{A2}$, corresponding to the hypothesis that the two-day breaks yield lower returns. This was indeed the case, and significantly so except during the 1950s.

Similarly, the last column shows the coefficient $b_{B1}-b_{B2}$, corresponding to the hypothesis that the market return is higher before a two-day break in trading than a one-day break. The results indicate this was the case in the first three decades, and the coefficient is significantly positive. During the 1980s, this effect was slightly negative, but the coefficient is not significantly different from zero.

Weekly Pattern of Returns Greatly Affected by Saturday Trading

An interesting aspect of the day-of-the-week effect is that Tuesdays tend to have negative returns following a one-day weekend, and Mondays decline after two-day weekends. Exhibit 10 shows this effect. The calculations are for data from April 1978 to June 1987 when there was Saturday trading for the first and fourth weeks (and the fifth if there was one).

The effects of Saturday trading from 1949 to 1988 are very interesting. First, Saturdays were extremely positive. Second, Saturdays were even more positive if the previous month had Saturday trading during the first week of the month in the sample period. Third, Mondays were negative if the previous Saturday was not a trading day (the third and fourth weeks), and even more negative if the third had no Saturday trading. However, Mondays were positive if the previous Saturday had trading, especially so if the second week of the month had no Saturday trading.

As of the beginning of February 1989, Saturday trading in Japan ceased. The preliminary evidence since that time for the two-day weekends is broadly consistent with U.S. data and the results presented here, namely, negative Mondays and positive Tuesdays. For example, for the four months February to May in 1989, there were negative Mondays, -0.14%, positive Tuesdays, $+0.17\%$, strongly positive Wednesdays, $+0.38\%$, mildly negative Thurdays, -0.03%, and positive Fridays, $+0.14\%$.

EXHIBIT 9:   Estimated Coefficient Values for Equation (1) for the Four Decade Periods.

	bmon	btue	bwed	bthu	bfri	bsat	bB1	bB2	bA1	bA2	bA1−bA2	bB1−bB2
49–59												
est	−1.083	−0.0356	0.0935	0.1466	0.0433	0.0797	0.1504	0.2329	−0.0555	0.1718	−0.22704***	−0.0825***
t-stat	−0.708	−0.732	1.9310	3.0260	0.8930	0.5230	1.0230	0.9410	−0.3760	0.7020	−44.881	16.171
60–69												
est	−0.0333	0.0629	−0.0063	0.1149***	0.0104	−0.1682	0.2256	0.3611	−0.0106	0.1710	0.1604	0.1355
t-stat	−0.283	1.611	−1.1610	2.9550	0.2660	−1.4440	2.0180	1.762	−0.0940	−0.8470	37.953	37.953
70–79												
est	0.1551	−0.0900*	0.1713***	0.0122	0.03807	0.0259	0.0901	0.1673*	−0.1576*	−0.2322**	0.074**	0.0772***
t-stat	1.5570	−2.340	4.4510	0.318	0.925	0.2500	0.2500	1.888	−1.6530	−2.0430	27.076	31.652
80–88												
est	−0.113	−0.1067***	0.2157***	0.0450	0.0621	0.554	0.1046	0.1004	0.1163	0.0266	0.0898***	−0.0043
t-stat	−1.095	−2.7590	5.5980	1.1650	1.394	0.5280	1.0470	1.253	1.1790	0.2290	29.7240	−1.6830

*, **, or *** indicate that the coefficient is not equal to zero at the 10%, 5%, or 1% level, respectively.

William T. Ziemba

EXHIBIT 10: Effects of Saturday Trading on the Topix, April 4, 1978, to June 18, 1987, Mean Daily Returns in Percent.

Week	Trading Ends		Mon	Tues	Wed	Thur	Fri	Sat	F	Sample Size
	This Week	Last Week								
1st, 5th A1	Sat	Sat	0.0198	−0.1072	0.1790	0.0581	0.0605	0.1678	8.67**	1406
4th A2	Sat	Fri	−0.1008	−0.1102	0.1074	0.0306	0.1582	0.0793	2.53*	649
2nd B1	Fri	Sat	0.1135	−0.0649	0.0980	0.0933	0.1341		4.05**	539
3rd B2	Fri	Fri	−0.3489	0.1931	0.2479	0.2609	0.2193		0.46	58
All Weeks			0.0039	−0.0902	0.1449	0.0648	0.1049	0.1397		
Sample Size			449	464	464	465	467	343		2652

*and **indicate significance at the 1% and 5% levels, respectively, for rejection of the hypothesis that the mean returns are equal across days of the week.

Source: Kato, Schwartz, and Ziemba (1990) and Kato (1990).

These results are based on data before the stock market decline of 1990–1992. Empirical anomalies such as the weekend effect tend to persist during periods when cash flow and institutional and individual investor behavior and constraints are functioning in a relatively smooth fashion. During extreme market declines and volatility such as the 63% drop in the NSA from January 1990 to August 1992, these anomalies are not as strongly present as investor fear and uncertainty prevent the usual behavior. Stone and Ziemba (1993) and Ziemba (1993) discuss this.

References

Admati, A. and P. Pfleiderer (1988). A theory of intrady patterns: Volume and price variability. *Review of Financial Studies*, 1, 3–40.

――――(1989). Divide and conquer: A theory of intraday and day-of-the-week mean effects. *Review of Financial Studies*, 2, 189–223.

Dimson, E. and P. Marsh (1986). Event study methodologies and the size effect: The case of U.K. press recommendations. *Journal of Financial Economics*, 17, 113–142.

French, K. R. (1980). Stock returns and the weekend effect. *Journal of Financial Economics*, 8, 55–70.

Gibbons, M. R. and P. Hess (1981). Day of the week effects and asset returns. *Journal of Business*, 54, 579–596.

Groth, J. C., W. Lewellen, G. Schlarbaum and R. Lease (1979). An analysis of brokerage house security recommendations. *Financial Analysis Journal*, 32–40.

Jaffe, J. and R. Westerfield (1985). Patterns in Japanese common stock returns: Day of the week and turn of the year effects. *Journal of Financial and Quantitative Analysis*, 20, 243–260.

Kato, K. (1990). Weekly patterns in Japanese stock returns. *Management Science*, 36, 1031–1043.

Kato, K., S. L. Schwartz and W. T. Ziemba (1990). Day of the week effects in Japanese securities markets. In E.J. Elton and M.J. Gruber (eds.), *Japanese Capital Markets*. New York: Harper and Row, pp. 249–281.

Keim D. B. and M. Smirlock (1987). The behavior of intraday stock index futures prices. *Advances in Futures and Options Research*, 2, 143–166.

Lakonishok, J. and E. Maberly (1990). The weekend effect: Trading patterns of individual and institutional investors. *Journal of Finance*, 45, 231–243.

Miller, E. M. (1988). Why a weekend effect? *Journal of Portfolio Management*, 15, 42–48.

Osborne, M. F. M. (1962). Periodic structure in the Brownian motion of the stock market. *Operations Research*, 10, 345–379.

Ritter, J. (1988). The buying and selling behavior of individual investors at the turn of the tear. *Journal of Finance*, 43, 701–717.

Stoll, H. R. and R. E. Whaley (1983). Transactions costs and the small firm effect. *Journal of Financial Economics*, 12, 57–79.

Stone, D. and W. T. Ziemba (1993). Land and stock prices in Japan. Forthcoming in *Journal of Economics perspectives*, 7(3), 149–165.

Ziemba, W. T. (1989). Seasonality effects in Japanese futures markets. In S. Ghon Rhee and Rosita P. Chang (eds.), *Research on Pacific Basin Capital Market*. Amsterdam: North-Holland.

————(1991). Japanese security market regularities: Monthly, turn of the month and year. Holiday and golden week effects. *Japan and the World Economy*, 32, 119–146.

————(1994). World wide security market regularities. *European Journal of Operational Research*, 75, 198–229.

Ziemba, W. T., W. Bailey and Y. Hamao (eds.) (1991). *Japanese Financial Market Research*. Amsterdam: North-Holland.

Ziemba, W. T. and S. L. Schwartz (1991). *Invest Japan: The Structure, Performance and Opportunities of Japan's Stock, Bond and Fund Markets*. Chicago, IL: Probus Publishing.

Chapter 2

The Effect of Errors in Means, Variances, and Covariances on Optimal Portfolio Choice*

Vijay K. Chopra

Frank Russell Company

William T. Ziemba

University of British Columbia and Frank Russell Company

Good mean forecasts are critical to the mean-variance framework

There is considerable literature on the strengths and limitations of mean-variance analysis. The basic theory and extensions of MV analysis are discussed in Markowitz (1987) and Ziemba and Vickson (1975). Bawa, Brown and Klein (1979) and Michaud (1989) review some of its problems.

MV optimization is very sensitive to errors in the estimates of the inputs. Chopra (1993) shows that small changes in the input parameters can result in large changes in composition of the optimal portfolio. Best and Grauer (1991) present some empirical and theoretical results on the sensitivity of optimal portfolios to changes in means. This article examines the relative impact of estimation errors in means, variances, and covariances.

Kallberg and Ziemba (1984) examine the question of mis-specification in normally distributed portfolio selection problems. They discuss three

---

*Reprinted, with permission, from *Journal of Portfolio Management*, 1993. Copyright 1993 Institutional Investor Journals.

areas of misspecification: the investor's utility function, the mean vector, and the covariance matrix of the return distribution.

They find that utility functions with similar levels of Arrow–Pratt absolute risk aversion result in similar optimal portfolios irrespective of the functional form of the utility[1]; Thus, mis-specification of the utility function is not a major concern because several different utility functions (quadratic, negative exponential, logarithmic, power) result in similar portfolio allocations for similar levels of risk aversion.

Misspecification of the parameters of the return distribution, however, does make a significant difference. Specifically, errors in means are at least ten times as important as errors in variances and covariances.

We show that it is important to distinguish between errors in variances and covariances. The relative impact of errors in means, variances, and co-variances also depends on the investor's risk tolerance. For a risk tolerance of 50, errors in means are about eleven times as important as errors in variances, a result similar to that of Kallberg and Ziemba.[2] Errors in variances are about twice as important as errors in covariances.

At higher risk tolerances, errors in means are even more important relative to errors in variances and covariances. At lower risk tolerances, the relative impact of errors in means, variances, and covariances is closer. Even though errors in means are more important than those in variances and covariances, the difference in importance diminishes with a decline in risk tolerance.

These results have an implication for allocation of resources according to the MV framework. The primary emphasis should be on obtaining superior estimates of means, followed by good estimates of variances. Estimates of covariances are the least important in terms of their influence on the optimal portfolio.

---

[1]For an investor with utility function U and wealth W, the Arrow-Pratt absolute risk aversion is ARA $= -U''(W)/U'(W)$. Friend and Blume (1975) show that investor behavior is consistent with decreasing ARA; that is, as investors' wealth increases, their aversion to a given risk decreases.

[2]The risk tolerance reflects the investor's desired trade-off between extra return and extra risk (variance). It is the inverse slope of the investor's indifference curve in mean–variance space. The greater the risk tolerance, the more risk an investor is willing to take for a little extra return. Under fairly general input assumptions, a risk tolerance of 50 describes the typical portfolio allocations of large US pensions funds and other institutional investors. Risk tolerances of 25 and 75 characterize extremely conservative and aggressive investors, respectively.

Theory

For a utility function U and gross returns $r - i$ (or return relatives) for assets $i = 1, 2, \ldots, N$, an investor's optimal portfolio is the solution to:

$$\text{maximize } Z(x) = E\left[U\left(W_0 \sum_{i=1}^{N}(r_i)x_i \right) \right]$$

$$\text{such that } x_i > 0, \quad \sum_{i=1}^{N} = 1,$$

where $Z(x)$ is the investor's expected utility of wealth, W_0 is the investor's initial wealth, the returns r_i have a distribution $F(r)$, and x_i are the portfolio weights that sum to one.

Assuming a negative exponential utility function $U(W) = -\exp(-aW)$ and a joint normal distribution of returns, the expected utility maximization problem is equivalent to the MV-optimization problem:

$$\text{maximize } Z(x) = \sum_{i=1}^{N} E[r_i]x_j - \frac{1}{t}\sum_{i=1}^{N}\sum_{j=1}^{N} x_i x_j E[\sigma_{ij}]$$

$$\text{such that } x_i > 0, \quad \sum_{i=1}^{N} x_i = 1,$$

where $E[r_i]$ is the expected return for asset i, t is the risk tolerance of the investor, and $E[\sigma_{ij}]$ is the covariance between the returns on assets i and j.[3]

A natural question arises: How much worse off is the investor if the distribution of returns is estimated with an error? This is an important consideration because the future distribution of returns is unknown. Investors rely on limited data to estimate the parameters of the distribution, and estimation errors are unavoidable. Our investigation assumes that the distribution of returns is stationary over the sample period. If it is time-varying or non-stationary, the estimated parameters will be erroneous.

To measure how close one portfolio is to another, we compare the cash equivalent (CE) values of the two portfolios. The cash equivalent of a risky portfolio is the certain amount of cash that provides the same utility as

---

[3] Although the exponential utility function is convenient for deriving the MV problem with normally distributed returns, the MV framework is consistent with expected utility maximization for any concave utility function, assuming normality.

the risky portfolio, that is, $U(\text{CE}) = Z(x)$ or $\text{CE} = U^{-1}[Z(x)]$ where, as defined before, $Z(x)$ is the expected utility of the risky portfolio.[4] The cash equivalent is an appropriate measure because it takes into account the investor's risk tolerance and the inherent uncertainty in returns, and it is independent of utility units. For a risk-free portfolio, the cash equivalent is equal to the certain return.

Given a set of asset parameters and the investors risk tolerance, a MV-optimal portfolio has the largest CE value of any portfolio of those assets. The percentage cash equivalent loss (CEL) from holding an arbitrary portfolio, x instead of an optimal portfolio o is

$$\text{CEL} = \frac{\text{CE}_o - \text{CE}_x}{\text{CE}_o}$$

where CE_o and CE_x axe the cash equivalents of portfolio o and portfolio x respectively.

Data and Methodology

The data consist of monthly observations from January 1980 through December 1989 on ten randomly selected Dow Jones Industrial Average (DJIA) securities. We use the Center for Research in Security Prices (CRSP) database, having deleted one security (Allied–Signal, Inc.) because of lack of data prior to 1985. Each of the remaining twenty–nine securities had an equal probability of being chosen. The securities are listed in Exhibit 1.

MV optimization requires as inputs forecasts for: mean returns, variances, and covariances. We computed historical means ($\bar{r}_i$), variances (σ_{ii}), and covariances (σ_{ij}), and assumed that these are the 'true' values of these parameters. Thus, we assumed that $E[r_i] = \bar{r}_i$, $E[\sigma_{ii}] = \sigma_{ii}$, and $E[\sigma_{ij}] = \sigma_{ij}$. A base optimal portfolio allocation is computed on the basis of these parameters for a risk tolerance of 50 (equivalent to the parameter $a = 0.04$).

---

[4]For negative exponential utility, Freund (1956) shows that the expected utility of portfolio x is $Z(x) = 1 - \exp(-aE[x] + (a^2/2)\text{Var}[x])$, where $E[X]$ and $\text{Var}[x]$ are the expected return and variance of the portfolio. The cash equivalent is $\text{CE}_x = (1/a)\log(1 - Z(x))$. If returns are assumed to have a multivariate normal distribution, this is also the cash equivalent of an MV-optimal portfolio. See Dexter, Yu and Ziemba (1980) for more details.

EXHIBIT 1:   List of Ten Randomly Chosen
DJIA Securities.

1.   Aluminum Co. of America
2.   American Express Co.
3.   Boeing Co.
4.   Chevron Co.
5.   Coca Cola Co.
6.   E.I. Du Pont De Nemours & Co.
7.   Minnesota Mining and Manufacturing Co.
8.   Procter & Gamble Co.
9.   Sears, Roebuck & Co.
10. United Technologies Co.

Our results are independent of the source of the inputs. Whether we use historical inputs or those based on a complete forecasting scheme, the results continue to hold as long as the inputs have errors.

Exhibit 2 gives the input parameters and the optimal base portfolio resulting from these inputs. To examine the influence of errors in parameter estimates, we change the true parameters slightly and compute the resulting optimal portfolio. This portfolio will be suboptimal for the investor because it is not based on the true input parameters.

Next we compute the cash equivalent values of the base portfolio and the new optimal portfolio. The percentage cash equivalent loss from holding the suboptimal portfolio instead of the true optimal portfolio measures the impact of errors in input parameters on investor utility.

To evaluate the impact of errors in means, we replaced the assumed true mean $\bar{r}_i$ for asset i by the approximation $\bar{r}_i(l + kz_i)$ where z_i has a standard normal distribution. The parameter k is varied from 0.05 through 0.20 in steps of 0.05 to examine the impact of errors of different sizes. Larger values of k represent larger errors in the estimates. The variances and covariances are left unchanged in this case to isolate the influence of errors in means.

The percentage cash equivalent loss from holding a portfolio that is optimal for approximate means $\bar{r}_i(1 + kz_i)$ but is suboptimal for the true means r, is then computed. This procedure is repeated with a new set of z values for a total of 100 iterations for each value of k.

To investigate the impact of errors in variances each variance forecast σ_{ii} was replaced by $\sigma_{ii}(1 + kZ_j)$. To isolate the influence of variance errors, the means and covariances are left unchanged.

Finally, the influence of errors in covariances is examined by replacing each covariance $\sigma_{ij}(i \neq j)$ by $\sigma_{ij} + kz_{ij}$ where z_{ij} has a standard

Vijay K. Chopra and William T. Ziemba

EXHIBIT 2: Inputs to the Optimization and the Resulting Optimal Portfolio for a Risk Tolerance of 50 (January 1980–December 1989).

	Alcoa	Amex	Boeing	Chev.	Coke	Du Pont	MMM	P&G	Sears	U Tech
Means (% per month)	1.5617	1.9477	1.907	1.5801	2.1643	1.6010	1.4892	1.6248	1.4075	1.1537
Std. Dev. (% per month)	8.8308	8.4585	10.040	8.6215	5.988	6.8767	5.8162	5.6385	8.0047	8.212
Correlations										
Alcoa	1.0000									
Amex	0.3660	1.0000								
Boeing	0.3457	0.5379	1.0000							
Chev.	0.1606	0.2165	0.2218	1.0000						
Coke	0.2279	0.4986	0.4283	0.0569	1.0000					
Du Pont	0.5133	0.5823	0.4051	0.3609	0.3619	1.0000				
MMM	0.5203	0.5569	0.4492	0.2325	0.4811	0.6167	1.0000			
P&G	0.2176	0.4760	0.3867	0.2289	0.5952	0.4996	0.6037	1.0000		
Sears	0.3267	0.6517	0.4883	0.1726	0.4378	0.5811	0.5671	0.5012	1.0000	
U Tech	0.5101	0.5853	0.6569	0.3814	0.4368	0.5644	0.6032	0.4772	0.6039	1.0000
Optimal Port. Weights	0.0350	0.0082	0.0	0.1626	0.7940	0.0	0.0	0.0	0.00	0.00

normal distribution, while retaining the original means and variances. The procedure is repeated 100 times for each value of k, each time with a new set of z values, and the cash equivalent loss computed. The entire procedure is repeated for risk tolerances of 25 and 75 to examine how the results vary with investors' risk tolerance.

Results

Exhibit 3 shows the mean, minimum, and maximum cash equivalent loss over the 100 iterations for a risk tolerance of 50. Exhibit 4 plots the average CEL as a function of k. The CEL for errors in means is approximately eleven times that for errors in variances and over twenty times that for errors in covariances. Thus, it is important to distinguish between errors in variances and errors in covariances.[5] For example, for $k = 0.10$, the CEL is 2.45 for errors in means, 0.22 for errors in variances, and 0.11 for errors in covariances.

Our results on the relative importance of errors in means and variances are similar to those of Kallberg and Ziemba (1984). They find that errors in

EXHIBIT 3: Cash Equivalent Loss (CEL) for Errors of Different Sizes.

k (size of error)	Parameter with Error	Mean CEL	Min. CEL	Max. CEL
0.05	Means	0.66	0.01	5.05
0.05	Variances	0.05	0.00	0.34
0.05	Covariances	0.02	0.00	0.25
0.10	Means	2.45	0.01	15.61
0.05	Variances	0.22	0.00	1.39
0.10	Covariances	0.11	0.00	0.66
0.15	Means	5.12	0.15	24.35
0.15	Variances	0.55	0.00	3.35
0.15	Covariances	0.27	0.00	1.11
0.20	Means	10.16	0.17	36.09
0.20	Variances	0.90	0.01	4.16
0.20	Covariances	0.47	0.00	1.94

[5]The result for covariances also applies to correlation coefficients, as the correlations differ from the covariances only by a scale factor equal to the product of two standard deviations.

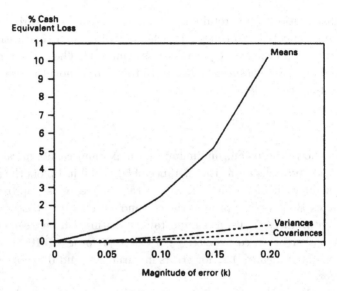

EXHIBIT 4:   Mean Percentage Cash Equivalent Loss Due to Errors in Inputs.

EXHIBIT 5:   Average Ratio of CELs for Errors in Means, Variances, and Covariances.

Risk Tolerance	Errors in Means versus Variances	Errors in Means versus Covariances	Errors in Variances versus Covariances
25	3.22	5.38	1.67
50	1.98	22.50	2.05
75	21.42	56.84	2.68

means are approximately ten times as important as errors in variances and covariances considered together (they do not distinguish between variances and covariances).

Our results show that for a risk tolerance of 50 the importance of errors in covariances is only half as much as previously believed. Furthermore, the relative importance of errors in means, variances, and covariances depends upon the investor's risk tolerance.

Exhibit 5 shows the average ratio (averaged over errors of different sizes, k) of the CELs for errors in means, variances, and covariances. An investor with a high risk tolerance focuses on raising the expected return of the portfolio and discounts the variance more relative to the expected return. To this investor, errors in expected returns are considerably more important than errors in variances and covariances. For an investor with a risk tolerance of 75, the average CEL for errors in means is over twenty–one times that for errors in variances and over fifty–six times that for errors in covariances.

Minimizing the variance of the portfolio is more important to an investor with a low risk tolerance than raising the expected return. To this investor, errors in means are somewhat less important than errors in variances and covariances. For an investor with a risk tolerance of 25, the average CEL for errors in expected returns is about three times that for errors in variances and about five times that for errors in covariances.

Most large institutional investors have a risk tolerance in the 40 to 60 range. Over that range, there is considerable difference in the relative importance of errors in means, variances, and covariances. Irrespective of the level of risk tolerance, errors in means are the most important, followed by errors in variances. Errors in covariances are the least important in terms of their influence on portfolio optimality.

Implications and Conclusions

Investors have limited resources available to spend on obtaining estimates of necessarily unknowable future parameters of risk and reward. This analysis indicates that the bulk of these resources should be spent on obtaining the best estimates of expected returns of the asset classes under consideration.

Sometimes, investors using the MV framework to allocate wealth among individual stocks set all the expected returns to zero (or a non-zero constant). This can lead to a better portfolio allocation because it is often very difficult to obtain good forecasts for expected returns. Using forecasts that do not accurately reflect the relative expected returns of different securities can substatially degrade MV performance.

In some cases it may be preferable to set all forecasts equal.[6] The optimization then focuses on minimizing portfolio variance and does not suffer from the error-in-means problem. In such cases it is important to have good estimates of variances and covariances for the securities, as MV optimizes only with respect to these characteristics.

---

[6]This approach is in the spirit of Stein estimation and is discussed in Chopra, Hensel, and Turner (1993). As a practical matter, it should be used for assets that belong to the same asset class. e.g., equity indexes of different countries or stocks within a country. It would be inappropriate to apply it to financial instruments with very different characteristics; for example, stocks and T-bills.

Of course, if investors truly believe that they have superior estimates of the means, they should use them. In this case it may be acceptable to use historical values for variances and covariances.

For investors with moderate to high risk tolerance, the cash equivalent loss for errors in means is an order of magnitude greater than that for errors in variances or covariances. As variances and covariances do not much influence the optimal MV allocation (relative to the means), investors with moderate-to-high risk tolerance need not expend considerable resources to obtain better estimates of these parameters.

References

Bawa, V. S., S. J. Brown and R. W. Klein (1979). Estimation risk and optimal portfolio choice. *Studies in Bayesian Econometrics*, Bell Laboratories Series. Amsterdam: North Holland.

Best, M. J. and R. R. Grauer (1991). On the sensitivity of means-variance-efficient portfolios to changes in asset means: Some analytical and computational results. *Review of Financial Studies*, 4, No. 2, 315–342.

Chopra, V. K. (1991). Mean-variance revisited: Near-optimal portfolios and sensitivity to input variations. *Russell Research Commentary*.

Chopra, V. K., C. R. Hensel and A. L. Turner (1993). Massaging mean-variance inputs: Returns from alternative global investment strategies in the 1980's. *Management Science*, (July): 845–855.

Dexter, A. S., J. N. W. Yu and W. T. Ziemba (1980). Portfolio selection in a lognormal market when the investor has a power utility function: Computational results. In *Proceedings of the International Conference on Stochastic Programming*, M.A.H. Dempster (ed.), New York: Academic Press, pp. 507–523.

Freund, R. A. (1956). The introduction of risk into a programming model. *Econometrica*, 24, 253–263.

Freund, L. and M. Blume (1975). The demand for risky assets. *The American Economic Review*, December, 900–922.

Kallberg, J. G. and W. T. Ziemba (1984). Mis-specification in portfolio selection problems. In *Risk and Capital*, G. Bamberg and K. Spremann (eds.), Lecture Notes in Econometrics and Mathematical Systems. New York: Springer-Verlag.

Klein, R. W. and V. S. Bawa (1976). The effect of estimation risk on optimal portfolio choice. *J. of Financial Economics*, 3 (June), 215–231.

Markowitz, H. M. (1987). *Mean-Variance Analysis in Portfolio Choice and Capital Markets*. New York: Basil Blackwell.

Michaud, R. O. (1989). The markowitz optimization enigma: Is optimized optimal? *Financial Analysts Journal*, 45 (January–February), 31–42.

Ziemba, W. T. and R. G. Vickson (eds.) (1975). *Stochastic Optimization Models in Finance*. New York: Academic Press.

Chapter 3

The Turn-of-the-Month Effect in the U.S. Stock Index Futures Markets, 1982–1992*

Chris R. Hensel

Frank Russell Company, 909 A Street, Tacoma, WA 98401

Gordon A. Sick

Faculty of Management, University of Calgary, Calgary, Alberta T2N IN4 Canada

William T. Ziemba

Faculty of Commerce, University of British Columbia, Vancouver, BC V6T 1Y8 Canada

The mean return for small and large capitalized stocks in the cash and futures markets was positive in the first half of the month and negative in the second half of the month during the 10-year period of futures trading from May 1982–April 1992. The mean return in the cash and futures markets for small and large capitalized stocks at the turn-of-the-month five-day trading period was significantly greater than average. There was partial anticipation of the cash turn-of-the-month effect in the futures markets on the previous three trading days. There was seasonality in the monthly return patterns, with the first and last quarter exhibiting higher returns at the turn-of-the-month and in the first half of the month. These results are an

*This research was partially supported by the Social Sciences and Humanities Research Council of Canada and the Frank Russell Company. Without implicating them, we would like to thank Gayle Nolte for computational assistance and Michael Brennan and Richard Thaler for helpful comments on an earlier draft of this paper. Proofs and reprint orders should be sent to William Ziemba.

out-of-sample confirmation of the turn-of-the-month anomaly Ariel (1987) reported for the cash market in the earlier period 1963–1981. The anomaly appears in the cash and futures markets, ruling out many explanations of the cash market anomaly that are based on trading frictions.

1. Introduction

There is considerable belief in the investment profession that there is a turn-of-the-month effect in US and other security markets. Market advisors such as Merrill (1966), Fosback (1976), and Hirsch (1986) have argued that stocks advance at the turn-of-the-month. The five days consisting of the last trading day of the previous month (−1) and the first four trading days of the new month (+1 to +4) are referred to as the turn of the month. Roll (1983) has documented that there were significant positive returns during the years 1963 to 1978 in January at the turn of the month and, in particular, that the small-capitalized stocks significantly outperformed the large capitalized stocks on these days.

Ariel (1987) documented the turn-of-the-month and first-half-of-the-month effects (trading days −1 to +9) for small and large capitalized US-traded stocks in the 19 years from 1963–1981, using equal- and value-weighted indexes of all NYSE stocks. His research showed there were very high returns at the turn of the month. The rest of the market gains during 1963–81 occurred in the second week of the month. The first half of the month had all the gains, and the second half of the month had negative returns.

Lakonishok and Smidt (1988) reported that over the 90-year period, 1897–1986, the large-capitalized Dow Jones Industrial Index rose 0.475% during the four day period −1 to +3 each month, whereas the average gain for a four-day period is 0.061%. The average gain per month over these 90 years was 0.349%. Hence, aside from these four days at the turn of the month, the DJIA had negative returns.

The reasons for the turn-of-the-month effect are several, but they are largely cash flow and institutionally based. For example, the US economy often has cash payments to private investors of salaries and debt interest on the −1 day of the month. In addition, there are institutional corporate and pension fund purchases at the turn of the month. These cash flows vary by month and lead to higher average returns in January, which has the highest cash flow. Odgen (1990) presents some empirical support of this hypothesis and related monetary actions for US markets. For example,

70% (90%) of the interest and principal payments on corporate (municipal) debt are payable on the first or last days of the month. Moreover, 45% (65%) of dividends on common (preferred) stock are payable on these dates. Another factor in this effect seems to be behavioral. One manifestation is that bad news such as that relating to earnings announcements is delayed and announced late in the month, while good news is released promptly at the beginning of the month [see Penman (1987)].

Evidence from Japan by Ziemba (1989, 1991) and Canada, the United Kingdom, Australia, Switzerland, and West Germany by Cadsby and Ratner (1991) provides further support for the cash flow hypothesis. In Japan most salaries are paid from the 20th to the 25th of the month, with the majority on the 25th. Security firms can invest for their own accounts based on their capitalization, which results in buying commencing on the −3 day with their three-day settlement. Individual investors buy mutual funds with their pay, which they receive on calendar days 15 to 25 of the month; the funds are then invested in stocks with a lag. Employee stock-holding plans and mutual funds also receive money in this period to invest during the turn of the month.

Using data from 1949 to 1988, Ziemba (1991) found that the turn of the month in Japan is similar to that in the US. However, the dates change, with the turn of the month being trading days −5 to +2 with +3 to +7 the rest of the first half of the month. Ziemba also found that each of the days −5 to +2 had significantly positive returns. Moreover, all the gains in the stock market were in the first half of the month. The securities firms have some information regarding these trading patterns and plan their monthly sales efforts during the −5 to +7 period.

Ziemba (1989) investigated the futures market trading outside Japan on the Simex in Singapore at the turn of the month in Japanese security markets during the period September 1986 to September 1988, before there was futures trading on the NSA or Topix in Japan. The spot effect was consistent with past data, so the futures market did not alter the effect. However, the futures market in Singapore anticipated the effect on days −8 to −5 with a total average rise of 2.8%. Then, when the effect occurred on days −5 to +2 and the spot market gained 1.7%, the futures market had zero returns.

Cadsby and Ratner (1991) investigated turn-of-the-month and holiday effects in Canada, the United Kingdom, Australia, Switzerland, West Germany, Japan, Hong Kong, Italy, and France. Their use of −1 to +4 as the turn of the month in all these countries makes their results hard to interpret, as there may be cash flow and institutional constraint date alterations as in Japan. Still, they find a significant turn of the month in most countries. Ziemba (1993a) also confirms the existence of a significant turn-of-the-month effect in the United Kingdom cash and futures markets.

In this paper we investigate the turn-of-the-month and first-half-of-the-month effects in the 10-year period of trading in US index futures from May 1982 to April 1992. Results are presented for the cash and futures markets for small-capitalized stocks proxied by the Value Line Composite Index and for large-capitalized stocks proxied by the S&P 500 Index. The results are broadly consistent with those of Ariel (1987) in that all the gains in the stock market for small and large-capitalized US securities occur in the first half of the month. For small and large-capitalized stocks there were significant positive returns in the cash and futures markets at the turn and first half of the month. These returns were significantly greater than average during the turn of the month.

Mean returns were lower than average in the second half of the month and significantly so for the small-capitalized stocks in the cash market. There is a strong monthly seasonality effect, particularly for the small-capitalized stocks. The returns were significantly higher than average at the turn and first half of the month in January, February, March, and November for large-capitalized stocks. Mean returns are greater than zero during the turn of the month in each of the first and last three months of the year and above, but not significantly greater than, average. The month-by-month returns for the large-capitalized stocks have similar patterns to the small-capitalized stocks, but the mean returns are not as large in the first half of the month or as negative in the second half of the month.

Ariel found abnormally large returns starting only on day -1 in his early cash market sample. We find abnormally large returns starting on day -4 in both the cash and futures markets in our later, non-overlapping sample. Perhaps this is a result of speculative activity on the futures market anticipating a cash market gain starting on day -1, which moves the anomaly ahead to day -4. Index arbitrage may then be forcing the anomaly to appear on day -4 in the S&P cash market as well, although it is not statistically significant. This is consistent with the greater index arbitrage activity for the S&P 500 contract.

The results in this paper add to the literature on seasonal anomalies in security markets, of which the following are some of the important references. Discussion of the day-of-the-week effect appears in French

(1980), Gibbons and Hess (1981), Jaffe and Westerfield (1985ab), Kato, Schwartz and Ziemba (1989), Lakonishok and Maberly (1990), Solnik (1990), and Ziemba (1993b). Holiday effects are analyzed by Ariel (1990), Cadsby and Ratner (1991), Pettengill (1989), and Ziemba (1991). Monthly effects are studied by Gultekin and Gultekin (1983), Brown, Kleidon, and Marsh (1983), Jacobs and Levy (1988), Hawawini (1991), Jaffe and Westerfield (1989), and Cadsby (1992). Harris (1986) studied time-of-day effects. January and size effects are analyzed by Rozeff and Kinney (1976), Banz (1981), Reinganum (1981), Keim (1983, 1989), Roll (1983), Ritter (1988), Ritter and Chopra (1989), and Jaffe, Keim, and Westerfield (1989). Surveys of this literature appear in Thaler (1987ab), Ziemba (1993a), and Hawawini and Keim (1993).

Section 2 presents the results in the futures and cash markets for the 10 years from May 1982 to April 1992, and section 3 provides concluding remarks.

2. The Monthly Return Patterns in the Cash and Futures Markets

The data used in this study consist of the daily cash and futures closing prices for the Value Line Composite and S&P 500 Index contracts for the 10-year period May 1982 to April 1992. The futures contracts were chosen as those contracts with the nearest expiry date. The rollover into the next contract does not occur in the day -4 to day $+4$ period that is the focus of this study, and hence cannot explain any of the anomaly. This period was chosen to not overlap with Ariel's (1987) study, which used cash data from 1963–1981, and to include the entire period of index futures trading. The Value Line Composite is an equally weighted index of about 1,650 stocks and is used as a proxy for small stocks. It is currently arithmetically weighted. However, it was geometrically weighted from May 1982 until January 1988. Futures contracts expiring in March, June, September, and December are traded on the Kansas City Board of Trade. Futures options on this index are traded on the Philadelphia stock exchange. The S&P 500 Index is a value-weighted index of 500 large-capitalized stocks and serves as the large-capitalized index. S&P 500 futures contracts with the same maturity as the Value Line are traded on the Chicago Mercantile Exchange, and futures options are traded at the Chicago Board of Trade. Daily volume in the S&P 500 futures contracts is in the 40,000–100,000 contracts range, with a contract being $500 times the index value. A substantial portion of this volume is associated with various types of program trading, including index arbitrage.

Daily volume in the Value Line Composite futures contract is less than 1,000 contracts per day. This includes little if any index arbitrage trading. Figure 1 shows the small and large-capitalized returns in the cash and futures markets for the period May 1982 to April 1992 by trading day of the month. Figure 1 shows percentage rates of return for both the cash and futures markets. Since the investment in a futures contract is $0, this is not a return in the investment sense. However, it is a useful scaling of the dollar

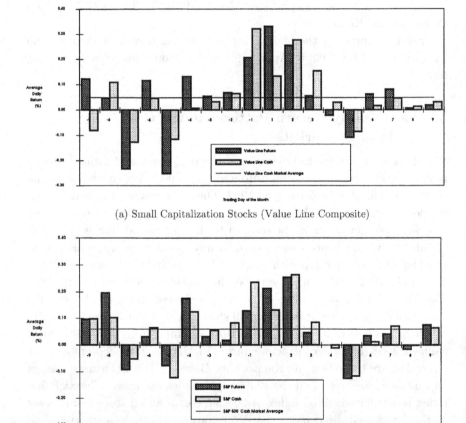

(a) Small Capitalization Stocks (Value Line Composite)

(b) Large Capitalization Stocks (S&P 500)

Figure 1:   Average Daily Returns in the Cash and Futures Market for Small and Large-Capitalized Stocks by Trading Day of the Month, May 1982–April 1992.

profit accruing to the daily mark-to-market, adjusting for contract size and price.

There were high returns on trading days -1 to $+3$ in the cash and -1 to $+2$ in the futures markets. Some, but not all of these days had returns significantly above average. This is consistent with the results documented for the cash market in the earlier period by Ariel in a paper that was published at the mid point of the time interval of our data sample. That is, the cash anomaly was well-known for part but perhaps not all of our data period and our results are an out-of-sample confirmation of Ariel's results. Unlike Ariel, we also find some anticipation of the turn-of-the-month, particularly on day -4 in the futures markets. The effect was more pronounced with the S&P 500 cash market. This is consistent with speculation on the futures markets anticipating the cash market gains starting on day -1 as documented by Ariel. The high degree of index arbitrage on the S&P contract carries the effect into that cash market. To the extent that the speculative anticipation by the futures markets is a type of intertemporal index "arbitrage," the anticipation effect is stronger for the S&P futures contract than for the Value Line contract, because of the greater arbitrage activity with that contract, which has fewer and more heavily traded stocks in its index.

The comparison of the turn-of-the-month anomaly for cash and futures markets also allows us to study another potential explanation of the anomaly in the cash market. If ex-dividend dates do not occur evenly through the month, there will be a tendency for the cash (indices) to fall on those dates when there is a high incidence of ex-dividend activity. This could contribute to a seasonal anomaly in the indices, since they are not adjusted for dividends. However, the futures are essentially adjusted for dividends, because rational investors know the expiry date of the futures and can anticipate accurately the dividends to be paid to the index each day. Hence, they will set futures prices to reflect the distribution of this final ex-dividend index value. Thus, if the turn-of-the-month anomaly is an artifact of ex-dividend price drops in the cash index, it should vanish in the futures market. Since the anomaly still appears in the futures market, the ex-dividend explanation does not hold.

From Ariel's analysis, the cash market is known to exhibit the anomalous turn-of-the-month behavior in which high profits are earned at the turn-of-the-month. One might hypothesize that speculators would adopt trading strategies at the turn-of-the-month that would drive these profits to zero. By going to a period subsequent to that of Ariel, we find that this anomalous turn-of-the-month behavior still arises in the cash market, although it may have been moved ahead in time. Thus, the anomalous behavior does not arise because of an ignorance of the speculative opportunity. This means that cash market frictions are sufficiently large to make the speculative behavior unrewarding. The fact that the Value Line anomaly is more pronounced that the S&P anomaly might suggest that it is more difficult to speculate in the small-capitalized stocks, due to higher bid-ask spreads, for example.

Transactions costs and other frictions on the futures markets are lower and some researchers (e.g., Kleidon and Whaley (1992)) have suggested that the superior efficiency of order execution in futures trading mechanisms can allow decoupling between the futures and cash markets. This suggests the hypothesis that the turn-of-the-month anomaly will be less pronounced in the futures market than in the cash market. To the extent that the more-pronounced Value Line anomaly is a result of greater frictions in the small-capitalized cash market, one might further hypothesize that any attenuation of the anomaly in the futures market will be more noticeable with the Value Line futures than the S&P futures. Neither of these hypotheses seem to hold. An examination of Figure 1 and Table 1 shows that the futures market anomalies are just as pronounced as the cash market anomalies. The Value Line futures anomaly is more pronounced than the S&P futures anomaly, with no evidence of attenuation.

One might also hypothesize that the futures market anomalies would anticipate the cash market anomalies because the futures market has lower frictions and because of delays in the settlement process. Indeed, the futures market anomalies are larger on day -4 and smaller on day -1. However, the futures market anomaly is also larger on day $+1$, suggesting that the futures market has not fully anticipated the profits in the cash market.

The effects of seasonality by month and period of the month are investigated in Table 2. Average daily logarithmic returns were computed during the turn-of-the-month (trading days -1 to $+4$), called TOM, the first half of the month (trading days -1 to $+9$), called FH, and the rest of the month (trading days $+10$ to -2), called ROM. The average returns and t-values for the hypothesis of positive returns and returns above average are given by month, and for all months with and without January, for the cash and futures data.

There is a strong monthly seasonality effect shown in the mean returns during the turn-of-the-month, the first half of the month, and rest of the month shown in Table 2. As expected, January has very high small-stock

Table 1: Average Daily Returns (Log Values) in the Cash and Futures
Markets for Small and Large-Capitalized Stocks by Trading Day of the Month,
along with t-values for the Hypothesis that the Day's Return Differs from the
Mean Return, May 1982–April 1992. In this and Succeeding Tables, t-values
Significant at the 5% Level (Two-tailed) are in Bold Type.

Trading Day	Average Daily Return (%)		Value Line t-value	S&P 500 t-value
	Value Line	S&P 500		
(a) Cash Market Data				
−9	−0.0813	0.0992	−1.33	0.43
−8	0.1101	0.1025	0.63	0.35
−7	−0.1281	−0.0527	**−2.40**	−1.28
−6	0.0470	0.0652	−0.03	0.06
−5	−0.1163	−0.1239	−1.61	−1.68
−4	0.0077	0.1246	−0.64	0.83
−3	0.0333	0.0548	−0.24	−0.08
−2	0.0655	0.0838	0.24	0.27
−1	0.3218	0.2361	**3.74**	**2.03**
1	0.1342	0.1309	1.34	0.79
2	0.2769	0.2637	**3.52**	**2.74**
3	0.1554	0.0852	1.46	0.27
4	0.0303	−0.0123	−0.25	−0.79
5	−0.0862	−0.1181	−1.84	−1.95
6	0.0174	0.0124	−0.51	−0.61
7	0.0463	0.0716	−0.04	0.13
8	0.0148	0.0003	−0.51	−0.69
9	0.0320	0.0647	−0.25	0.05
Average −9 to 9	0.0489	0.0604		
(b) Futures Data				
−9	0.1230	0.0973	0.68	0.38
−8	0.0465	0.1959	−0.04	0.76
−7	−0.2346	−0.0932	**−2.68**	−1.37
−6	0.1176	0.0317	0.65	−0.28
−5	−0.2533	−0.0779	**−2.13**	−1.12
−4	0.1329	0.1757	0.95	1.31
−3	0.0553	0.0315	0.03	−0.31
−2	0.0695	0.0184	0.19	−0.39
−1	0.2082	0.1285	1.82	0.72
1	0.3314	0.2122	**2.72**	1.54
2	0.2567	0.2541	**2.11**	**2.18**
3	0.0572	0.0467	0.04	−0.10
4	−0.0217	0.0000	−0.72	−0.53
5	−0.1087	−0.1276	−1.44	−1.61
6	0.0637	0.0354	0.12	−0.25
7	0.0822	0.0410	0.29	−0.16
8	0.0083	−0.0163	−0.47	−0.72
9	0.0190	0.0759	−0.32	0.18
Average −9 to 9	0.05295	0.0572		

Table 2: Average Daily Returns and *t*-values for the Hypothesis that Returns are Greater than Zero and the Mean Return, Respectively, in the Cash and Futures Markets for Small and Large Capital Stocks During the Turn of the Month, First Half of the Month, and Rest of the Month, May 1992–April 1992.

	Average Daily Returns (%)				t-values (Ho: return = 0)				t-values (Ho: ret diff = 0)			
	TOM −1 to 4	FH −1 to 9	ROM 10 to −2	All Days −1 to −1	TOM −1 to 4	FH −1 to 9	ROM 10 to −2	All Days −1 to −1	TOM −1 to 4	FH −1 to 9	ROM 10 to −2	All Days −1 to −1
(a) Cash Market Data												
Value Line Index									Avg Daily VL Index Ret = 0.0388			
January	0.5483	0.2547	0.1087	0.1769	**4.40**	**2.61**	1.42	**2.89**	**4.08**	**2.21**	0.91	**2.26**
February	0.3839	0.2479	0.1030	0.1784	**4.00**	**3.61**	1.56	**3.72**	3.59	**3.04**	0.97	**2.91**
March	0.3229	0.1712	0.0099	0.0842	3.99	2.94	0.18	2.11	3.51	2.28	−0.53	1.14
April	0.0054	0.0161	0.0051	0.0104	0.06	0.22	0.09	0.22	−0.36	−0.31	−0.57	−0.61
May	0.1464	0.1147	−0.0084	0.0494	**1.96**	**2.16**	−0.14	1.20	1.44	1.43	−0.77	0.26
June	0.2203	0.0709	0.0006	0.0336	**2.63**	1.18	0.01	0.75	2.16	0.53	−0.58	−0.12
July	0.0278	0.0416	−0.0927	−0.0291	0.31	0.68	−1.59	−0.69	−0.12	0.05	**−2.26**	−1.60
August	−0.0212	0.0036	0.0864	0.0493	−0.15	0.04	1.07	0.81	−0.42	−0.38	0.59	0.17
September	0.0495	−0.0804	−0.0801	0.0802	0.53	−1.04	−1.40	−1.68	0.11	−1.54	**−2.07**	**−2.49**
October	0.1272	0.0422	−0.3121	−0.1518	1.34	0.55	−1.61	−1.35	0.93	0.04	−1.81	−1.70
November	0.3421	0.2321	−0.0711	0.0768	**2.33**	**2.46**	−1.07	1.32	**2.06**	**2.05**	−1.65	0.65
December	0.0521	0.0170	0.1410	0.0819	0.39	0.22	1.70	1.44	0.10	−0.28	1.23	0.76
All Months	0.1837	0.0943	−0.0112	0.0388	**5.84**	**4.30**	−0.44	**2.27**	**4.61**	**2.53**	−1.95	0.00
All except Jan	0.1506	0.0797	−0.0225	0.0261	**4.70**	**3.59**	−0.83	1.47	**3.49**	1.84	**−2.26**	−0.72

(Continued)

Table 2:   (*Continued*)

	Average Daily Returns (%)				t-values (Ho: return = 0)				t-values (Ho: ret diff = 0)			
	TOM -1 to 4	FH -1 to 9	ROM 10 to -2	All Days -1 to -1	TOM -1 to 4	FH -1 to 9	ROM 10 to -2	All Days -1 to -1	TOM -1 to 4	FH -1 to 9	ROM 10 to -2	All Days -1 to -1
S&P 500 Index									Avg Daily S&P Index Ret = 0.0501			
January	0.2730	0.0716	0.1371	0.1065	1.75	0.58	1.46	1.40	1.43	0.17	0.93	0.74
February	0.2116	0.1471	0.0909	0.1202	1.79	1.68	1.01	1.93	1.36	1.11	0.46	1.12
March	0.2220	0.0987	0.0297	0.0615	**2.01**	1.28	0.41	1.16	1.56	0.63	-0.28	0.22
April	0.0308	0.0432	0.0680	0.0560	0.24	0.42	0.82	0.86	-0.15	-0.07	0.22	0.09
May	0.1393	0.0872	0.0377	0.0609	1.35	1.15	0.48	1.11	0.86	0.49	-0.16	0.20
June	0.2074	0.0579	0.0521	0.0548	1.70	0.67	0.65	0.94	1.29	0.09	0.03	0.08
July	-0.0456	0.0348	-0.0332	-0.0009	-0.37	0.44	-0.44	-0.02	-0.78	-0.19	-1.11	-0.94
August	0.0234	0.0540	0.1129	0.0865	0.15	0.54	1.11	1.21	-0.17	0.04	0.62	0.51
September	0.0138	-0.0961	-0.0443	-0.0698	0.10	-0.97	-0.56	-1.11	-0.26	-1.48	-1.19	-1.90
October	0.2029	0.1256	-0.1763	-0.0397	1.43	1.24	-0.69	-0.27	1.08	0.74	-0.89	-0.61
November	0.2776	0.1500	-0.0718	0.0364	1.89	1.38	-0.78	0.51	1.55	0.92	-1.33	-0.19
December	0.1323	0.1073	0.1531	0.1313	0.78	1.05	1.66	1.91	0.48	0.56	1.11	1.18
All Months	0.1407	0.0734	0.0290	0.0501	**3.59**	**2.65**	0.88	**2.30**	**2.31**	0.84	-0.64	0.00
All except Jan	0.1287	0.0736	0.0188	0.0449	**3.19**	**2.62**	0.54	1.98	1.95	0.84	-0.89	-0.23

(*Continued*)

Table 2: (Continued)

	Average Daily Returns (%)				t-values (Ho: return = 0)				t-values (Ho: ret diff = 0)			
	TOM −1 to 4	FH −1 to 9	ROM 10 to −2	All Days −1 to −1	TOM −1 to 4	FH −1 to 9	ROM 10 to −2	All Days −1 to −1	TOM −1 to 4	FH −1 to 9	ROM 10 to −2	All Days −1 to −1
(b) Futures Market Data												
Value Line Index									Avg Daily VL Index Ret = 0.0321			
January	0.5367	0.1926	0.1327	0.1606	**3.43**	1.32	1.27	1.82	**3.22**	1.10	0.96	1.46
February	0.3537	0.2115	0.0859	0.1510	**2.38**	**2.02**	0.93	**2.15**	**2.17**	1.72	0.58	1.70
March	0.2795	0.1467	−0.0165	0.0584	**2.25**	1.84	−0.21	1.05	1.99	1.44	−0.63	0.47
April	0.0419	0.0186	−0.0247	−0.0039	0.26	0.15	−0.25	−0.05	0.06	−0.11	−0.58	−0.45
May	0.1362	0.1228	−0.0043	0.0551	1.36	1.62	−0.05	0.99	1.04	1.20	−0.45	0.41
June	0.1601	0.0709	−0.0067	0.0298	1.29	0.80	−0.07	0.47	1.03	0.44	−0.42	−0.04
July	0.0204	0.0715	−0.1144	−0.0267	0.13	0.68	−1.36	−0.40	−0.07	0.38	−1.74	−0.88
August	−0.1085	−0.0306	0.0844	0.0329	−0.52	−0.24	0.75	0.39	−0.67	−0.50	0.47	0.01
September	−0.0024	−0.0974	−0.0996	−0.0985	−0.02	−0.90	−1.06	−1.38	−0.24	−1.19	−1.41	−1.83
October	0.1516	0.0853	−0.3130	−0.1336	0.94	0.74	−1.12	−0.82	0.74	0.46	−1.24	−1.02
November	0.2528	0.2404	−0.1097	0.0602	1.36	**1.99**	−1.08	0.76	1.19	1.72	−1.40	0.35
December	0.1488	0.0318	0.1833	0.1115	1.02	0.35	1.80	1.63	0.80	0.00	1.48	1.16
All Months	0.1642	0.0887	−0.0186	0.0321	**3.69**	**2.82**	−0.51	1.32	**2.97**	1.80	−1.39	0.00
All except Jan	0.1304	0.0792	−0.0328	0.0202	**2.82**	**2.50**	−0.85	0.80	**2.13**	1.49	−1.68	−0.47

(Continued)

Table 2: (Continued)

	Average Daily Returns (%)				t-values (Ho: return = 0)				t-values (Ho: ret. diff = 0)			
	TOM −1 to 4	FH −1 to 9	ROM 10 to −2	All Days −1 to −1	TOM −1 to 4	FH −1 to 9	ROM 10 to −2	All Days −1 to −1	TOM −1 to 4	FH −1 to 9	ROM 10 to −2	All Days −1 to −1
									Avg Daily S&P Index Ret = 0.0360			
S&P 500 Index												
January	0.2437	0.0485	0.1186	0.0859	1.38	0.33	1.13	0.98	1.18	0.09	0.79	0.57
February	0.2042	0.1396	0.0738	0.1079	1.47	1.38	0.77	1.55	1.21	1.03	0.39	1.03
March	0.1839	0.0743	−0.0060	0.0308	1.62	0.90	−0.07	0.53	1.30	0.47	−0.52	−0.09
April	0.0111	0.0170	0.0480	0.0331	0.07	0.14	0.52	0.44	−0.16	−0.15	0.13	−0.04
May	0.1235	0.0871	0.0254	0.0542	1.15	1.07	0.30	0.91	0.81	0.63	−0.12	0.31
June	0.1585	0.0484	0.0493	0.0489	1.11	0.49	0.52	0.72	0.86	0.12	0.14	0.19
July	−0.0053	0.0566	−0.0649	−0.0073	−0.03	0.59	−0.79	−0.12	−0.26	0.21	−1.23	−0.69
August	−0.0243	0.0383	0.0987	0.0716	−0.13	0.33	0.89	0.89	−0.32	0.02	0.57	0.44
September	−0.0163	−0.1185	−0.0529	−0.0852	−0.10	−1.03	−0.56	−1.15	−0.33	−1.34	−0.95	−1.64
October	0.1708	0.1284	−0.1972	−0.0505	1.02	1.07	−0.55	−0.25	0.80	0.77	−0.65	−0.42
November	0.2680	0.1499	−0.1122	0.0150	1.49	1.18	−1.07	0.18	1.29	0.90	−1.41	−0.25
December	0.2097	0.1094	0.1494	0.1303	1.22	1.05	1.45	1.78	1.01	0.70	1.10	1.29
All Months	0.1273	0.0649	0.0100	0.0360	**2.83**	**2.03**	0.24	1.34	**2.03**	0.91	−0.62	0.00
All except Jan	0.1167	0.0664	−0.0002	0.0314	**2.51**	**2.06**	0.00	1.11	1.74	0.94	−0.80	−0.16

returns during TOM. The results for 1982–1992 are consistent with Roll's (1983) results for 1963–1978 that the small stocks greatly outperformed the large-capitalized stocks on trading days −1 to +4 in January.

In addition, the t-statistics indicate higher than average returns for the Value Line Cash Index during TOM and the FH during February, March, June, and November. The returns are also high in these months for the S&P 500, but the t's are not significant. July and September and the category "all months except January" also have Value Line cash returns that are significantly below the average returns during the second half of the month.

Also, all the months except January, February, August, and December have negative or negligible ROMs. The S&P 500 Index is similar but less pronounced. The data suggest that the seasonality in small stocks is much greater than in large stocks.

The returns during TOM and ROM are significantly higher than average for the small stocks. Moreover, the small stocks have significantly lower than average returns during ROM. The cash effect was stronger during these periods for the small stock Value Line Index in the cash market because there was some anticipation in the futures market. The large-capitalized S&P 500 Index results are broadly similar. However, the t-values are lower and not significant at the 5% level during FH and ROM.

Although the futures market results in Table 2 are similar to those in the cash market, the futures markets have fewer significant t-values. This is probably due to the greater ease with which speculative trading can take place to anticipate and mitigate the effect at the turn-of-the-month. The speculative anticipation, while not statistically significant, has the effect of reducing the TOM and FH returns in the futures markets and therefore, the number of significant t-values.

Table 3 shows similar results using regression models with dummy variables for the TOM, second week (SW), and ROM periods. It is not possible to run a regression with all three subperiods because they are linearly dependent. Hence, separate regressions using each period as a dummy $(0, 1)$ variable were run to isolate the different effects.

The TOM variable is always highly significant for the small-capitalized stocks and either significant or nearly significant for the large-capitalized stocks. The second week and the rest of the month have insignificant returns when TOM and the mean return are accounted for. When TOM is excluded, then both the second week of the month and the rest of the month have returns significantly below the mean return.

Table 3: Regression Results for Turn-of-the-Month Effects for Cash and Futures Markets.

	Intercept	TOM	SW	ROM
Value Line				
Cash	−0.000062331	0.001899		
	(−0.320)	(4.756)		
Futures	−0.00008773	0.00173		
	(−0.315)	(3.025)		
Cash	−0.000112	0.00195	0.000161	
	(−0.480)	(4.639)	(0.383)	
Futures	−0.0000186	0.001828	0.000317	
	(−0.555)	(3.039)	(0.526)	
Cash	0.000048697	0.001788		−0.000161
	(0.140)	(3.625)		(−0.383)
Futures	0.000131	0.00070706		0.00060164
	(0.262)	(2.138)		(−0.526)
Cash	0.001837		−0.001788	−0.00195
	(0.527)		(−3.625)	(−4.639)
Futures	0.001642		−0.001511	−0.001828
	(3.285)		(−2.138)	(−3.039)
S&P 500				
Cash	0.000219	0.001188		
	(0.879)	(2.325)		
Futures	0.000076605	0.001196		
	(0.249)	(1.894)		
Cash	0.00029	0.001117	−0.000228	
	(0.966)	(2.078)	(−0.424)	
Futures	0.000099614	0.001173	−0.000074205	
	(0.269)	(1.766)	(−0.112)	
Cash	0.000061797	0.001345		0.000228
	(0.138)	(2.131)		(0.424)
Futures	0.000025409	0.001247		0.000074205
	(0.046)	(1.599)		(0.112)
Cash	0.001407		−0.001345	−0.001117
	(3.152)		(−2.131)	(−2.078)
Futures	0.001273		−0.001247	−0.001173
	(3.285)		(−1.599)	(−1.766)

Table 4 shows the growth of one dollar over the 10 years of our sample in the cash and futures market for small and large-capitalized stocks during the turn, first half, and rest of the month as well as during all days by month. These values show the compounded effects of monthly as well as

Table 4:   Growth of $1 Investment for Small and Large Capitalized Stocks in Various Periods, May 1982–April 1992.

	Growth of $1 Investment					Growth of $1 Investment			
Cash Market	TOM −1 to 4	FH −1 to 9	ROM 10 to −2	All Days −1 to −1	Futures	TOM −1 to 4	FH −1 to 9	ROM 10 to −2	All Days −1 to −1
Value Line Cash Market					Value Line Futures				
January	1.31539	1.29004	1.13193	1.46024	January	1.30778	1.21245	1.16484	1.41232
February	1.21160	1.28128	1.09938	1.40861	February	1.19347	1.23555	1.08313	1.33826
March	1.17520	1.18676	1.01164	1.20057	March	1.15000	1.15802	0.98069	1.13566
April	1.00272	1.01623	1.00556	1.02187	April	1.02119	1.01872	0.97369	0.99192
May	1.07595	1.12155	0.99050	1.11089	May	1.07050	1.13062	0.99508	1.12506
June	1.11645	1.07345	1.00064	1.07413	June	1.08334	1.07348	0.99250	1.06542
July	1.01399	1.04248	0.90220	0.94053	July	1.01023	1.07409	0.87976	0.94495
August	0.98944	1.00359	1.11211	1.11610	August	0.94718	0.96987	1.10945	1.07602
September	1.02506	0.92279	0.92078	0.84969	September	0.99882	0.90723	0.90159	0.81795
October	1.06565	1.04312	0.68550	0.71505	October	1.07876	1.08907	0.68255	0.74335
November	1.18652	1.26119	0.92802	1.17041	November	1.13476	1.27172	0.89022	1.13211
December	1.02641	1.01711	1.16779	1.18778	December	1.07725	1.03228	1.22568	1.26524
All months	3.01108	3.10035	0.86112	2.66979	All months	2.67908	2.89817	0.77980	2.26000
All except Jan	2.28912	2.40330	0.76076	1.82832	All except Jan	2.04856	2.39034	0.66945	1.60020

(Continued)

Table 4: (Continued)

S&P 500 Cash Market

Cash Market	Growth of $1 Investment			
	TOM −1 to 4	FH −1 to 9	ROM 10 to −2	All Days −1 to −1
January	1.14627	1.07421	1.16913	1.25589
February	1.11162	1.15848	1.08725	1.25956
March	1.11741	1.10378	1.03535	1.14280
April	1.01551	1.04413	1.07551	1.12298
May	1.07212	1.09108	1.04347	1.13851
June	1.10926	1.05961	1.06061	1.12383
July	0.97746	1.03546	0.96383	0.99801
August	1.01177	1.05548	1.14891	1.21266
September	1.00693	0.90834	0.95544	0.86786
October	1.10680	1.13381	0.80792	0.91603
November	1.14888	1.16187	0.92741	1.07753
December	1.06837	1.11331	1.18344	1.31753
All months	2.32626	2.41413	1.46965	3.54792
All except Jan	2.02942	2.24736	1.25705	2.82503

S&P 500 Futures

Futures	Growth of $1 Investment			
	TOM −1 to 4	FH −1 to 9	ROM 10 to −2	All Days −1 to −1
January	1.12958	1.04971	1.14479	1.20169
February	1.10752	1.14983	1.07107	1.23154
March	1.09629	1.07711	0.99291	1.06948
April	1.00554	1.01716	1.05318	1.07125
May	1.06369	1.09100	1.02936	1.12303
June	1.08250	1.04955	1.05734	1.10973
July	0.99736	1.05826	0.93050	0.98471
August	0.98791	1.03906	1.12911	1.17321
September	0.99191	0.88827	0.94693	0.84112
October	1.08913	1.13696	0.78618	0.89386
November	1.14337	1.16170	0.88791	1.03148
December	1.11057	1.11560	1.17858	1.31482
All months	2.14628	2.17926	1.14223	2.48922
All months Jan	1.90007	2.07606	0.99777	2.07143

intramonth seasonality during the TOM, FH, and ROM subperiods and the futures anticipation.

In interpreting the results in Table 4, one must consider the number of trading days in each period: TOM had 5, FH had 10, ROM had about 10–12, and the whole month had about 20–22. The highest dollar returns in the cash and futures market were during the short time at the turn-of-the-month. The January small stock effect is seen in the high Value Line futures returns in the second half of December (partial anticipation) and the turn-of-the-month for January. There were extremely low returns in the second half of September and October in the cash and futures markets.

A normality test was made and the results are shown in Table 5. In the cash market the normality of the first-half price changes cannot be rejected, but the returns were non-normal during the turn-of-the-month and the rest of the month. The high returns during TOM and low returns during ROM in the cash market apparently lead to the rejection of normality because of their skewness. The smoothing effect of the futures anticipation yields distributions that are not skewed enough to reject the normality hypothesis.

The distributions of returns in the futures market in the three parts of the month are shown in Figure 2. The results show that there are differences in the mean return during the turn, first half, and rest of the month that affect the total returns during these periods as discussed above. As Ariel (1987) found for the 1963–1981 cash data, the higher returns during

Table 5:   Results of Normality Tests.

	P-values*		
	TOM	FH	ROM
Value Line			
Futures	0.45	0.08	0.00
Cash Market	0.00	0.12	0.00
S&P 500			
Futures	0.79	0.29	0.00
Cash Market	0.01	0.39	0.00

*The P-value is the probability of rejecting the null hypothesis that the input data values are a random sample from a normal distribution when true. The test used calculates the Shapiro-Wilks W statistic, with small values of W leading to rejection of the null hypothesis.

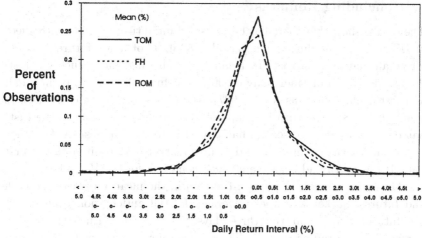

(a) Small Capitalized Stocks (Value Line)

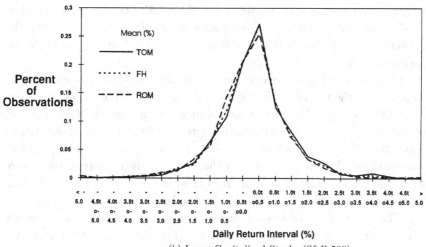

(b) Large-Capitalized Stocks (S&P 500)

Figure 2:   Relative Frequency Return Distribution in the Futures Markets for Small and Large-Capitalized Stocks, May 1982–April 1992.

TOM and ROM were caused by a slight shifting of the return distribution and not by a few outliers. These graphs are for the entire period and aggregate the stronger effects of individual months. The cash distributions, though slightly more skewed to the right, are similar and show the same effects.

3. Concluding Remarks

The results show that there has been a substantial turn-of-the-month effect in US stock prices during the period 1982–1992 of index futures trading for small and large stocks. To avoid data snooping biases such as those discussed by Lo and MacKinlay (1990), we defined the turn to be first half and rest of the month as Ariel (1987) did in his study of the cash markets from 1963–1981. The turn is composed of trading days −1 to 4, the first-half days −1 to +9, and second-half days +10 to −2. The results show that the mean returns in the cash and futures market were positive in the first half of the month and negative in the second half for the Value Line.

Moreover, during the turn-of-the-month, the mean return in the cash and futures market was above average. Partial anticipation occurred in the futures market on the three days prior to the turn-of-the-month, particularly on trading day −4. This anticipation was larger for the large-capitalized S&P 500 Index futures than for the small-capitalized Value Line futures. Moreover, it carries over to the S&P cash market, even though is does not appear in the Value Line cash market. This is consistent with the existence of considerable index arbitrage in the S&P 500 and virtually no such arbitrage in the Value Line.

Monthly seasonality effects were strong, with high returns occurring in January and the rest of the first quarter during the turn of the month. May, June, October, and November also had high returns during TOM. The rest of the month generally had negative returns, with the lowest returns in September, October and November. The media's widely discussed negative returns in October are supported by the data, but the negative returns were all in the ROM, while the TOM and FH were positive. The shift in mean return was larger for the small than for the large-capitalized stocks.

The cumulative effects of investment during various time periods magnify the effects. The results indicate that the total return over this 10-year period was mostly received during the turn-of-the-month in the cash and futures markets for small and large-capitalized stocks. There were small gains during the rest of the month for the large stocks and losses for the small stocks. These gains for the large stocks were essentially a result of the anticipation of the turn-of-the-month cash gains in the futures market on the previous three days.

The return distributions during the three parts of the month show that the larger returns at the beginning of the month and lower returns the second half of the month were not due to several large outliers but were instead due to a shift in the mean return and a skewness of the distribution.

References

Ariel, R. A. (1987). A monthly effect in stock returns. *Journal of Financial Economics*, 18, 161–174.

Ariel, R. A. (1990). High stock returns before holidays: Existence and evidence on possible causes. *Journal of Finance*, 45, 1611–1626.

Banz, R. (1981). The relationship between return and market value of common stock. *Journal of Financial Economics*, 9, 3–18.

Brown, P., A. W. Kleidon and T. A. Marsh. (1983). New evidence on the nature of size-related anomalies in stock prices. *Journal of Financial Economics*, 12, 33–56.

Cadsby, C. B. and M. Ratner (1991). Turn-of-Month and Pre-Holiday Effects on Stock Returns: Some International Evidence. Mimeo, University of Guelph.

Cadsby, C. B. (1992). The CAPM and the calendar: Empirical anomalies and the risk-return relationship. *Management Science*, November.

Fosback, N. (1976). *Stock Market Logic*. The Institute for Economic Research, Fort Lauderdale, FL.

French, K. R. (1980). Stock returns and the weekend effect. *Journal of Financial Economics*, 8, 55–70.

Gibbons, M. R. and P. Hess (1981). Day of the week effects in assets returns. *Journal of Business*, 54, 579–596.

Gultekin, M. N. and N. B. Gultekin (1983). Stock market seasonality: International evidence. *Journal of Financial Economics*, 12, 469–482.

Harris, L. (1986). A transaction data study of weekly and intradaily patterns in stock returns. *Journal of Financial Economics*, 16, 99–117.

Hawawini, G. (1991). Stock market anomalies and the pricing of equity on the Tokyo stock exchange. In William T. Ziemba, Warren Bailey and Yasushi Hamao (eds.), *Japanese Financial Market Research*, Amsterdam: North-Holland.

Hawawini, G. and D. Keim (1993). On the predictability of common stock returns: World-wide evidence. In Robert Jarrow, V. Maksimovic and William T. Ziemba (eds.), *Finance*, Amsterdam: North-Holland.

Hirsch, Y. (1986). *Don't Sell Stocks on Monday*. New York: Penguin.

Jacobs, B. I. and K. N. Levy (1988). Calendar anomalies: Abnormal returns at calendar turning points. *Financial Analysts Journal*, 44, 28–39.

Jaffe, J., D. B. Keim and R. Westerfield (1989). Earnings yields, market values and stock returns. *Journal of Finance*, 44, 135–148.

Jaffe, J. and R. Westerfield (1985a). The week-end effect in common stock returns: The international evidence. *Journal of Finance*, 40, 432–454.

Jaffe, J. and R. Westerfield (1985b). Patterns in Japanese common stock returns: Day of the week and turn of the year effects. *Journal of Financial and Quantitative Analysis*, 20, 261–272.

Jaffe, J. and R. Westerfield (1989). Is there a monthly effect in stock market returns? Evidence from foreign countries. *Journal of Banking and Finance*, 13, 237–244.

Kato, K., S. L. Schwartz and W. T. Ziemba (1989). Day of the Week Effects in Japanese Stocks. In E. J. Elton and M. J. Gruber (eds.), *Japanese Capital Markets*. New York: Harper and Row.

Keim, D. B. (1983). Size related anomalies and stock return seasonality: Further empirical evidence. *Journal of Financial Economics*, 12, 13–32.

Keim, D. B. (1989). Trading patterns, bid-ask spreads, and estimated security returns: The case of common stocks at calendar turning points. *Journal of Financial Economics*, 25, 75–98.

Kleidon, A. W. and R. E. Whaley (1992). One market? Stocks, futures, and options during October 1987, *Journal of Finance*, 47(3), 851–877.

Lakonishok, J. and S. Smidt (1988). Are seasonal anomalies real? A ninety-year perspective. *Review of Financial Studies*, 1, 403–425.

Lakonishok, J. and E. Maberly (1990). The weekend effect: Trading patterns of individual and institutional investors. *Journal of Finance*, 45: 231–243.

Lo, A. W. and A. C. MacKinlay (1990). Data-snooping biases in tests of financial asset pricing models, *Review of Financial Studies*, 3: 431–467.

Merrill, A. A. (1966). Behavior of prices on wall street. *Journal of Finance*.

Ogden, J. P. (1990). Turn-of-month evaluations of liquid profits and stock returns: A common explanation for the monthly and january effects. *Journal of Finance*, 45, 1259–1272.

Penman, S. H. (1987). The distribution of earnings news over time and seasonalities in aggregate stock returns. *Journal of Financial Economics*, 16.

Pettengill, G. N. (1989). Holiday closings and security returns. *Journal of Financial Research*, 12, 57–67.

Reinganum, M. R. (1981). A misspecification of capital asset pricing: Empirical anomalies based on earnings yields and market values. *Journal of Financial Economics*, 9, 19–46.

Ritter, J. R. (1988). The buying and selling behavior of individual investors at the turn of the year. *Journal of Finance*, 43, 701–717.

Ritter, J. R. and N. Chopra (1989). Portfolio rebalancing and the turn of the year effect. *Journal of Finance*, 44, 149–166.

Roll, R. (1983). The turn of the year effect and the return premia of small firms. *Journal of Portfolio Management*, 9 (Winter), 18–28.

Rozeff, M. S. and W. R. Kinney, Jr. (1976). Capital market seasonality: The case of stock returns. *Journal of Financial Economics*, 3, 379–402.

Solnik, B. (1990). The distribution of daily stock returns and settlement procedures: The Paris bourse. *Journal of Finance*, 45, 1601–1609.

Thaler, R. H. (1987a). The January turn of the year small firm effect. *Journal of Economic Perspectives*, 1(1), 197–201.

Thaler, R. H. (1987b). Seasonal movements in security prices II: Weekend, holiday, turn-of-the-month, and intraday effects. *Journal of Economic Perspectives*, 1(2), 169–177.

Ziemba, W. T. (1989). Seasonality effects in Japanese futures markets. (eds.) Ghon H. Rhee and Rosita P. Chang. In *Research on Pacific Basin Security Markets*. Amsterdam: North-Holland.

Ziemba, W. T. (1991). Japanese security market regularities: Monthly, turn-of-the-month and year, holiday and golden week effects. *Japan and the World Economy*, 3, 146.

Ziemba, W. T. (1993a). World wide anomalies in security markets. *European Journal of Operational Research*, 74, 198–229.

Ziemba, W. T. (1993b). Why a weekend effect? *Journal of Portfolio Management*, 19(2), 93–99.

Chapter 4

Stock Ownership Decisions in Defined Contribution Pension Plans*

Julian Douglass, Owen Wu, William Ziemba

University of British Columbia

This paper considers the risk of employee pension accounts when there is a large weighting in own company stock. The effect of reduced diversification and job related risk are considered. Mean-variance and scenario-based stochastic programming models are used for the analysis. The stochastic programming formulation allows for fat tailed return distributions. Company stock is only optimal for employees with very low risk aversion or with very high return expectations for company stock. These conclusions are further strengthened when the possibility of job loss associated with poor company stock performance is included in the model. High observed weightings in company stock in DC pension plans are not explained by rational one-period models. Employees are bearing high levels of risk that is not rewarded, and that can lead to disastrous consequences.

Introduction

Enron corporation collapsed in late 2001. The stock price fell 99% to under one dollar. Many employees lost their jobs and much of their pensions. Enron employees lost over a billion dollars in total, some 60% of their 401(k) pensions. Enron's collapse was a stark illustration of the potential consequences of holding one's pension fund largely in one asset, especially when that asset is correlated with one's income.

---

*This paper was presented at European Investment Review conference, London School of Economics, September 2002, and at the University of British Columbia, January 2003. This research was supported by NSERC. Without implicating them, thanks go to Frank Fabozzi and John Mulvey for comments on an earlier version of this paper.

Table 4.1:   Percentage of DC Plan Assets in Company Stock.

Company	Company stock percentage, 2001	Share price performance 2001, %	2002, %	2003, %
Proctor & Gamble (PG)	94.7	3.1	11.3	11.3
Pfizer (PFE)	85.5	−12.5	−22.2	17.8
Coca Cola (KO)	81.5	−21.5	−5.5	18.2
General Electric (GE)	77.4	−15.1	−37.7	30.7
Enron (ENRNQ)	57.7	−99.0	−89.7	−54.8
Texas Instruments (TXN)	75.7	−40.8	−46.2	96.6
McDonald's (MCD)	74.3	−21.5	−38.4	56.8
Ford (F)	57.0	−30.1	−38.9	78.6
Qwest (Q)	53.0	−65.5	−64.6	−13.6
AOL Time Warner (TWX)	52.0	−7.8	−59.2	37.3

(*Sources*: *The Economist*, December 15, 2001, Morningstar.com).

The plight of employees following Enron's spectacular collapse has focused attention on portfolio choices of individual investors. Enron sponsored a defined contribution (DC) pension plan. Under the rules of such plans, individual employees make their own investment decisions. Enron employees had placed themselves in the risky position that cost them so dearly. With large holdings in own company stock, Enron employees accepted excess exposure, relative to the market, to idiosyncratic risk of their employer's stock. Enron is no isolated case.[1] Many DC plans are heavily overweighted in company stock; see Table 4.1. For example, in November 2001, employees at Proctor and Gamble had 94.7% of their 401(k) assets in company shares.

Why would investors choose a large weighting in the stock of the company at which they are employed? The apparent overinvestment is puzzling when considered with respect to portfolio choice decisions predicted by the Markowitz mean-variance model. Employees are taking on greater risk than necessary by concentrating ownership in company stock. This behaviour is rendered even more puzzling when contrasted with results of surveys of investor behaviour. Generally, these studies conclude that a large part of the population does not invest in stocks [Mankiw and Zeldes, 1991]. Most investors take on less risk than is predicted by

---

[1]Leland (2004) discusses the fortunes of two Corning employees. One moved his million dollar plus pension which was mostly in Corning stock to bonds near the 2000 stock market peak. Another, scheduled to retire later, lost virtually all his pension when the stock fell from $113 to about $1 in late 2000 when telecom companies, the customers for Corning's fibre optic cables, stopped placing orders.

a mean-variance model. Not only do employees take on more risk than predicted by mean-variance theory, they take on more risk than typical individual investors.

The risk associated with holding company stock is great. Three major risk factors limit the weight of company stock in portfolio choice models. First, return properties of own-company stock are often unfavourable when compared to a market index. The volatility of individual stocks is two to three time that of the market. Under the assumptions of the Capital Asset Pricing Model, any excess return of company stock over the market portfolio only compensates for the non-idiosyncratic portion of the stock volatility. Any remaining risk is eliminated by diversification within the market portfolio. Thus, an optimizing investor that is not faced with trading constraints will not hold company stock beyond that included in their optimal market holding. Second, individual stocks can crash. It is not uncommon for companies that enter bankruptcy to lose over 90% of their value in a few months. Small though it is, this "torpedo" risk can significantly decrease the optimal holding of own-company stock. For example, United Airlines (UAL Corp.) stock fell below ten dollars in July 2002, and under one dollar in early December as the company filed for bankruptcy protection. Third, employees' wages are affected by company performance, thereby magnifying the risk of company stock ownership. An employee faces increased risk of lower bonuses, reduced return on stock options and even layoff during periods of poor company performance. The employee can be viewed as being in a long term relationship (employment) with a counterparty who may default (by terminating employment). Loss of wealth following termination has two main causes. First, an employee may lose income over some period of time. The magnitude of this loss depends on the outside market for his services and the length of any severance package. Second, termination following bankruptcy is likely to reduce the value of an employee's future income stream. If one assumes that employees remain at an organization because they have no better, higher utility choice in the market, the loss of that job will negatively effect the value of their expected future utility.

Despite the risk of the strategy, it is possible for company stock to be a rational portfolio choice for pension plan investors. DC pension plans are usually structured such that the investor chooses between a small number of investment options. Short selling of assets within DC plans is not permitted. However, hedging outside the plan is possible for some of the assets depending upon the asset mix, although there may well be correlation mismatching. The cost to an employee of acquiring the expertise to hedge properly is usually enough to deter such activity so it is rarely done. Given these constraints, company stock can become a favored option for a less risk averse investor. In addition, employees may have higher expectation for the return of company stock than the market.

We investigate employee investment decisions predicted by rational models of portfolio choice. We postulate a representative investment scenario, and consider portfolio choice under various parameter specifications. We investigate the problem using two models of portfolio choice: the Markowitz mean-variance approach and a scenario based, stochastic programming formulation. The mean-variance approach explores optimal portfolio choice under the assumption of normally distributed asset returns. The stochastic programming approach explores portfolio decisions when the normality assumption is violated, such as when we include a reasonable probability of a disastrous outcome for company stock. We also include job risk as a function of company stock performance. Portfolio choice models include non-observable parameters such as investor risk aversion and return expectations of investors. We consider portfolio choice over a range of parameters.

Our results demonstrate that the short selling constraint is not sufficient to overcome the additional risk associated with owning company stock. High company stock weightings such as those in Table 4.1 can only be explained by some combination of low risk aversion and/or high return expectations for company stock. These results hold with or without including extreme events. The inclusion of labour income risk in the models further reduces the optimal holding in company stock. Meulbroek (2002) calculates the cost to employees of foregone diversification. She compares employee portfolio choices to those of an unconstrained investor. Hence, her estimates are an upper bound on cost, and do not demonstrate that observed overinvestment in company stock is costly. Ramaswamy (2002) calculates a quantitative measure of the cost of choosing a portfolio that deviates from the most efficient (in the mean variance sense) portfolio constructed from assets available to a pension plan investor. The cost is determined by calculating the cost of buying insurance against poor outcomes from underdiversification.

In the next section, we introduce the investment scenario, and consider the investor's problem in the static mean variance framework. Then, we formulate the investment problem as a stochastic program. This model provides for more flexibility in choosing distributions of random variables, and setting policy, legal and other constraints. We then model expected losses to human capital as a function of company stock performance.

Static Portfolio Choice

The portfolio allocation problem for a utility maximizing investor is to select holdings that maximize expected lifetime utility

$$\max_{x \in K} \quad E[U(W)],$$

where K is a convex set. The x are portfolio weights, W is wealth and U is an increasing, concave utility function. To simplify the problem, we assume normally distributed returns, thereby permitting the use of mean-variance utility, $U(W) = E(W) - R_A/2 * \text{var}(W)$, where R_A is the investor's Arrow-Pratt risk aversion index. In addition to the wealth constraint, short selling is not permitted, since most DC plans do not permit this activity. The employee's problem is considered in a one period context. Since the time horizon for pension investments is on the order of decades, not allowing for intervening trading is an oversimplification. To validate a one period model, the investor is either assumed to be barred from further trading, or their investment decisions are myopic. Despite its simplicity, the static mean variance framework is commonly used in analysis of portfolio choice. For comparison, we also present optimal solutions for a utility function with the variance penalty replaced by a shortfall penalty. Shortfall is defined as the maximum of zero and the difference between a wealth target and the realized return. The investor's utility is penalized by subtracting the expected mean square shortfall. More elaborate models are often limited in the types of constraints that can be included.[2]

For illustrative purposes a simple investment scenario is parameterized. The investor chooses between four assets: market index, bond index, cash and company stock. The small number of assets is not atypical for DC plan investors. Such plans usually offer a relatively small set of investment choices, including a few stock and bond mutual funds, a money market

---

[2]See Campbell and Viceira (2002) for an extensive theoretical study of the individual investor's portfolio choice problem. For a continuous time approach to the pension investor's problem including liabilities, see Rudolf and Ziemba (2004). Ziemba (2003) discusses the scenario stochastic programming approach to asset liability management with applications to individual and retirement portfolios, insurance company and pension and hedge fund management.

investment and company stock. Each asset is given typical return and volatility parameters. Let vector and matrix indices 1 to 4 correspond to a market index, bond, cash, and company stock, respectively. The parameters of our base model are

$$\bar{R} = \begin{bmatrix} 1.10 & 1.05 & 1.00 & 1.125 \end{bmatrix} \tag{4.1}$$

$$\sigma = \begin{bmatrix} 0.20 & 0.04 & 0.01 & 0.50 \end{bmatrix} \tag{4.2}$$

$$\rho = \begin{bmatrix} 1.000 & 0.750 & 0.058 & 0.500 \\ 0.750 & 1.000 & 0.250 & 0.550 \\ 0.058 & 0.250 & 1.000 & 0.029 \\ 0.500 & 0.550 & 0.029 & 1.000 \end{bmatrix} \tag{4.3}$$

where $\bar{R}$, σ and ρ are asset mean returns, volatilities and correlations. Returns for other assets are relative to cash. Values used are based on *ex − post* calculations of mean returns, volatilities and correlations of monthly data series obtained from Datastream. We used seventeen years of data (1985 to 2002) for the U.S. The coefficients in (4.1)–(4.3) are similar to historical values for Dow stocks, the S&P 500 index which is commonly used as a proxy for the market, and two bond indices: Lehman Brothers U.S. aggregate and U.S. Long Bond.

This simple model is intended to illustrate the problems of own company stock ownership in individual pension portfolios. The assumption of a general bond index with 75% correlation with the stock index represents typical average behavior. The models here are static one-period analyses. In multi-period models, one might include future scenarios that yield negative correlation of stocks and bonds in certain periods, such as we had in 2000–2002 in the US. Also inflation linked bonds are a variable asset class to include in such models since future liabilities are a direct function of inflation. Models such as those in Geyer *et al.* (2003) and Ziemba (2003) include these features. These more complex models would only give further support to our conclusion that many individuals place too much confidence in their own company. Just ask them about the probability that the company will have a problem.

The stock price volatility is set to two and a half times that of the market, a level that is fairly high for large cap stocks but not atypical for mid-size companies (Mitchell and Utkus, 2002). The model parameters are also generally consistent with those measured from long run, multi-decade data in the literature (Dimson, Marsh and Staunton, 2002, Siegel, 2002, Constantinides, 2002). The return properties for company stock are chosen to satisfy the Capital Asset Pricing Model (CAPM),

$$r_w - r_f = \frac{\rho_{wM}\sigma_w}{\sigma_M}(r_M - r_f) \qquad (4.4)$$

where r_w, r_M and r_f are returns on own-company stock, market and risk-free rate, σ_w and σ_M are volatilities of own-company stock and market, and ρ_{wM} is correlation of returns of own-company stock with the market.

To specify a risk aversion parameter for the base case scenario, we assume that, in aggregate, investment advisors provide customers with portfolio recommendations that satisfy their needs. Professional investment advice often contradicts recommendations of economic models of portfolio choice. However, progress is being made towards reconciling practice and economic theory (Campbell and Viceira, 2002). We take a calibration approach to choosing k to reconcile portfolio weights based on our simplified model with typical investment advice. We assume an investor who is best off with a portfolio mix of 40% in bonds and 60% in the stock market index. The optimal portfolio of stocks, bonds and cash are plotted as a function of risk aversion parameter, R_A, in Figure 4.1a. The optimal holding of stock reaches 60% when R_A is 8. The remaining 40% is divided between bonds and cash. Thus, R_A for the base case is 8.

The optimal portfolio has no company stock holdings. In a CAPM economy, this is as one would expect, since the excess return of the stock is insufficient to compensate for the undiversifiable portion of the stock risk. With no trading constraints, company stock will never be held in an employee portfolio. However, for investor's faced with trading constraints, such as the inability to short sell, company stock can appear as an optimal choice. For example, company stock appears as an optimal portfolio choice if investor's risk aversion is very low or their expected return for the stock is high. At a risk aversion of five, the short-selling constraint becomes binding and the optimal portfolio begins to shift to the riskier stock investment (Figure 4.1b). However, to obtain company stock holdings above 50%, as observed in Table 4.1, requires a risk aversion parameter below 0.5. Alternatively, company stock holding of 50% is obtained if the employee is presumed to have an expected return for company stock over 50% (Figure 4.1c).

The expected stock return used for the base case is consistent with unconditional expectations in a CAPM type economy. However, employees of a company might have information that causes them to expect greater return from their company than is reflected by market valuation. Optimal

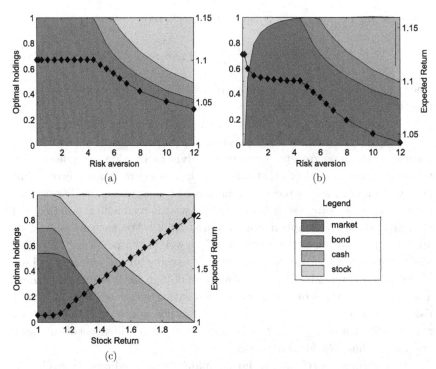

Figure 4.1: Results of the mean-variance model of portfolio choice. Properties of the optimal portfolio are plotted as a function of risk aversion (a-b) and expected return on company stock (c). Shaded regions indicate portfolio weights (left scale). The line represents the expected return on the optimal portfolio (right scale). Diamonds indicate values of independent variable for which calculations were performed. Plots are interpolated between calculated points. Results for the three asset case, with no company stock, are plotted in (a). Results for the four asset case are plotted in (b) and (c).

portfolio choices are plotted as a function of expected return on company stock in Figure 4.1c. Company stock enters the optimal portfolio as return expectations approach 20%; which is double the market index. The expected return must be greater than 50%, that is five times the market index for the optimal allocation to reach 50%. Given the standard deviation parameters in (4.2), this equates to a Sharpe ratio of one for company stock, which is twice the ratio for the market asset and four times that anticipated based on the CAPM.

So far we have assumed that all employee wealth is contained in the company pension plan. This assumption is reasonable considering that many North Americans save little beyond what enters their tax sheltered accounts. However, Figure 4.1b shows what proportion of wealth would have to be held outside the plan in order to support a 50% holding within the plan. An employee with risk aversion of 8 and 50% of their pension plan in company stock would have to have 50% of their retirement savings outside the company plan.

The effect of human capital on investment choice is modeled as an additional risky asset in the employee's portfolio. The value of the asset is determined by assuming an expected starting annual income, i_0, and income growth rate g. The value of the asset is

$$v_{hc} = \left(i_0 * \sum_{j=0}^{t-1} g^j \right)^{1/t} . \tag{4.5}$$

For an employee with twenty years to retirement and starting income equal to twenty percent of wealth (in the retirement plan), the present value of human capital is 1.12 times wealth. For the base case scenario, assume a 20% income volatility and 80% correlation between income and return on company stock. Optimal asset choices as a percentage of income versus risk aversion are plotted in Figure 4.2a, and of expected stock return in Figure 4.2b. The parameter choices required to obtain high company

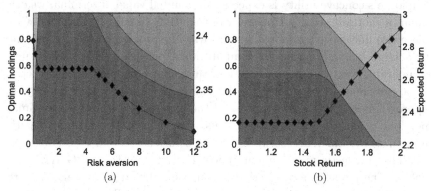

(a)   (b)

Figure 4.2:   Results of the mean-variance model when human capital is modeled as an untradeable asset. Optimal portfolio properties are plotted as a function of risk aversion (a) and expected return on company stock (b). Shaded regions indicate portfolio weights (left scale). The line represents the expected return on the optimal portfolio (right scale). Diamonds indicate values of independent variable for which calculations were performed. Plots are interpolated between calculated points. See Figure 4.1 for the legend.

stock holding become more extreme with inclusion of the untradeable asset. This result confirms findings of Viceira [2001], who concluded, in a continuous-time setting, that investor's with an untradeable asset tended to hold less risky portfolios.

In a mean-variance portfolio setting, high company stock holdings can only be explained by extreme values of risk aversion or expected return for company stock. These values only become more extreme once certain restrictive assumptions required for mean variance analysis are relaxed.

A Stochastic Programming Model for Portfolio Choice

The mean-variance approach relies on distributional assumptions that must be relaxed to study the portfolio choice problem for pension plan investors. The normal distribution does not fit stock returns well in the tails, particularly returns sampled at quarterly or greater frequency. This is especially true for individual stocks. The probability that an individual stock will experience an extreme negative event, such as bankruptcy, is greater than is predicted by a best fitting normal distribution.[3] Human capital can only be included in a mean-variance model as an asset that follows the same distributional assumptions as the financial assets.

As an alternative to mean variance analysis we develop a discrete time stochastic optimization model of the employee's investment problem. The employee's concave utility is expected discounted value of terminal wealth minus a shortfall penalty. Concavity of the utility function is obtained with piecewise linear convex shortfall penalties. The problem is then equivalent to a large linear program for computational purposes. To obtain results comparable with the previous section, the penalty function is constructed to approximate a quadratic in the shortfall. The expected penalty is approximately half the variance when the expected return on the optimal portfolio equals the wealth target. Thus, a judicious choice of target wealth minimizes the difference between the two solutions.

The stochastic programming model is similar to that of Geyer et al. [2003]. The model is a one period formulation. The decision variables are the purchases and sales for N assets in each scenario. The investor chooses

---

[3]Longin (1996), using 105 years of data for the S& P 500 and equivalent predecessors, argues that the distribution of return outliers is best fit with a Fréchet distribution, yielding tails that are much fatter than those of normal or lognormal distributions.

an asset allocation at time 0, and receives investment proceeds at time 1. The problem is

$$\max E \left[\sum_{i=1}^{N} W_{i1} - \lambda c(M) \right], \qquad (4.6)$$

where W_{it} is wealth in asset i at time t. λ is a coefficient of risk aversion, and $c(M)$ is a convex function of wealth shortfall at time 1, M. At time zero, the investor faces N balance constraints and a budget constraint

$$W_{i0} - P_{i0} + S_{i0} = E_i, \qquad i = 1, \dots, N, \qquad (4.7)$$

$$\sum_{i=1}^{N} [P_{i0}(1 + t) - S_{i0}(1 - t)] = 0. \qquad (4.8)$$

The E_i are endowments of each asset. P_i and S_i are purchases and sales respectively of asset i, and t represents transaction costs. The time 1 constraints are

$$W_{i1} = W_{i0}R_i, \qquad i = 1, \dots, N, \qquad (4.9)$$

$$\sum_{i=1}^{N} W_{i1} + M \geq \bar{W}_t, \qquad (4.10)$$

where $\bar{W}_t$ is the threshold for determining wealth shortfall, and the R_i are the realized returns.

Approximation of return distributions is a significant challenge in stochastic programming. The solution of (4.6–4.10) requires a means of approximating the expectations that appear in the objective function. The usual method is to perform a discrete approximation to the integral, by replacing a continuous multivariate distribution with a discrete distribution. For multiperiod problems, the discrete distribution takes the form of a scenario tree. With T time steps and V realizations per node, the number of scenarios increases as V^T on a non-recombinant scenario tree. The number of nodes increases at the same rate. The power law relationship between number of nodes and realizations per node limits feasible problem size, since computational time is proportional to number of nodes. Solution of a stochastic program effectively requires the solution of a linear program at each node. Hence, even for small problems, computational restrictions limit V and T to magnitudes of order 10. Berkalaar *et al.*(2002) list some event trees used in the literature. These previous applications, each involving three to seven assets, have employed scenario trees with at most ten time steps and one hundred scenarios per node. Gondzio and Kouwenberg (2001) develop algorithms that allow them to solve problems with almost five million scenarios. They show that solutions to a seven stage asset allocation problem do not stabilize even with thirteen scenarios per node.

One method of creating scenarios is to generate V realizations of the random variables, and use these as sample points for estimating the expectation. However, less than one hundred realizations is a very crude approximation to a multi-dimensional integral. We employ two methods to partially overcome this issue. First, we employ pseudorandom sequences in place of random deviates. The random generation of scenarios is equivalent to a Monte Carlo integral approximation. Such approximations are improved significantly by the use of pseudorandom sampling (Press *et al.*, 1997). We use a multi-dimensional Sobol sequence to generate scenario returns (see Pennanen and Koivu (2002) for another discussion of this approach). Second, a potentially significant source of bias is eliminated by adjusting scenario returns to reflect model means and variances. Chopra and Ziemba (1993) show that return mean and variance plays the greatest role in determining portfolio allocations, with solutions ten times more sensitive to the mean than the variance with covariances half again as important. In stability tests, we find that thirty scenarios is the minimum required to reach a stable solution.

A serious issue arises when continuous return distributions are approximated with scenario trees is the possibility of arbitrage (Berkalaar *et al.*, 2002; Klaassen, 2002). Arbitrage occurs if a costless asset allocation exists that guarantees zero return in all states and that produces a profit in at least one state, or if a negative cost asset allocation can be found that produces a non-negative return in all future states. Arbitrage occurs almost certainly if the number of assets exceeds the number of return realizations. With just four assets and thirty scenarios per node, arbitrage does not affect our solutions.

Portfolio decisions for the base scenario are plotted in Figure 4.3a. The overall pattern of the solution is similar to that obtained by mean-variance (Figure 4.1b). Since mean-variance penalizes excess returns as well as losses, mean variance solutions for risk aversion equal to R_A, will correspond to mean-shortfall solutions with penalty parameter, $\lambda = 2R_A$. In both cases company stock disappears from the portfolio completely for risk aversions above five.

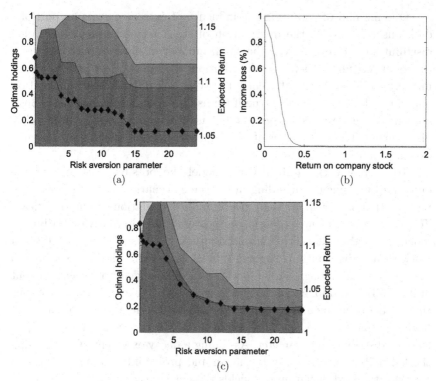

Figure 4.3:   Solution of employee's problem formulated as stochastic program. Figure (a) correponds to the base case discussed in the text. Portfolio properties obtained when human capital returns are modeled as a logit function of wealth are plotted in (c). The logit function used in the model is plotted in (b). In (a) and (c), portfolio weights (shaded regions/right scale) and expected return on the optimal portfolio (line/right scale) are plotted as a function of the risk aversion parameter, λ. The plots are interpolated between λ values indicated by diamonds. In (b), probability of job retention is plotted *versus* company stock return. See Figure 4.1 for the legend.

Portfolio Choice with Extreme Events and Job Loss

A major risk factor for the employee is the possibility of a crash of the company stock held in their pension portfolio. Normal distribution models of stock returns place inadequate weight in distribution tails. But increasing the weight in the tails of the distribution has a disproportionately large negative effect on the expected utility for risk averse investors. For example, for mean-variance investors, the weight given to extreme events increases as the square of the distance of the extreme outcome from the mean.

One method of capturing the influence of extreme events on portfolio decisions is to model the distribution of stock returns using a fat tailed distribution. However, given the small number of discrete outcomes used to model the full multi-variate distribution, the tails of the distribution are unlikely to be sampled sufficiently to reveal any difference in the solution outcomes. This is especially true if we use pseudorandom sequences. Such sequences are designed to give a balanced sampling of the probability distribution. The early terms of the sequence are guaranteed not to sample extreme values.

To overcome this difficulty we model the possibility of an extreme outcome by explicitly including an extreme scenario. Extreme events are returns that occur more than two standard deviations from the mean. To specify the extreme scenario, we postulate an alternative distribution function for the left tail of the distribution. Studies of extreme values of stock return distributions suggest that stock return distributions obey a power law decay. Longin (1996) and Cont (2000) suggest a decay exponent of 2.5 to 3. The implication is that stock returns have finite variance, but that higher order moments do not exist. The t-distribution follows a power law decay path in the tails. The exponent of the power law decay is equal to the t-distribution parameter. Assuming a decay exponent of n and using the t-distribution to specify the mean and probability mass of returns in the two standard deviation tail yields the extreme scenario

$$ r_m^e = \int_{-\infty}^{-2} xt(x; n)/T(-2; n)dx, \qquad p(r_m^e) = T(-2; n), $$

where r_m^e is the extreme stock return, $t(x; n)$ and $T(x; n)$ are probability and cumulative distribution functions for the t-distribution.

Our results demonstrate no significant effect of extreme scenarios on portfolio decisions. When plotted as a function of risk aversion, the portfolio decisions closely resemble the solutions obtained without extreme events (Figure 4.3a). This result confirms conclusions by Chopra and Ziemba (1993) who demonstrate that portfolio choice decisions are most sensitive to first and then second moments of return distributions.

The stochastic programming model examines the effect of job loss on portfolio choice. The probability of job loss increases if the company has serious difficulties. The employee is terminated with scenario dependent probability $\gamma_t(s_t)$. Employee termination does not necessarily have to be accompanied by company default or *vice-versa*. Thus, we do not explicitly model company default. Instead, we assume that probability of termination is a non-linear function of the stock price factors, increasing rapidly as the stock price approaches zero. A logit function models the probability of termination: $\gamma = 1/(1 + a\exp(br))$, where a and b are parameters and r is the stock return. The probability of termination approaches 1 as the return approaches zero. Thus, the parameter, a, takes on a small value. The b sets the rate at which termination probability decays as the return falls.

We consider a scenario in which the employee receives an income, i, equal to ten percent of starting wealth. The expected income in each scenario is calculated as i multiplied by probability of job retention: $1 - logit(r; a, b)$, where r is return on company stock. Parameters, a and b are chosen to yield significant job loss properties once company stock return drops below 0.5, rapidly rising to almost certain job loss in the case of zeros return or bankruptcy (Figure 4.3b). We assume the employee considers loss of labour income as an addition to any shortfall. The portfolio choices are calculated for our returns parameters. The results indicate a shift to a more conservative portfolio when potential loss of labour income is included in the portfolio choice problem (Figure 4.3c). At low levels of risk aversion, company stock holdings are replaced by holdings in the market. At higher risk aversion, the total holdings of bonds and cash are much higher than those observed when potential income loss is not included in the analysis.

Discussion

Various risk factors that dictate against the holding of company stock has led most previous studies to presume that employee investment decisions are the result of behavior that is inconsistent with rational portfolio choice. For example, employers, as plan fiduciaries, may be in a position to influence employee decisions and steer them towards company stock (Mitchell and Utkus, 2002). Employees may interpret the channeling of employer contributions into company stock as an endorsement of that investment (Mitchell and Utkus, 2002). Alternatively, employees may choose company stock simply because it is a listed investment option. Benartzi and Thaler (1999) found that many DC plan investors follow some version of the $1/n$ strategy; i.e. they divide their contributions evenly across plan offerings. In addition, employees may be myopic when evaluating risk of company stock. John Hancock (2001), in a survey of DC plan participants during a period of stock market growth, reported that DC plan participants rated company stock as less risky than an equity mutual fund. Other factors, such as loyalty and peer pressure considerations may also influence employee investment decisions.

Trading constraints have also been discussed as explanations for high company stock holdings. For example, many companies that match contributions to pension plans, deposit company stock. Often, an employee is restricted from trading this stock. However, the interest of this paper has been in exploring potential explanations for extremely high company stock weights such as those listed in Table 4.1. In most cases, any minimum holding constraint for company stock is not binding. Employees hold more company stock than they have to (Mitchell and Utkus, 2002).

Our results reinforce the conclusion that large holdings of company stock in pension accounts cannot be explained by traditional models of rational portfolio choice. As a result, explanation of the exceptionally high observed holdings continues to rely on behavioral explanations. The problem with behavioral explanations of company stock holdings is that they presuppose some ignorance on the part of the employee or an ability of the employer to dupe the employee. However, large holding in company stock is a phenomenon that has persisted for decades. Thus, employees would appear to have been making the same errors in their portfolio choices for a long time.[4] One would expect the irrationality of employee choices to lessen over time as employees learn from previous actions and consequences. This leads us to suspect that there is some factor(s) that need to be included in rational choice models to explain company stock holdings. This is a topic for future research.

References

Benartzi, S. (2001). Excessive extrapolation and the allocation of 401(k) accounts to company stock. *Journal of Finance*, 56(5), 1747–1764.

Benartzi, S. and R. Thaler (2001). Naive diversification strategies in defined contribution saving plans. *American Economic Review*, 91(1), 79–98.

Berkelaar, A., H. Hoek and A. Lucas (2002). Arbitrage and sampling uncertainty in financial stochastic programming models. Working Paper, Erasmus University.

Campbell, J. Y. and L. M. Viceira (2001). Who Should Buy Long-term Bonds? *American Economic Review*, 91(1), 99–127.

---

[4]Causes for the excess investment in company stock include incentives from the company such as discounted or easy to buy stock or options, inertia by the individual to do things that are simple, overconfidence that the company will continue to survive and investing in a familiar company. Many employees take the view: if it's good enough for the employer to match, it's good enough for me. This is another example where individuals do no always make wise or optimal decisions without assistance.

Campbell, J. Y. and L. M. Viciera (2002). *Strategic Asset Allocation: Portfolio Choice for Long-Term Investors*. Oxford, UK: Oxford University Press.

Chopra, V. K. and W. T. Ziemba (1993). The effect of errors in mean, variance and covariance estimates on optimal portfolio choice. *Journal of Portfolio Management*, 6–11.

Cont, R. (2001). Empirical properties of asset returns: Stylized facts and statistical issues. *Quantitative Finance*, 1(2), 223–236.

Constantinides, G. M. (2002). Rational asset prices. *Journal of Finance*, 57(4), 1567–1591.

Dimson, E., P. Marsh and M. Staunton (2002). *Triumph of the Optimists: 101 Years of Global Investment Returns*. Princeton, NJ: Princeton University Press.

Fleten, S.-E., K. Hoyland and S. W. Wallace (2002). The performance of stochastic dynamic and fixed mix portfolio models. *European Journal of Operational Research*, 140(1), 37–49.

Geyer, A., W. Herold, K. Kontriner and W. T. Ziemba (2003). The innovest Austrian Pension Fund financial planning model InnoALM. Working Paper, University of British Columbia.

Leland, J. (2004). All the nest eggs in one company basket. *Wall Street Journal*, April 11.

Longin, F. M. (1996). The asymptotic distribution of extreme stock market returns. *Journal of Business*, 69(3), 383–408.

Mankiw, N. G. and S. P. Zeldes (1991). The Consumption of stockholders and non-stockholders. *Journal of Financial Economics*, 7(1), 265–296.

Meulbroek, L. (2002). Company stock in pension plans: How costly is it?. Working Paper, Harvard Business School.

Mitchell, O. S. and S. P. Utkus (2002). Company stock and retirement plan diversification. Working Paper, Wharton School.

Pennanen, T. and M. Koivu (2002). Integration quadratures in discretization of stochastic programs. Stochastic Programming E-Print Series.

Press W. H., S. A. Teukolsky, W. T. Vetterling, B. P. Flannery (1997). *Numerical Recipes in C*. Cambridge, UK: Cambridge University Press.

Ramaswamy, K. (2002). Company stock and pension plan diversification. Pension Research Council, Wharton School, Working Paper.

Rudolf, M. and W. T. Ziemba (2004). Intertemporal surplus management. *Journal of Economic Dynamics and Control*, 28(5), 975–990.

Siegel, J. J. *Stocks for the Long Run: The Definitive Guide to Financial Market Returns and Long-Term Investment Strategies*. New York: McGraw-Hill.

Viceira, Luis M. (2001). Optimal portfolio choice for long-horizon investors with nontradable labor income. *Journal of Finance*, 56(2), 433–470.

Ziemba, W. T. and J. M. Mulvey (eds.) (1998). *Worldwide Asset and Liability Management*. Cambridge, UK: Cambridge University Press.

Ziemba, W. T. (2003). *The Stochastic Programming Approach to Asset Management*. Charlottesville, VA: AIMR.

Chapter 5

The Symmetric Downside-Risk Sharpe Ratio and the Evaluation of Great Investors and Speculators

William T. Ziemba*

*Alumni Professor of Financial Modeling
and Stochastic Optimization Emeritus
Sauder School of Business
University of British Columbia,
2053 Main Mall, Vancouver, B.C., Canada V6T 1Z2
and
Visiting Professor of Finance
Sloan School of Management, 50 Memorial Drive E52-410
Massachusetts Institute of Technology
Cambridge, MA 02142
July 4, 2005*

The Sharpe ratio is a very useful measure of investment performance. However, it is based on mean-variance theory and thus is basically valid only for quadratic preferences or normal distributions. Hence skewed investment returns can lead to misleading conclusions. This is especially true for superior investors such as Warren Buffett and others with a large number of high returns. Many of these superior investors use capital growth wagering ideas to implement their strategies which leads to higher growth rates but also higher variability of wealth. A simple modification of the Sharpe ratio to assume that the upside deviation is identical to the downside risk provides a useful modification that gives more realistic results.

---

*Thanks are due to Larry Siegel of the Ford Foundation for the data used in this article and for helpful comments; see his AIMR monograph (Siegel, 2003) for the role of benchmarks and indices in portfolio management worldwide, to Lawrence Booth, Andrew Lo and John Mulvey for comments on earlier drafts of this paper and to Sandra Schwartz for research assistance and valuable discussions.

Figure 5.1: Growth of Assets, Various High Performing Funds, Monthly Data, December 1985 to April 2000.

5.1. Introduction

Figure 5.1 plots the wealth levels using monthly data from December 1985 to March 2000 for the Windsor Fund of George Neff, the Ford Foundation, the Tiger Fund of Julian Robertson, the Quantum Fund of George Soros and Berkshire Hathaway, the fund run by Warren Buffett, as well as the S&P500 total return index, US Treasuries and T-bills. The yearly data is shown in Table 5.1.

The means, standard deviations and Sharpe (1966, 1994) ratios of these six funds, based on monthly, quarterly and yearly net arithmetic and geometric total return data are shown in Table 5.2. Also shown here is data from the Harvard endowment (quarterly) plus that of US Treasuries, T-bills and US inflation and the number of negative months and quarters. The top panel of Table 5.2 shows the data of Figure 5.1 which illustrates the large mean returns of Berkshire Hathaway and the Tiger Fund's and that the Ford Foundation's standard deviation was about a third of Berkshire's. The Ford Foundation actually trailed the S&P500 mean return. Observe the much lower monthly and quarterly Sharpe ratios compared to the annualized values based on monthly, quarterly and yearly data.

Table 5.1: Yearly Return Data in Percent.

Date	Windsor	Berkshire Hathaway	Quantum	Tiger	Ford Ford	Harvard	S&P500 Total	US Trea	US T-bills	US Infl
Yearly data, 14 years										
Neg years	2	2	1	0	1	1	1	2	0	0
Dec-86	20.27	14.17	42.12	26.83	18.09	22.16	18.47	15.14	6.16	1.13
Dec-87	1.23	4.61	14.13	7.28	5.20	12.46	5.23	2.90	5.47	4.41
Dec-88	28.69	59.32	10.13	15.76	10.42	12.68	16.81	6.10	6.35	4.42
Dec-89	15.02	84.57	35.21	24.72	22.15	15.99	31.49	13.29	8.37	4.65
Dec-90	-15.50	-23.05	23.80	5.57	1.96	-1.01	-3.17	9.73	7.81	6.11
Dec-91	28.55	35.58	50.58	37.59	22.92	15.73	30.55	15.46	5.60	3.06
Dec-92	16.50	29.83	6.37	8.42	5.26	4.88	7.67	7.19	3.51	2.90
Dec-93	19.37	38.94	33.03	24.91	13.07	21.73	9.99	11.24	2.90	2.75
Dec-94	-0.15	24.96	3.94	1.71	-1.96	3.71	1.31	-5.14	3.90	2.67
Dec-95	30.15	57.35	38.98	34.34	26.47	24.99	37.43	16.80	5.60	2.54
Dec-96	26.36	6.23	-1.50	8.03	15.39	26.47	23.07	2.10	5.21	3.32
Dec-97	21.98	34.90	17.09	18.79	19.11	20.91	33.36	8.38	5.26	1.70
Dec-98	0.81	52.17	12.46	11.21	21.39	12.14	28.58	10.21	4.86	1.61
Dec-99	11.57	-19.86	34.68	27.44	27.59	23.78	21.04	-1.77	4.68	2.68

Table 5.2: Fund Return Data: Yearly Means and Standard Deviations (in Percent) and Sharpe Ratios for Various High Yielding Funds versus the S&P500, Treasuries, T-bills and Inflation Using Monthly and Quarterly and Yearly Data with Arithmetic and Geometric Means, December 1985 to April 2000.

	Windsor	Berkshire Hathaway	Quantum	Tiger	Ford Found	Harvard	S&P500 Total	US Trea	US T-bills	US Infl
Monthly data, 172 months Neg months	61	58	53	56	44	na	56	54	0	13
arith mean, mon	1.17	2.15	1.77	2.02	1.19	na	1.45	0.63	0.44	0.26
st dev, mon	4.70	7.66	7.42	6.24	2.68	na	4.41	1.32	0.12	0.21
Sharpe, mon	0.157	0.223	0.180	0.54	0.80	na	0.230	0.145	0.000	−0.827
arith mean	14.10	25.77	21.25	24.27	14.29	na	17.44	7.57	5.27	3.14
st dev	16.27	26.54	25.70	21.62	9.30	na	15.28	4.58	0.43	0.74
Sharpe, yr	0.543	0.773	0.622	0.879	0.970	na	0.797	0.504	0.000	−2.865
geomean, mon	1.06	1.87	1.48	1.83	1.16	na	1.35	0.62	0.44	0.26
geo st dev,mon	4.70	7.67	7.42	6.25	2.69	na	4.41	1.32	0.12	0.21
Sharpe, mon	0.133	0.186	0.140	0.222	0.267	na	0.208	0.139	0.000	−0.828
geo mean, yr	12.76	22.38	17.76	21.92	13.86	na	16.25	7.47	5.27	3.14
geo st dev, yr	16.27	26.56	25.72	21.63	9.30	na	15.28	4.58	0.43	0.74
Sharpe, yr	0.460	0.644	0.486	0.770	0.924	na	0.719	0.482	0.000	−2.868

(*Continued*)

Table 5.2: (Continued)

	Windsor	Berkshire Hathaway	Quantum	Tiger	Ford Found	Harvard	S&P500 Total	US Trea	US T-bills	US Infl
Quarterly data, 57 quarters										
Neg quarters	14	15	16	11	11	11	10	15	0	1
mean, qtly	3.55	6.70	5.70	4.35	3.68	3.86	4.48	1.93	1.32	0.79
st dev, qtly	8.01	14.75	12.67	7.70	4.72	4.72	7.52	2.67	0.36	0.49
mean, yr	14.20	26.81	22.79	17.42	14.71	15.44	17.91	7.73	5.29	3.16
st dev, yr	16.03	29.50	25.33	15.40	9.43	9.45	15.05	5.34	0.73	0.97
Sharpe, yr	0.556	0.729	0.691	0.788	0.999	1.074	0.839	0.456	0.000	-2.188
geomean, qtly	3.23	5.67	4.94	4.07	3.57	3.75	4.20	1.90	1.32	0.79
geo st dev,qtly	8.02	14.79	12.69	7.70	4.72	4.73	7.53	2.67	0.36	0.49
geo mean, yr	12.90	22.67	19.78	16.28	14.29	15.01	16.80	7.59	5.29	3.16
geo st dev, yr	16.04	29.58	25.38	15.41	9.43	9.45	15.06	5.34	0.73	0.97
Sharpe, yr	0.475	0.588	0.571	0.713	0.954	1.029	0.764	0.431	0.000	-2.190
Yearly Data, 14 years										
Neg years	2	2	1	0	1	1	1	2	0	0
mean,	14.63	28.55	22.93	18.04	14.79	15.47	18.70	7.97	5.40	3.14
st dev,	13.55	30.34	16.17	11.40	9.38	8.52	12.88	6.59	1.50	1.35
Sharpe, yrly	0.681	0.763	1.084	1.109	1.001	1.181	1.033	0.390	0.000	-1.673
geom mean	13.83	24.99	21.94	17.54	14.43	15.17	18.04	7.78	5.39	3.13
st dev	13.58	30.57	16.20	11.41	9.39	8.53	12.90	6.59	1.50	1.35
Sharpe	0.621	0.641	1.022	1.064	0.962	1.146	0.981	0.362	0.000	-1.672

By the Sharpe ratio, the Harvard endowment and the Ford Foundation had the best performance, followed by the Tiger Fund then the S&P500 total return index, Berkshire Hathaway Quantum, Windsor and US Treasuries. The basic conclusions are the same with monthly or quarterly data and with arithmetic and geometric means. Because of data smoothing, the Sharpe ratios with yearly data usually exceed those with quarterly data which in turn exceed the monthly calculations.

The reason for this ranking is that the Ford Foundation and the Harvard endowment, while they had less growth, they also had much less variability. Indeed, these funds have different purposes, different investors, different portfolio managers, and different fees, so such differences are not surprising.

Clifford, Kroner and Siegel (2001) have similar calculations for a larger group of funds. They also show that starting from July 1977 to March 2000, Berkshire Hathaway's Sharpe ratio was 0.850 versus Ford's 0.765 and the S&P500 was 0.676. The geometric mean returns were 32.07% (Buffett), 14.88% (Ford), and 16.71% (S&P500). See also Siegel, Kroner and Clifford (2001) for additional calculations and discussion. Table 5.3 shows Buffett's returns on a yearly basis in terms of increase in per share book value of Berkshire Hathaway versus the S&P500 total return yearly index values for the 40 years 1965 to 2004. Buffett's geometric and arithmetic means were 22.02% and 22.84% respectively versus 10.47% and 11.83% for the S&P500. This measure does not fully reflect trading prices of Berkshire Hathaway shares and thus yearly net returns but it does indicate that Buffett has easily beaten the S&P500 over these 40 years with a 286,841% increase versus the S&P500's 5,371% increase.

Typically the Sharpe ratio is computed using arithmetic returns. This is because the basic static theories of portfolio investment management such as mean-variance analysis and the capital asset pricing model are bassed on arithmetic means. These are static one period theories. However, for asset returns over time, the geometric mean is a more accurate measure of average performance since the arithmetic mean is biased upwards. The geometric mean helps mitigate the autocorrelated and time varying mean and other statistical properties of returns that are not iid. For example, if one has returns of +50% and −50% in two periods, then the arithmetic mean is zero which does not correctly reflect the fact that 100 became 150 and then 75. The geometric mean which is −13.7% is the correct measure to use. For investment returns in the 10–15% range, the arithmetic returns are about 2% above the geometric returns. But for higher returns this

Table 5.3:   Increase in Per Share Book Value of Berkshire Hathaway Versus Returns
on the S&P500 with Dividends Included, 1965–2004, in Percent.

Year	BH	S&P500	Diff	Year	BH	S&P500	Diff
1965	23.8	10.0	13.8	1985	48.2	31.6	16.6
1966	20.3	(11.7)	32.0	1986	26.1	18.6	7.5
1967	11.0	30.9	(19.9)	1987	19.5	5.1	14.4
1968	19.0	11.0	8.0	1988	20.1	16.6	3.5
1969	16.2	(8.4)	24.6	1989	44.4	31.7	12.7
1970	12.0	3.9	8.1	1990	7.4	(3.1)	10.5
1971	16.4	14.6	1.8	1991	39.6	30.5	9.1
1972	21.7	18.9	2.8	1992	20.3	7.6	12.7
1973	4.7	(14.8)	19.5	1993	14.3	10.1	4.2
1974	5.5	(26.4)	31.9	1994	13.9	1.3	12.6
1975	21.9	37.2	(15.3)	1995	43.1	37.6	5.5
1976	59.3	23.6	35.7	1996	31.8	23.0	8.8
1977	31.9	(7.4)	39.3	1997	34.1	33.4	.7
1978	24.0	6.4	17.6	1998	48.3	28.6	19.7
1979	35.7	18.2	17.5	1999	.5	21.0	(20.5)
1980	19.3	32.3	(13.0)	2000	6.5	(9.1)	15.6
1981	31.4	(5.0)	36.4	2001	(6.2)	(11.9)	5.7
1982	40.0	21.4	18.6	2002	10.0	(22.1)	32.1
1983	32.3	22.4	9.9	2003	21.0	28.7	(7.7)
1984	13.6	6.1	7.5	2004	10.5	10.9	(0.04)

Overall Gain	286,841	5,371					
Arithmetic Mean	22.84	11.83	11.01				
Geometric Mean	22.02	10.47	10.07				

Source: Berkshire Hathaway 2004 Annual Report and in Hagstrom (2004). Data are
for calendar years except 1965 and 1966, year ended 9/30; 1967,15 months ended
12/31. Starting in 1979, accounting rules required insurance companies to value the
equity securities they hold at market rather than at the lower of cost or market,
which was previusly the requirement. In this table, Berkshire's results through 1978
have been restated to conform to the changed rules.

The S&P500 numbers are pre-tax whereas the Berkshire numbers are after-tax. If a
corporation such as Berkshire were simply to have owned the S&P500 and accrued
the appropriate taxes, its results would have lagged the S&P500 in years when that
index showed a positive return, but would have exceeded the S&Pin years when the
index showed a negative return. Over the years, the tax costs would have caused the
aggregate lag to be substantial.

approximation is not accurate. Hence, geometric means as well as more
typical arithmetic means are used in this paper. Lo (2002) points out that
care must be used in Sharpe ratio estimations when the investment returns
are not iid, which they are for the investors discussed here. For dependent
but stationary returns he derives a correction of the Sharpe ratios that

Figure 5.2: Ford Foundation and Harvard Investment Corporation Returns, Quarterly Data, June 1977 to March 2000.

deflates artificially high values back to correct values using an estimation of the correlation of serial returns. See also Miller and Gehr (1978) and Knight and Satchell (2005) who derive exact statistical properties of the Sharpe ratio with normal and lognormal assets, respectively. The Sharpe ratios are almost always lower when geometric means are used rather than arithmetic means with the difference between these two measures a function of return volatility. However, the basic conclusions of the paper such as the relative ranking of the various funds, are the same for the arithmetic and geometric means.

Figure 5.2 shows that the Harvard Investment Company, that great school's endowment, had essentially the same wealth record over time as the Ford Foundation. This is based on quarterly data which is all I have on Harvard. Harvard beats Ford by the ordinary Sharpe ratio but Ford is superior by the symmetric downside risk measure discussed later in the paper (see Tables 5.2, 5.9–5.11). Throughout this paper some graphs have log scales and some arithmetic based on what data I have and the best way to present the data.

Before evaluating positive and negative returns performances of these various funds using the Sharpe ratio and my modified version, it is useful to discuss how these funds got their outstanding but sometimes volatile records.

Table 5.4: Summary Over Funds of Negative Observations and Arithmetic and Geometric Means

Number of negative	Windsor	Berkshire Hathaway	Quantum	Tiger	Ford Found	Harvard	S&P Tota	US Treasl
...months out of 172	61	58	53	56	44	na	56	54
...quarters out of 57	14	15	16	11	10	11	10	15
...years out of 14	2	2	1	0	1	1	1	2

5.2. Some Great Investors and Their Use of the Capital Growth Criterion and Its Variants

The Sharpe ratio penalizes high return but volative records. However, ideally we would want to penalize only losses such as those shown in Table 5.4 while rewarding positive returns.

In the theory of optimal investment over time, it is not quadratic (the utility function behind the Sharpe ratio) but log that yields the most long term growth. But the elegant results on the Kelly (1956) criterion, as it is known in the gambling literature and the capital growth theory as it is known in the investments literature, see the surveys by Hakansson and Ziemba (1995), Ziemba (2003) and MacLean and Ziemba (2005), that were proved rigorously by Breiman (1961) and generalized by Algoet and Cover (1988) are long run asymptotic results. However, the Arrow-Pratt absolute risk aversion of the log utility criterion

$$R_A(w) = \frac{-u''(w)}{u'(w)} = 1/w$$

is essentially zero, where u is the utility function of wealth w, and primes denote differentiation. Hence, in the short run, log can be an exceedingly risky utility function with wide swings in wealth values because the optimal bets can be so large.

Long run exponential growth is equivalent to maximizing the one period expected log of that period's returns. To illustrate how large Kelly (expected log) bets are, consider the simplest case with Bernoulli trials where you win with probability p and lose with probability $q = 1 - p$.

Log utility is related to negative power utility, namely, αw^α for $\alpha < 0$ since negative power converges to log when $\alpha \to 0$. Kelly (1956) discovered that log utility investors were in possession of the best utility function provided they were very long run investors. The asymptotic rate of asset growth is

$$G = \lim_{N \to \infty} log \left(\frac{w_N}{w_0} \right)^{\frac{1}{N}},$$

where w_0 is initial wealth and w_N is period N's wealth. Consider Bernoulli trials that win $+1$ with probability p and lose -1 with probability $1 - p$. If we win M out of N of these independent trials, then the wealth after period N is

$$w_N = w_0(1 + f)^M(1 - f)^{N-M}$$

where f is the fraction of our wealth bet in each period. Then

$$G(f) = \lim_{N \to \infty} \left[\frac{M}{N} log(1 + f) + \frac{N - M}{N} log(1 - f) \right]$$

which by the strong law of large numbers is

$$G(f) = plog(1 + f) + qlog(1 - f) = E(logw).$$

Hence, the criterion of maximizing the long run exponential rate of asset growth is equivalent to maximizing the one period expected logarithm of wealth. Hence, to maximize long run (asymptotic) wealth maximizing expected log is the way to do it period by period.

The optimal fractional bet, obtained by setting the derivative of $G(f)$ to zero, is $f^* = p - q$ which is simply the investor's edge or expected gain on the bet.[1] If the bets are win $O + 1$ or lose 1, that is the odds are O to 1 to win, then the optimal Kelly bet is $f^* = \frac{p-q}{O}$ or the $\frac{edge}{odds}$. Since edge is a mean concept and odds is a risk concept you wager more with higher mean and less with higher risk.

In continuous time

$$f^* = \frac{\mu - r}{\sigma^2} = \frac{edge}{risk(odds)}$$

---

[1] If there are two independent wagers and the size of the bets does not influence the odds, then an analytic expression can be derived, see Thorp (1997, 19–20). In general, to solve for the optimal wagers in cases where the bets influence the odds, there is dependence, or for cases with three or more wagers, one must solve a non-convex nonlinear program, see Ziemba and Hausch (1984, 1987) for technique. This gives the optimal wager taking into account the effect of our bets on the odds (prices).

with optimal growth rate

$$G^* = \frac{1}{2}\left(\frac{\mu - r}{\sigma}\right)^2 + r = \frac{1}{2}(\text{Sharpe Ratio})^2 + \text{ risk free asset,}$$

where μ is the mean portfolio return, r is the risk free return and σ^2 is the portfolio return variance. So the ordinary Sharpe ratio determines the optimal growth rate.

Kelly bets can be large. Consider Bernoulli trials where you win 1 or lose 1 with probabilities p and $1 - p$, respectively, then

p	0.5	0.51	0.6	0.8	0.9	0.99
$1 - p$	0.5	0.49	0.4	0.2	0.1	0.01
f^*	0	0.02	0.2	0.6	0.8	0.98.

So if the edge is 98%, the optimal bet is 98% of ones fortune. With longer odds bets the wagers are lower.

The Kelly bettor is sure to win in the end if the horizon is long enough. Breiman (1960, 1961) was the first to clean up the math from Kelly's 1956 and Latane's 1957 heuristic analyses. He proved that

$$\lim_{N \to \infty} \frac{w_{KB}(N)}{w_B(N)} \to \infty,$$

where $w_{KB}(N)$ and $w_B(N)$ are the wealth levels of the Kelly bettor and another essentially different bettor after N play, that is, the Kelly bettor wins infinitely more than bettor B and moves further and further ahead as the long time horizon becomes more distant.[2]

Breiman also showed that the expected time reach a pre assigned goal in asymptotically the least with an expected log strategy. Moreover, the ratio of the expected log bettor's fortune to that of any other essentially different investor goes to infinity. So the log investor gets all the money in the end if one plays forever.

Hensel-Ziemba (2000) calculated that from 1942 to 1997 a 100% long investor solely in large cap stocks with Republican administrations and solely in small cap stocks with Democrats had 24.5 times as much wealth

---

[2]Bettor B must use an *essentially different* strategy than our Kelly bettor for this to be true. This means that the strategies differ infinitely often. For example, they are the same for the first 10 years, then every second trial is different. This is a technical point to get proofs correct but nothing much to worry about in practice since non-log strategies will differ infinitely often.

as a 60-40 large cap-bond investor. That's the idea more or less. Keynes and
Buffett are essentially Kelly bettors, see Figures 5.6 and 5.1, respectively.
Kelly bettors will have bumpy investment paths but, most of the time, in
the end accumulate more money than other investors.

Ziemba and Hausch (1986) performed a simulation to show *medium*
run properties of log utility and half Kelly betting (namely using the $-w^{-1}$
utility function). Starting with an initial wealth of $1000 and considering
700 independent wagers with probability of winning 0.19 to 0.57 all with
expected values of $1.14 per dollar wagered, they computed the final wealth
profiles over 1000 simulations. These wagers corresponded to odds of 1-1,
2-1, 3-1, 4-1 and 5-1. The results show that the log bettor has more than
100 times initial wealth 16.6% of the time and more than 50 times as much
30.2% of the time. This shows the great power of log betting since the half
Kelly strategy had extremely few such high outcomes. However, this high
return comes at a price. Despite making 700 independent bets, each with a
14% success rate, the investor could have lost more than 98% of his initial
wealth of $1000; see Table 5.5 which contains the simulation results. The
Ziemba-Hausch simulation used the data in Table 5.6. The edge over odds
gives f^* equal to 0.14 down to 0.028 for the optimal Kelly wagers for 1-1
versus 5-1 odds bets.

Table 5.5: Distributions of Final Wealth for Kelly and Half Kelly Wagers in the
Ziemba-Hausch (1986) Simulation.

Final Wealth Strategy	Min	Max	Mean	Median	>500	>1000	>10,000	>50,000	>100,000
					Number of times the final wealth out of 1000 trials was				
Kelly	18	483,883	48,135	17,269	916	870	598	302	166
Half Kelly	145	111,770	13,069	8,043	990	954	480	30	1

Table 5.6: Value of Odds on Wagers in the Ziemba-Hausch (1986) Simulation.

Probability of Winning	Odds	Probability of Being Chosen in the Simulation at Each Decision Point	Optimal Kelly Bets Fraction of Current Wealth
0.57	1-1	0.1	0.14
0.38	2-1	0.3	0.07
0.285	3-1	0.3	0.047
0.228	4-1	0.2	0.035
0.19	5-1	0.1	0.028

The 18 in the first column shows that it is possible for a Kelly bettor to make 700 independent wagers all with a 14% edge having 19% to 57% chance of winning each wager and still lose over 98% one's wealth. Even with half Kelly, the minimum starting with $1000 was $145, or a 85.5% loss. This shows the effect of a sequence of very bad scenarios which are unlikely but possible. However, the last column shows that 16.6% of the time the Kelly bettor more than 100-folds initial wealth. The half Kelly strategy is much safer since the chance of being ahead after the 700 wagers is 95.4% versus 87% for full Kelly. But the growth rate is much lower since the 16.6% chance of hundred plus folding is only 0.1% for half Kelly wagerers. The Kelly bettor accumulates more wealth but with a much riskier time path of wealth accumulation. Additional details of this and many other Kelly and fractional Kelly comparisons appear in Ziemba (2003) and MacLean and Ziemba (2005). The Kelly bettor can take a long time to get ahead of another bettor. See the discussion of properties in MacLean and Ziemba (2005) and Thorp (1997).

What one wants is to have those swings in the right direction. And who better, it seems, at predicting these swings than Warren Buffett. Chopra and Ziemba (1993) showed that in portfolio problems, errors in estimating means, variance and co-variances impact on investment performance roughly in the ratio 20:2:1. When risk aversion is lower, as it is with log, then the errors are even larger. In this case, the effect on portfolio performance of mean errors can be 100 times the errors in co-variances.

Who then would use a log utility function if it is so risky or use a toned down log utility function by mixing the log utility investment fraction of one's wealth with cash? These so-called fractional Kelly strategies are actually mathematically equivalent to negative power utility when the assets are log normally distributed and approximately so otherwise, see MacLean, Ziemba and Li (2005).

The difference in wealth paths between Kelly and half Kelly strategies is illustrated in Figure 5.3. This shows the wealth level histories from place and show betting on the Kentucky Derby, 1934–1994 with the Dr Z system utilizing a 4.00 dosage index breeding filter rule with full and half Kelly wagering and from $200 flat bets on the favorite, initial wealth of $2500. Starting with $2500, full Kelly yields a final wealth of $16,861 while half Kelly, with a much smoother path has final wealth of $6945. Here, we have bets on the Kentucky Derby with these two strategies which are winning ones compared to the losing strategy of betting on the favorite which turns the $2500 into $480.

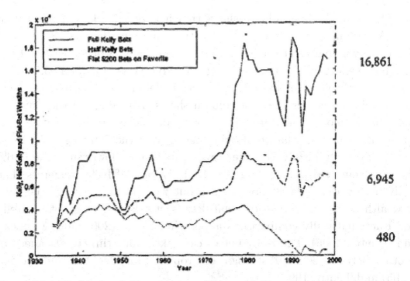

Figure 5.3:   Wealth Level Histories from Place and Show Betting on the Kentucky Derby, 1934–1994 with Kelly, Half Kelly and Betting on the Favorite Strategies. Source: Bain, Hausch and Ziemba (2005), Data in MacLean and Ziemba (1999).

Some rather good investors, including four I have worked with or consulted with have used the Kelly and fractional Kelly approach to turn humble beginnings into a fortune of hundreds of millions. One was the world's most successful racetrack better, see Benter's article in Hausch, Lo and Ziemba (1994). Another was a trend following futures trader in the Caribbean for whom I designed a Kelly betting system for the 90 liquid futures markets he traded. The Kelly system added $9 million extra profits per year to his already good betting system based on an ad hoc but sound probability of success approach. Another was an options trader eaking out nickels and dimes with slightly mispriced optons in Chicago. The fourth was the popularizer of the Kelly approach in sports betting, Edward O. Thorp. Thorp's fund Princeton-Newport had a net mean return of 15.1%, the S&P500's was 10.2% and T-bills returned 8.1%. Interest rates were very high in 1968–88 while Thorp was running his fund. Thorp had no losing quarters, only three losing months, and a most impressive yearly standard deviation of 4%.

To show the differences between the *gamblers* and other investors, Figure 5.4 shows Benter's racetrack betting record from 1989 up to 1994 and from 1989 to 2001, and Figure 5.5 which shows Thorp's record from

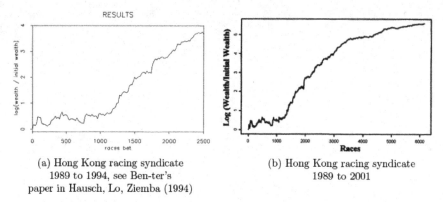

(a) Hong Kong racing syndicate
1989 to 1994, see Ben-ter's
paper in Hausch, Lo, Ziemba (1994)

(b) Hong Kong racing syndicate
1989 to 2001

Figure 5.4: The *Gamblers* Like Smooth Wealth Paths Using Fractional Kelly Strategies.

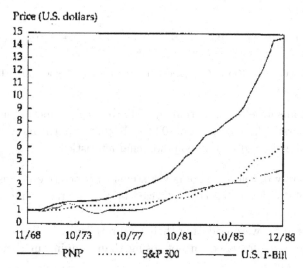

Figure 5.5: Princeton Newport Partners, L.P., Cumulative Results, November 1968–December 1988.

1968 to 1988. Compare these rather smooth graphs with the brilliant but quite volatile record of the eminent economist John Maynard Keynes who ran the King's College Chest Fund, the college's endowment from 1927 until his death in 1945, see Figure 5.6. Keynes lost more than 50% of his fortune during the difficult years of the depression around the 1929 crash in 1928 to 1931. This bad start was followed by many years of outperformance on

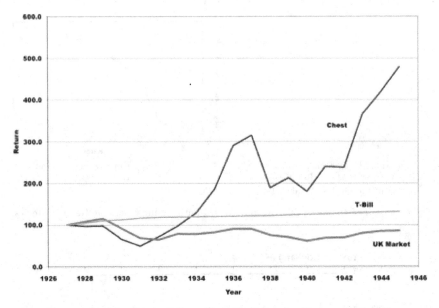

Figure 5.6: The King's College Chest Fund Run by Keynes, 1927–1945.

relative and absolute terms so that by 1945 Keynes' geometric mean return was 9.12% versus the UK index of -0.89%. Keynes' Sharpe index was 0.385. The gamblers had several common characteristics:

- they carefully developed anomaly systems with positive means;
- they carefully developed computerized betting systems that automated the betting process;
- they constantly were updating their research, and
- they were more focussed on not losing than winning in their carefully done risk control.

In a masterful paper on various mathematical properties and his own use of the Kelly criterion, Thorp (1997) shows that the Buffett trades are actually very similar to those of a Kelly trader. In Ziemba (2003) I found that Keynes is well approximated as a fractional Kelly bettor with 80% Kelly and 20% cash; that is equivalent to the negative power utility function $-w^{-0.25}$. Recall log is when the power coefficient goes to zero and that log is the most risky utility function that should ever be considered. Positive power utility has less growth and more risk so is not an acceptable utility function.

5.3. The Symmetric Downside Sharpe Ratio Performance Measure

Now back to the records of the funds in Figure 5.1. The reader has been patient so far and now demands that we disclose how we feel that these various investors be compared. And especially we want to determine if Warren Buffett really is a better investor than the rather good but lesser funds mentioned here, especially the Ford Foundation and the Harvard endowment, in some fair way.

The idea is presented in Figure 5.7 where we have plotted the Berkshire Hathaway and Ford Foundation monthly returns as a histogram and show the losing months and the winning months in a smooth curve. We want to penalize Warren for losing but not for winning. So define the downside risk as

$$\sigma_{x_-}^2 = \frac{\sum_{i=1}^n (x_i - \bar{x})_-^2}{n-1},$$

where our benchmark $\bar{x}$ is zero, i is the index on the n months in the sample and the x_i taken are those below $\bar{x}$, namely those m of the n months with losses. This is the downside variance measured from zero, not the mean, so it is more precisely the downside risk. To get the total variance we use

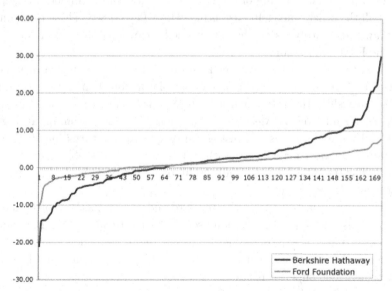

Figure 5.7: Berkshire Hathaway versus Ford Foundation, Monthly Returns Distribution, January 1977 to April 2000.

Table 5.7: Comparison of Ordinary and Symmetric
Downside Sharpe Yearly Performance Measures, Monthly
Data and Arithmetic Means.

	Ordinary	Downside
Ford Foundation	0.970	0.920
Tiger Fund	0.879	0.865
S&P500	0.797	0.696
Berkshire Hathaway	0.773	0.917
Quantum	0.622	0.458
Windsor	0.543	0.495

twice the downside variance namely $2\sigma_{x-}^2$ so that Buffett gets the symmetric gains added not his actual gains. Using $2\sigma_{x-}^2$, the usual Sharpe ratio with monthly data and arithmetic returns is

$$S_- = \frac{\bar{R} - R_F}{\sqrt{2}\sigma_{x-}}.$$

Table 5.7 gives the results for the ordinary and symmetric downside Sharpe ratios using monthly data and arithmetic means.

My measure moves Warren Buffett higher to 0.917 but not up to the Ford Foundation and not higher because of his high monthly losses. He did gain in the switch from ordinary Sharp to downside symmetric Sharpe while all the other funds fell. Ford is 0.920 and Tiger 0.865. These Berkshire Hathaway's monthly losses when annualized are over 64% versus under 27% for the Ford Foundation.

Figure 5.7 shows these rather fat tails on the upside and downside of Berkshire Hathaway versus the much less volatile Ford Foundation returns. When Berkshire Hathaway had a losing month it averaged -5.36% versus +2.15% for all months. Meanwhile, Ford lost 2.44% and won, on average, 1.19%. Figure 5.8 shows the histogram of quarterly returns for all funds including Harvard for which monthly data was not available. This figure shows that the distributions of all the funds lie between those of Berkshire Hathaway, Harvard and Ford.

Using the quarterly data, the Harvard endowment has a record almost as good as the Ford Foundation, see Tables 5.10 and 5.11. Berkshire Hathaway made the most money but took more risk and by either the Sharpe or downside Sharpe measures the Ford Foundation and the Harvard endowment had superior rewards.

I first used this measure in Ziemba and Schwartz (1991) to compare the results of superior investment in Japanese small capitalized stocks

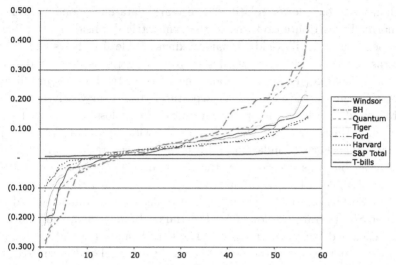

Figure 5.8: Return Distributions of All the Funds, Quarterly Returns Distribution, December 1985 to March 2000.

during the late 1980's. The choice of $\bar{x} = 0$ is convenient and has a good interpretation. Buth other $\bar{x}$'s are possible and might be useful in other applications. This measure is closely related to the Sortino ratio (see Sortino and van der Meer, 1991 and Sortino and Price, 1994) which considers downside risk only. That measure does not have the two sided interpertation of my measure and the $\sqrt{2}$ does not appear. The notion of focusing on downside risk is popular these days as it represents real risk better. I started using it in asset-liability models in the 1970s; see Kallberg, White and Ziemba (1982) and Kusy and Ziemba (1986) for early applications.[3] In the models we measure risk as the downside non-attainment of investment target goals which can be deterministic such as wealth growth over time or stochastic such as the non-attachment of a portfolio of weighted benchmark returns. See Geyer *et al.* (2003) for an application of this to the Siemens Austria pension fund.

Calculating the Sharpe ratio and the downside symmetric Sharpe ratio using quarterly or yearly data does not change the results much even though this smoothes the data since individual monthly losses are combined

---

[3]Others such as Roy (1952), Markowitz (1959), Mao (1970), Bawa (1975, 1977), Bawa and Lindenberg (1977), Fishburn (1977), Harlow and Rao (1989), and Harlow (1991) have used downside risk measures in portfolio theories alternative to those of Markowitz and Sharpe based on mean-variance and related analyses.

with gains to have lower volatility. The yearly data moves one back closer to normally distributed returns so the symmetric downside and ordinary Sharpe measures will yield similar rankings. Table 5.1 shows the yearly returns for the various funds and their Sharpe ratios computed using arithmetic and geometric means and the yearly data. There is insufficient data to compute the downside Sharpe ratios based on yearly data. The Ford Foundation had only one losing year and that loss was only -1.96%. Berkshire Hathaway had two losing years with losses of -23.1% and -19.9%. The Ford Foundation had a higher Sharpe ratio than Berkshire Hathaway but was exceeded by the Tiger and Quantum funds and the S&P500. Table 5.11 and Figure 5.9 summarize the annualized results using monthly, quarterly and yearly data. The Ford Foundation had the highest Sharpe ratio, followed by the Harvard Endowment and both of these exceeded Berkshire Hathaway. The Ford Foundation had the highest symmetric downside Sharpe ratio followed by Harvard and both exceeded Berkshire Hathaway and the other funds.

As Siegel, who works for the Ford Foundation, privately acknowledges, some of the Ford Foundation's high Sharpe ratio results from dividing by

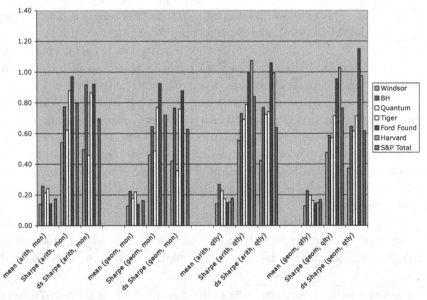

Figure 5.9: Summary of the Means Both Arithmetic and Geometric and the Sharpe and Downside Sharpes for the Monthly, Quarterly, and Yearly Data, All Annualized, December 1985 to March 2000.

The Symmetric Downside-Risk Sharpe Ratio

Table 5.8: Asset Allocation of Harvard Endowment to June 2004.

Harvard's Holdings By Sector	Annual Returns 1-Year, %	10-Year, %	Weight In Endowment, %
Domestic Equities	22.8	17.8	15
Foreign Equities	36.1	8.5	10
Emerging Markets	6.6	9.7	5
Private Equity	20.8	31.5	13
Hedge Funds	15.7	n.a	12
High Yield	12.4	9.7	5
Commodities	19.7	10.9	13
Real Estate	16.0	15.0	10
Domestic Bonds	9.2	14.9	11
Foreign Bonds	17.4	16.9	5
Inflation-indexed Bonds	4.2	n.a.	6
Total Endowment	21.1	15.9	105%*

*includes slight leverage

Source: Barron's, February 1, 2005.

an artificially smoothed standard deviation, due to that institution's high private equity allocation whose market prices do not reflect actual volatility. This is also true of Harvard. Table 5.8 shows the Harvard endowment's asset allocation. Their 10-year 15.9% performance of their $22.6 billion portfolio was 3.1% better than the median of the 25 largest university endowments up to June 2004. Harvard has continued its good performance and has extensively used private equity and other non-traditional investments. Ford's performance in 2001-2 was poor and Berkshire Hathaway has doubled in price since the 2000 lows so these rankings based on more data, which I do not have, may well change.

Tables 5.4, 5.9–5.11 give a short overview of key data. The numbers in italic indicate the worst outcomes and those in bold, the best. Windsor had the most negative months and negative years (tied with Berkshire Hathaway) and the lowest means. Berkshire Hathaway had the highest annual mean returns.

My measure is ad hoc as all performance measures are and adds to, but does not close, the debate on this subject.

Hodges (1998), see also the discussion in Ziemba (2003), proposed a generalized Sharpe measure where some of the paradoxes that the Sharpe measure leads to are eliminated. It uses a constant absolute risk return exponential utility function and general return distributions. When the returns are normally distributed, this is the usual Sharpe ratio since that portfolio problem is equivalent to a mean-variance model. A better

Table 5.9: Yearly Sharpe and Symmetric Downside Sharpe Ratios Computed from Monthly Return Data Using Arithmetic and Geometric Means and Standard Deviations (in Percent), for the 172 Months from December 1985 to April 2000 in Percent.

	Windsor	Berkshire Hathaway	Quantum	Tiger	Ford Found	Harvard	S&P Total	US Trea	T-bills	US Infl
Neg months	61	58	53	56	44	na	56	54	0	13
arith mean, neg	-3.54	-5.36	-5.65	-4.41	-2.24	na	-3.31	-0.87	na	-0.14
arith mean, mon	1.17	2.15	1.77	2.02	1.19	na	1.45	0.63	0.44	0.26
ds st dev, mon	5.15	6.46	10.08	6.34	2.83	na	5.05	1.06	0.00	0.19
arith mean, yr	14.10	25.77	21.25	24.27	14.29	na	17.44	7.57	5.27	3.14
ds st dev, yr	17.85	22.36	34.91	21.97	9.81	na	17.49	3.66	0.00	0.64
ds Sharpe	0.495	0.917	0.458	0.865	0.920	na	0.696	0.631	na	-3.320
geomean, neg	-3.62	-5.48	-5.95	-4.53	-2.26	na	-3.38			
geomean, mon	1.06	1.87	1.48	1.83	1.16	na	1.35	0.62	0.44	0.26
ds geo st dev,mon	5.15	6.46	10.09	6.34	2.83	na	5.05	0.60	0.00	0.00
geo mean, yr	12.76	22.38	17.76	21.92	13.86	na	16.25	7.47	5.27	3.14
ds geo st dev, yr	17.86	22.37	34.94	21.98	9.81	na	17.49	2.09	0.00	0.00
ds Sharpe	0.420	0.765	0.358	0.758	0.876	na	0.628	1.053		

Table 5.10: Yearly Sharpe and Symmetric Downside Sharpe Ratios Computed from Quarterly Return Data Using Arithmetic and Geometric Means and Standard Deviations (in Percent), December 1985 to April 2000.

	Windsor	Berkshire Hathaway	Quantum	Tiger	Ford Found	Harvard	S&P Total	Trea
qtly data, 57 quarters								
neg qts	14	15	16	11	10	11	10	15
mean, neg	−6.69	−10.50	−7.77	−6.26	−3.59	−2.81	−6.92	−1.35
mean, qtly	3.55	6.70	5.70	4.35	3.68	3.86	4.48	1.93
ds st dev, qtly	10.52	14.00	12.09	8.18	4.44	5.12	9.89	1.35
mean, yr	14.20	26.81	22.79	17.42	14.71	15.44	17.91	7.73
ds st dev, yr	21.04	28.00	24.17	16.35	8.89	10.24	19.78	2.70
ds Sharpe	0.424	0.769	0.724	0.742	1.060	0.991	0.638	0.903
geomean, qtly	3.23	5.67	4.94	4.07	3.57	3.75	4.20	1.90
ds geo st dev, qtly	10.20	13.49	11.80	7.71	3.91	4.99	9.34	1.28
geo mean, yr	12.90	22.67	19.78	16.28	14.29	15.01	16.80	7.59
ds geo st dev, yr	20.41	26.97	23.60	15.43	7.83	9.97	18.68	2.56
ds Sharpe	0.373	0.644	0.614	0.712	1.150	0.975	0.616	0.900

utility function is the constant relative risk aversion negative power. See additional discussion in Ziemba (2003). Leland (1999) shows how to modify β's when there are fat tails into more correct β's in a CAPM framework.

Goetzmann *et al.* (2002) and Spurgin (2001) show how the Sharpe ratio may be manipulated using option strategies to obtain what looks like a superior record to obtain more funds to manage. Managers sell calls to cut off upside variance and use the proceeds to buy puts to cut off downside variance leading to higher Sharpe ratios because of the reduced portfolio variance. These options transactions may actually lead to poorer investment performance in final wealth terms even with their higher Sharpe ratios. For example, Tompkins, Ziemba and Hodges (2003) show how on average the calls sold and the puts purchased on the S&P500 both had negative expected values from 1985–2002.

I have not tried to establish when the symmetric downside risk Sharpe ratio might give misleading results in real investment situations nor to

William T. Ziemba

Table 5.11:   Summary of the Means, Both Arithmetic and Geometric (in Percent), and the Sharpe and Symmetric Downside Sharpe Ratios for the Monthly Quarterly and Yearly Data All Annualized.

	Windsor	Berkshire Hathaway	Quantum	Tiger	Ford Found	Harvard	S&P Total	Trea
mean (arith, mon)	14.10	25.77	21.25	24.27	14.29	na	17.44	7.57
Sharpe (arith, mon)	0.543	0.773	0.622	0.879	0.970	na	0.797	0.504
ds Sharpe (arith, mon)	0.495	0.917	0.458	0.865	0.920	na	0.696	0.631
mean (geom, mon)	12.76	22.38	17.76	21.92	13.86	na	16.25	7.47
Sharpe (geom, mon)	0.460	0.644	0.486	0.770	0.924	na	0.719	0.482
ds Sharpe (geom, mon)	0.420	0.765	0.358	0.758	0.876	na	0.628	1.053
mean (arith, qtly)	14.20	26.81	22.79	17.42	14.71	15.44	17.91	7.73
Sharpe (arith, qtly)	0.556	0.729	0.691	0.788	0.999	1.074	0.839	0.456
ds Sharpe (arith, qtly)	0.424	0.769	0.724	0.742	1.060	0.991	0.638	0.903
mean (geom, qtly)	12.90	22.67	19.78	16.28	14.29	15.01	16.80	7.59
Sharpe (geom, qlty)	0.475	0.588	0.571	0.713	0.954	1.029	0.764	0.431
ds Sharpe (geom, qtly)	0.373	0.644	0.614	0.712	1.150	0.975	0.616	0.900
mean (arith, yrly)	14.63	28.55	22.93	18.04	14.79	15.47	18.70	7.97
Sharpe (arith, yrly)	0.681	0.763	1.084	1.109	1.001	1.181	1.033	0.390
mean (geom, yrly)	13.83	24.99	21.94	17.54	14.43	15.17	18.04	7.78
Sharpe (geom, yrly)	0.621	0.641	1.022	1.064	0.962	1.146	0.981	0.362

establish its mathematical and statistical properties except for noting that it is consistent with an investor with utility based on the negative of the disutility of losses. It does seem to be a simple way to avoid penalizing superior performance so that a fairer performance can be evaluated. Another way will have to be found to measure and establish the superiority of Warren Buffett. One likely candidate is related to the Kelly way of evaluating investments which looks at compounded wealth over a long period of time which we know in the limit is attained by the log bettor which Buffet seems to be. After 40 years, most of us believe that Buffett is in the skill not luck category; after all $15 a share in 1965 became $87,000 in June 2005, but since he is a log bettor only more time will tell. For studies of dynamic Sharpe ratios, see Cvitanić, Lazrak and Wang (2004) and Nielsen and Vassalou (2004).

References

Algoet, P. and T. Cover (1988). Asymptotic optimality and asymptotic equipartition properties of log-optimum investment. *Annals of Probability*, 16, 876–898.

Bain, R., D. B. Hausch, and W. T. Ziemba (2005). An application of expert information to win betting on the Kentucky Derby, 1981–2005. Working paper, University of British Columbia.

Bawa, V. (1975). Optimal rules for ordering uncertain prospects. *Journal of Financial Economics*, 2, 95–121.

Bawa, V. (1978). Safety first, stochastic dominance and optimal portfolio choice. *Journal of Finance and Quantitative Analysis*, 13, 255–271.

Bawa, V. and E. Lindenberg (1977). Capital market equilibrium in a mean, lower partial moment framework. *Journal of Financial Economics*, 5, 189–200.

Breiman, L. (1960). Investment policies for expanding business optimal in a long-run sense. *Naval Research Logistics Quarterly*, 7, 647–651.

Breiman, L. (1961). Optimal gambling system for favorable games. *Proceedings of the 4th Berkeley Symposium on Mathematical Statistics and Probability*, 1, 63–8.

Chopra, V. K. and W. T. Ziemba (1993). The effect of errors in mean, variance and co-variance estimates on optimal portfolio choice. *Journal of Portfolio Management*, 19, 6–11.

Clifford, S. W., K. F. Kroner, and L. B. Siegel (2001). In pursuit of performance: the greatest return stories ever told. *Investment Insights, Barclays Global Investor*, 4(1), 1–25.

Cvitanić, J., A. Lazrak, and T. Wang (2004, April). Sharpe ratio as a performance measure in a multi-period setting. Technical report, University of British Columbia.

Fishburn, P. C. (1977). Mean-risk analysis with risk associated with below target returns. *American Economic Review*, 76, 116–126.

Geyer, A., W. Herold, K. Kontriner, and W. T. Ziemba (2003). The Innovest Austrian pension fund financial planning model InnoALM. Working paper, UBC.

Goetzmann, W., J. Ingersoll, M. Spiegel, and I. Welch (2002). Sharpening Sharpe ratios. Working paper, Yale School of Management.

Hagstrom, R. G. (2004). *The Warren Buffett Way*. New York, NY: Wiley.

Hakansson, N. H. and W. T. Ziemba (1995). Capital growth theory. In R. A. Jarrow, V. Maksimovic, and W. T. Ziemba (Eds.), *Finance Handbook*, pp. 123–44. Amsterdam: North-Holland.

Harlow, W. V. (1991). Asset allocation in a downside-risk framework. *Financial Analysts Journal*, 28–40.

Harlow, W. V. and R. K. S. Rao (1989). Asset pricing in a generalized mean-lower partial moment framework: theory and evidence. *Journal of Financial and Quantitative Analysis*, 24(3), 285–311.

Hausch, D. B., V. Lo, and W. T. Ziemba (Eds.) (1994). *Efficiency of Racetrack Betting Markets*. San Diego, CA: Academic Press.

Hensel, C. R. and W. T. Ziemba (2000). How did Clinton stand up to history? US stock market returns and presidential party affiliations. In D. B. Keim and W. T. Ziemba (Eds.), *Security Market Imperfections in World Wide Equity Markets*, pp. 203–217. Cambridge, UK: Cambridge University Press.

90   *William T. Ziemba*

Kallberg, J., R. White, and W. Ziemba (1982). Short term financial planning under uncertainty. *Management Science*, XXVIII, 670–682.

Kelly, J. (1956). A new interpretation of information rate. *Bell System Technology Journal*, 35, 917–26.

Knight, J. and S. Satchell (2005). A re-examination of Sharpe's ratio for log-normal prices. *Applied Mathematical Finance*, 12(1), 87–100.

Kusy, M. and W. Ziemba (1986). A bank asset and liability management model. *Operations Research*, XXXIV, 356–376.

Latane (1959). Criteria for choice among risky ventures. *Journal of Political Economy*, 38, 144–155.

Leland, H. (1999). Beyond mean-variance: performance measurement in a nonsymmetrical world. *Financial Analysts Journal*, 27–36.

Lo, A. W. (2002). The statistics of Sharpe ratios. *Financial Analysts Journal*, 56, 36–52.

MacLean, L. C. and W. T. Ziemba (1999). Growth versus security tradeoffs in dynamic investment analysis. *Annals of Operations Research*, 85, 193–227.

MacLean, L. C. and W. T. Ziemba (2005). Capital growth: theory and practice. In S. A. Zenios and W. T. Ziemba (Eds.), *Handbook of Asset-Liability Management, Volume 1: Theory and Methodology*. North Holland, in press.

MacLean, L. C., W. T. Ziemba, and Y. Li (2005). Time to wealth goals in capital accumulation and the optimal trade-off of growth versus security. *Quantitative Finance*, in press.

Mao, J. (1970). Models of capital budgeting, e-v vs. e-s. *Journal of Financial and Quantitative Analysis*, 5, 657–675.

Markowitz, H. M. (1959). *Portfolio Selection*. Wiley & Sons.

Miller, R. and A. Gehr (2005). Sample bias and Sharpe's performance measure: a note. *Journal of Financial and Quantitative Analysis*, 13, 943–946.

Nielson, L. T. and M. Vassalou (2004). Sharpe ratios and alphas in continuous time. *Journal of Financial and Quantitative Analysis*, 39(1), 103–114.

Roy, A. (1952). Safety first and the holding of assets. *Econometrica*, 20, 431–449.

Sharpe, W. (1966). Mutual fund performance. *Journal of Business*, 39, 119–138.

Sharpe, W. F. (1994). The Sharpe ratio. *Journal of Portfolio Management*, 21(1), 49–58.

Siegel, L. B. (2003). *Benchmarks and investment management*. AIMR.

Siegel, L. B., K. F. Kroner, and S. W. Clifford (2001). The greatest return stories ever told. *The Journal of Investing* (Spring), 1–12.

Sortino, F. A. and L. N. Price (1994). Performance measurement in a downside risk framework. *Journal of Investing* (Fall).

Sortino, F. A. and R. van der Meer (1991). Downside risk. *Journal of Portfolio Management* (Summer).

Spurgin, R. B. (2000). How to game your Sharpe ratio. *Journal of Alternative Investments*, 4(3), 38–46.

Thorp, E. O. (1997). The Kelly criterion in blackjack, sports betting and the stock market. Mimeo, Forthcoming in *Handbook of Asset Liability Management, Volume 1: Theory and Methodology*, S.A. Zenios and W.T. Ziemba (eds), Elsevier, North Holland, in press, 2005.

Tompkins, R., W. Ziemba, and S. Hodges (2003). The favorite-longshot bias in S&P500 futures options: the return to bets and the cost of insurance. Working paper, Sauder School of Business, UBC.

Ziemba, W. T. (2003). *The Stochastic Programing Approach to Asset Liability and Wealth Management.* AIMR.

Ziemba, W. T. and D. B. Hausch (1984). *Beat the Racetrack.* San Diego, CA: Harcourt.

Ziemba, W. T. and D. B. Hausch (1986). *Betting at the Racetrack.* DrZ Investments, Inc, San Luis Obispo, CA.

Ziemba, W. T. and S. L. Schwartz (1991). *Invest Japan.* Chicago, IL: Probus.

Chapter 6

The Predictive Ability of the Bond Stock Earnings Yield Differential Model*

Klaus Berge

Department of Economics, Dresden University of Technology,
D-01062 Dresden, Germany;
phone +49 (351) 463-34628, fax +49 (351) 463-35404,
email klaus.berge@tu-dresden.de

Giorgio Consigli

Department of Mathematics, Statistics and Computer Science,
University of Bergamo, 20147 Bergamo, Italy;
phone +39 (035) 2052685, fax +39 36 335 7373585,
email: giorgio.consigli@unibg.it

William T. Ziemba

Sauder School of Business, University of British Columbia,
Vancouver, 2053 Main Mall, Vancouver, BC V6T 1Z2, Canada;
phone +1 (604) 261-1343, fax +1 (604) 263-9572,
email ziemba@interchange.ubc.ca

This is a survey of the bond stock prediction model in international equity markets which is useful for predicting the time varying equity risk premium (ERP) and for strategic asset allocation of bond-stock equity mixes. The model has two versions. Beginning with Ziemba and Schwartz (1991), the BSEYD model our is the difference between the most liquid long bond, usually thirty or ten or five years, and the trailing equity yield. The idea is that asset allocation between stocks and bonds is related to their relative yields and, when the bond yield is too high, there is a shift out of stocks into bonds that can cause an equity market correction. This model predicted the 1987 US, the 1990 Japan, the 2000, 2002 and 2007 US corrections. The FED model

---

*We would like to thank, Sandra Schwartz and two anonymous referees for helpful comments on an earlier drafts of this paper. This research was supported by NSERC and MIUR(PRIN 2005139555002) grants.

is a special case of the BSYED model with bond and stock yields assumed to be equal. A ratio model and the FED model have origins in reports and statements from the Federal Reserve System under Alan Greenspan, from 1996. Hence the ERP can be negative or positive and is thus partially predictable. Despite its predictive ability, the bond-stock model has been criticized as being theoretically unsound because it compares a nominal quantity, the long bond yield, with a real quantity, the earnings yield on stocks. However, inflation and mis-conception arguments may justify the model. Theoretical models of fair priced equity indices can be derived and compared to actual index values to ascertain danger levels. This paper surveys this literature with a focus on their economic and financial implications and its application to the study of stock market strategies and corrections in five worldwide equity markets.

JEL Classification: G14; G15; G12

Keywords: market crash, yield differential, bond-stock yield ratio, over-under valuation, equity risk premium.

6.1. Introduction

The BSEYD and FED models provide a framework for discussing stock market over-under valuation. The FED model was introduced by market practitioners after Alan Greenspan's speech on market irrational exuberance in November 1996 in an attempt to understand and predict variations in the equity risk premium. The model relates the yield on stocks (measured by the ratio of earnings to stock prices) to the yield on nominal Treasury bonds. The theory behind the FED model is that an optimal asset allocation between stocks and bonds is related to their relative yields and when the bond yield is too high, a market adjustment is needed and there is a shift out of stocks into bonds. If the adjustment is large, it causes an equity market correction (a decline of 10% within one year). Hence, there is a short term negative ERP. This related BSEYD model predicted the 1987 US, the 1990 Japan and the 2000 and 2002 US corrections. The BSEYD valuation model with the 30-year long rate and the equity yield difference as the underlying measure of relative equity market valuation was suggested by Ziemba and Schwartz (1991); see also Ziemba (2003) and Koivu et al. (2005). The partial predictability of stock returns has been analysed and confirmed by Fama and French (1988b) and Poterba and Summers (1988). The ability of financial and accounting variables to predict individual stock prices and stock indices has been studied by Campbell (1987, 1990, 1993), Campbell and Shiller (1988), Campbell and Yogo (2006), Fama and French (1988a, 1989), Goetzmann and Ibbotson (2006), Jacobs and Levy (1988),

Lakonishok, Schleifer and Vishny (1994), Polk, Thompson and Vuolteenaho (2006), and Ziemba and Schwartz (1991, 2000).

The FED and BSEYD models have been successful in predicting market turns, but in spite of their empirical success and simplicity, they have been criticised. First they do not consider the role played by time varying risk premiums in the portfolio selection process while it does consider a risk free government interest rate as the discount factor of future earnings. More seriously, the inflation illusion (the possible impact of inflation expectations on the stock market) as suggested by Modigliani and Cohn (1979) is not taken into consideration. Secondly, the models assumes the comparability of earning price ratios, a real quantity, with a nominal, bond induced, interest rate (Campbell and Vuolteenaho, 2004). Asness (2000, 2003), and Ritter and Warr (2002) discuss these issues. Consigli, MacLean, Zhao and Ziemba (2006) propose a stochastic model of equity returns based on an extension of the BSEYD model inclusive of a risk premium in which market corrections are endogenously generated by the bond-stock yield difference. The model accommodates both cases of prolonged yield deviations leading to a long series of small declines in the equity market and the case, peculiar of recent speculative bubbles, of a series of corrections over limited time periods. The inclusion of the yield differential as a key driver of the market correction process is tested and the model validated with market data in Section 5. Section 2 discusses the bond-stock valuation model and shows its original application to the October 1987 correction. Hence the ERP is not constant and thus is partially predictable. Section 3 discusses over valuation and possible forthcoming corrections. Section 4 discusses empirical evidence from the US, Japan, Germany, the UK and Canada. Section 5 analyzes endogenous instability, risk premiums and the nominal versus real variable issue. Section 6 concludes.

6.2. Valuation Model, Equity Yield and 10 Year Interest Rate

The FED model in its original 1996 form states the equivalence of a fair stock price level $\tilde{p}(t)$ at time t to the expected earnings $E(t)$ and the 10-year Treasury rate $r(t)$. Earnings expectations are fully incorporated in prices and discounted at the current 10 year risk free rate, for $t = 1, 2, \ldots$

$$\tilde{p}(t) = \frac{E(t)}{r(t)}. \qquad (6.1)$$

Earnings per share $y(t)$ are computed by equity investors as the expected earnings for given unit investment in the stock market with equity shares, $S(t)$

$$y(t) = \frac{E(t)}{S(t)}. \tag{6.2}$$

Then $S(t) = \frac{E(t)}{y(t)}$, and there is a direct relationship between the equity yield in (6.2) and the risk free rate in (6.1). The ratio of the current market value to the theoretical value is the *bond stock yield ratio* BSYR(t)

$$\frac{S(t)}{\tilde{p}(t)} = \left[\frac{\frac{E(t)}{y(t)}}{\frac{E(t)}{r(t)}} \right] = \frac{r(t)}{y(t)} = BSYR(t). \tag{6.3}$$

The *bond stock earnings yield differential* $BSEYD(t) = r(t) - y(t)$ is related to the (random) valuation measure and the equity yield

$$\frac{S(t)}{\tilde{p}(t)} - 1 = \frac{BSEYD(t)}{y(t)}. \tag{6.4a}$$

$$BSEYD(t) = [BSYR(t) - 1]y(t). \tag{6.4b}$$

The differential reflects the difference between the current market value and its theoretical value. As pointed out by a referee, a more theoretically sound motivation for the predictive ability of the BSEYD is using the basic Gordon formula, where E/P is the forward earnings yield (which Schwartz and Ziemba (2000) show is the best predictor of at least individual Japanese stock prices):

E/P – nominal yield = equity risk premium – real growth – inflation.

So the BSEYD can be used as a proxy for the unobservable right hand side economic variables.

For given equity yield the BSEYD and the BSYR can be used to identify zones of under and over valuation and forecast possible forthcoming market adjustments. Under the FED model assumptions we expect the market, even with prolonged deviations, to fluctuate around its theoretical value and thus from time to time the BSYR should converge to 1 and the BSEYD to 0. Alternatively a market risk premium should be accounted for and future earnings be accordingly discounted by an interest rate above the prevailing risk free rate (10 year maturity rates in the canonical FED assumption).

A classic example of the use of this model is the stock market correction in October 1987 as illustrated in Table 6.1. It is from this application that

Table 6.1:   Behavior of the BSEYD in the US around the Stock Market Correction in October 1987.

All data except for stock market return data are as of the end of the given months. The BSEYD is the difference between the 10-year bond yield and the E/P ratio.

Date	10Y T-Bond Yield	E/P Ratio	BSEYD	MSCI TRI Return in %
Sep-86	7.45	7.19	0.26	−8.50
Oct-86	7.43	6.81	0.62	5.68
Nov-86	7.25	6.78	0.47	2.35
Dec-86	7.11	7.07	0.04	−2.52
Jan-87	7.08	6.26	0.82	13.28
Feb-87	7.25	5.96	1.29	3.59
Mar-87	7.25	5.76	1.49	2.70
Apr-87	8.02	5.8	2.22	−0.90
May-87	8.61	5.85	**2.76**	0.56
Jun-87	8.40	5.59	**2.81**	5.18
Jul-87	8.45	5.36	**3.09**	4.75
Aug-87	8.76	4.88	**3.88**	3.94
Sep-87	9.42	5.03	**4.39**	−2.13
Oct-87	9.52	6.35	3.17	**−21.22**
Nov-87	8.86	7.38	1.48	−8.45
Dec-87	8.99	6.87	2.12	7.04
Jan-88	8.67	6.66	2.01	4.28
Feb-88	8.21	6.86	1.35	4.19
Mar-88	8.37	7.14	1.23	−3.35
Apr-88	8.72	7.08	1.64	0.92
May-88	9.09	7.51	1.58	0.86
Jun-88	8.92	7.29	1.63	4.65
Jul-88	9.06	7.32	1.74	−0.31
Aug-88	9.26	8.77	0.49	−3.35

Source: Berge and Ziemba (2006).

Ziemba's Yamaichi Research Institute study group in 1988 formulated the BSEYD measure as described in Ziemba and Schwartz (1991) and Ziemba (2003). The danger zone was entered in May 1987 and the correction occurred in October, four months later. During June, July and August investors kept rebalancing their portfolios from the bond to the equity market (MSCI TRI + 13.87% over the quarter) then the equity market fell −31.80% in the following quarter (September to November 1987) with the main decline in October. In order to validate the approach, Berge and Ziemba (2006) used eight different strategies to test the predictive ability of the BSEYD or, equivalently, the BSYR, see Table 6.2. The strategies are defined over either 5 or 10 year time data intervals, under normal or historical return distribution assumptions and different fractile levels on

Table 6.2:   Strategies Used to Evaluate the Robustness (Predictive Ability) of (the) BSEYD-based Strategies.

Strategy	Length of Determining Interval (Years)	Distribution Type	Fractile for Exit Threshold Level (α_1)	Fractile for Entry Threshold Level (α_2)
1	5	Historical	90%	80%
2	5	Historical	90%	70%
3	5	Normal	95%	85%
4	5	Normal	95%	75%
5	10	Historical	95%	85%
6	10	Historical	95%	75%
7	10	Normal	90%	85%
8	10	Normal	90%	80%

Source: Berge and Ziemba (2006).

such distributions for exiting and entering the equity market. The threshold levels were specified for the BSEYD measure.

These 60 or 120 observations, respectively, including the value of the current month define the threshold levels for the end of that month. As time evolves, the most recent monthly value is added and the oldest value is omitted. Moving intervals diminish the impact of changes in the regulatory framework of the economy on E/P ratios over time, since high past values of the BSEYD are eventually excluded. For the historical values of the BSEYD two different distributional concepts are used to define the predetermined exit and entry threshold levels, normality and historical. With normality, the mean and standard deviation of the historical range of BSEYDs are

$$\overline{BSEYD}_{t,d} = \frac{1}{d} \sum_{j=t-d+1}^{t} BSEYD_j, \qquad (6.4)$$

and

$$s_{BSEYD_{t,d}} = \sqrt{\frac{1}{d-1} \sum_{j=t-d+1}^{t} (BSEYD_j - \overline{BSEYD}_{t,d})^2}, \qquad (6.5)$$

respectively, where d is the length of the interval considered. The exit threshold levels is

$$TL_{t,d,\alpha_1}^{Out,ND} = \overline{BSEYD}_{t,d} + z_{\alpha_1} \cdot s_{BSEYD_{t,d}} \qquad (6.6)$$

and the entry threshold level is

$$TL_{t,d,\alpha_2}^{In,ND} = \overline{BSEYD}_{t,d} + z_{\alpha_2} \cdot s_{BSEYD_{t,d}}, \qquad (6.7)$$

where z_{α_1} and z_{α_2} are the α_1- and α_2-fractiles of the standard normal probability distribution, respectively. The second concept calculates the α_1- and α_2-fractiles of the historical distribution. The α-fractile of d observations is

$$\tilde{x}_\alpha = x_{(k)} + \left(x_{(k+1)} - x_{(k)}\right) \cdot (1 - \alpha), \tag{6.8}$$

where $k = d \cdot \alpha$ and $x_{(k)}$ is the k-smallest value of the d observations starting at the end of month $(t - d + 1)$ and ending at the end of month t.

The strategies are evaluated over the 1979–2005 period in five equity markets: the US, Germany, Canada, UK and Japan. The stock market index data are from Morgan Stanley Capital International (MSCI). These indices utilize a uniform methodology across all markets. The total return indices (TRI) are calculated with gross dividends (before taxes) reinvested to estimate the total return on the market that would be achieved by reinvesting one twelfth of the annual dividend reported at every month end. P/E ratios provided by MSCI refer to the companies in the respective MSCI TRI. They are the sum of the weighted latest share prices in local currency divided by the sum of the weighted most recent trailing twelve-month earnings (losses) per share. MSCI does not estimate future earnings so only past earnings are included in their data. Actual earnings are entered in the database as soon as they are reported at an adequately detailed level. The advantage of the MSCI indices over other indices is that even when the overall market experiences losses, P/E ratios, in this case negative, can be calculated. For cash equivalents the yield on 3-month T-Bills is used. Data for 3-month T-Bills are from Global Financial Data (GFD) and Thomson Financial Datastream.

Data on 10-year government bond yields come from various sources. The United States, data is from the Federal Reserve. Yields are of constant maturity interpolated from the daily yield curve. Data for Germany were supplied by the Deutsche Börse AG and are calculated in a similar way as for US data. Data for the United Kingdom and Japan come from GFD. These yields refer to government bonds with a maturity closest to ten years. Data for Japan are available beginning in May 1980. Japanese T-Bills data were not updated monthly until December 1981. Canadian government bond yields were obtained from the Bank of Canada.

For the first strategy, five years of monthly observations are used prior to 1979 to estimate the historical (or frequency) distribution of the 90% and 80% fractiles. Every month the data includes the realized monthly return and discards the oldest observation to keep the five year window constant.

Table 6.3: Required Exit and Re-Entry Fractiles for Strategy 6 for Optimal Performance*

Correction Number	Start Date	Value of BSEYD (Previous Month)/ Corresponding Required Exit Fractile	End Date	Value of BSEYD/ Corresponding Required Re-Entry Fractile
3	April 1981	1.74/97.5%	September 1981	2.04/96.5%
4	December 1981	1.26/87.5%	July 1982	0.00/65.0%
5	September 1987	3.88/99.0%	November 1987	1.48/55.0%
6	June 1990	2.31/77.0%	October 1990	1.40/41.0%
7	July 1998	1.83/62.0%	August 1998	0.96/25.0%
8	April 2000	2.99/94.0%	September 2001	1.11/18.5%
9	April 2002	2.39/84.0%	September 2002	−0.32/0.0%

*Corrections 1 and 2 predate April 1981, see Table A1 in the appendix.

Every strategy has well defined equity market entry and exit values: once in, the strategy suggests 100% in equities, once out 0%, i.e., a 0-1 stock-bond strategy. The Appendix contains results for the five markets for the 35-period, 1970–2005. Every fractiles pair defines the market *danger zone*, which are used in the definition of the optimal investment strategies and portfolio rebalancing.

Strategy 6 was preferable in terms of total return over the 25 years, 1980–2005, in the US market. Table 6.3 shows exiting and entering months according to these thresholds and the BSEYD signal in the previous month.

Tables A1–A10 in the Appendix show for the five countries, the stock market corrections (declines of 10% plus) and their durations and the results of the strategies in terms of percent of time in the stock market, mean log return, standard deviation, Sharpe ratio, mean excess return and terminal value all the comparison with the actual stock markets total returns in 1975–2005 for strategies 1–4 and 1980–2005 for strategies 5–8. Dimson *et al.* (2006a,b) present returns over more than 100 years but do not discuss partially predictive investment strategies as do Berge and Ziemba (2006).

The US had nine corrections and the terminal values, Sharpe ratios, etc. all suggest that the strategies added considerable value. The main test is: are you better off or not being out of the stock market when the BSEYD measure suggest you should be? For example, $100 grew to $4650 in the stock market and from $8480 to $10,635 with strategies 1–4 for the period 1975–2005. In addition, the portfolio variance was less because about 15–20% of the time one is out of the stock market. The period 1980–2005 had similar positive results for the various strategies.

Japan had seven corrections including the 31-month 56.2% decline starting in January 1990. Ziemba (2003) and Ziemba and Schwartz (1991) provide calculations showing that this correction was the most in the danger zone of any of the measures in the 42-year period 1948–1990. Ziemba and Schwartz (1991) found that every time during 1948–1988 that the BSEYD measure was in the danger zone, there was a correction of at least 10% from the current stock index level. There were no misses (12/12) but only 12 of the 20 corrections during 1948–88 were from this prediction. The other eight were from other causes. The results for Japan, like the US, are good for the measure: 100 yen grows to 213.88 yen with the market index from 1985–2005 but to 455.72 yen to 498.62 yen with strategies 1–4. Strategies 5–8 also had good prediction results for 1990–2005.

The results for the other three countries were not as good in terms of final wealth levels from 1975–2005. However, all the strategies were superior to buy and hold in terms of the Sharpe ratios and in the final wealth levels during 1980–2005. For the UK, most of the strategies outperformed the buy and hold stock market returns but there were some underperforming strategies and the outperformance of the winning strategies was minimal.

The UK had 15 corrections mostly of short duration but the 17.9% decline of September 2000 lasted 13 months and the April 2002 decline of 31.6% lasted 10 months.

Canada had similar results to the US with five of its 12 corrections having declines of over 20% including a 41.2% decline in September 2000 over 13 months. Germany also had similar results with 13 corrections with the March 2000 decline being −44% over 19 months and April 2002 −53.9% over 12 months.

The basic conclusion is that the bond-stock model has had positive predictive ability worked in these five countries especially in the 1980–2005 period with the results in the US and Japan the best: portfolio strategies based on the bond-stock relative valuation measure have produced superior returns relative to a buy and hold strategy.

6.3. Over Valuation and Forthcoming Corrections

The evidence shows that the effectiveness of the bond-stock yield difference measure differs from market to market and in general additional indicators may be required to generate robust strategies across markets and times. We focus here on the properties of the yield ratio as a signal of forthcoming market corrections, thus suggesting an immediate exit from the equity market. Investors will follow different strategies.

A critical view on the role of the bond stock yield differential as a predictive variable for future market adjustments depends on the market evidence. Consider the following alternative scenarios, from which an indirect economic validation of the approach can be derived:

1. The stock market is overvalued according to the bond-stock yield differential and a subsequent market correction is observed, this evidence supports the suggested approach.
2. Market corrections are observed even if the yield differential is within the no danger zone.
3. Even if the yield differential remains for an extended period in the danger zone, no market corrections occur.
4. Market corrections do not occur for an extended period of time and the yield differential is around zero.

The first and fourth market conditions support the BSEYD model and suggest that a high difference between the earnings-per-share at an aggregate level in the economy and the 10-year bond rate is a sufficient condition for a subsequent correction.

The second and third conditions suggest that investors act independently and do not rely on the bond-equity yield differentials to determine their portfolio strategies and the strategic bond-equity portfolio composition. If corrections are observed even if the yield differential is relatively low, this would imply that the yield differential may very well provide a sufficient but not a necessary condition for corrections. In this case other variables are determining the adjustment. Finally the absence of corrections in the presence of persistently high differentials would contradict the sufficient condition.

Following the suggestion of a referee, we test the short-term predictive power of the yield spread with respect to market returns directly, verifying the market response to diverging bond and stock yields observed in previous periods. A BSEYD in the upper tail of the frequency distribution should, in general, anticipate a market correction of varying intensity. To document short term predictability we use a simple predictive regression model based on monthly returns in the equity market and one, two and three months lagged yield spreads. The bivariate prediction equation for each market k (US, UK, Japan, Germany and Canada), is

$$\rho_k(t) = a_k + b_k \left[y_k(t-h) \geq z_{k,90\%}^{t-h} \right] + e_k(t) \quad h = 1, 2, 3 \quad k = 1, \ldots, 5$$

$$(6.9)$$

where:

$\rho_k(t)$ is the month-to-month log equity return for market k, over $(t-1, t)$, namely $\ln \left(\frac{s_k(t)}{s_k(t-1)} \right)$,

$y_k(t-h)$ is the *BSEYD* or *yield spread* at time $t - h$: one, two and three months earlier, and

$z_{k,90\%}^{t-h}$ is the 90th percentile of the yield spread historical distribution estimated at time $t - h$ over the market history $(t - h - H, t - h)$ where H defines a 15 year data history.

For every t, starting with the period Jan 1970 to Dec 1984, we estimate the frequency distribution on this window, and identify the 90% percentile and then move forward 1 month, identify the associated 90% percentile, and repeat with a constant time window.

Once such series of critical values have been identified, we test for $t =$ Jan 1985, ..., Dec 2004, whether the current yield spread falls above the current critical value, namely, $y_k(t-h) \geq z_{k,90\%}^{t-h}$. Then, conditional on the yield spread excess, we determine the market return one, two and three months ahead and identify the residuals for each month and market. In this way we estimate directly from the tail of the distribution the market specific coefficients a_k, b_k over the 20 years.

This procedure tests the market return dependence on the 1, 2 and 3 month lagged yield spread, conditionally on such spread being above the 90th yield percentile. A statistically significant relationship between $\rho_k(t)$ and $y_k(t-h), h = 1, 2, 3$ for market k, is not sufficient to assess the predictive power of the yield spread with respect to the equity return. A negative coefficient b_k is needed with residuals normally distributed with mean 0 and given variance, $e_k(t) \in N(0, \sigma_k^2)$. Table 6.4 reports the results; see also Figure 6.1 for the one-month predictive regressions in the US. In columns 2 and 3 the mean and standard deviations of monthly returns conditional on the yield spread being inside the time varying 10% upper tail. The regression results and the mean and variance of the computed residuals, on the selected sub-samples (which depend on the markets volatility).

Table 6.4: 1, 2, 3 Month Prediction Power of the BSEYD for Various EQUITY MARKETS (No Results are Reported for Canada Since No Yield Excesses were Reported Over the 20 years).

Jan 1985–Dec 2005 MSCI Monthly Data

$$y(t) = a + b\,z(t-j) + e(t); j = 1,2,3$$

	Conditional Mean	Conditional Std Dev	a	b	R^2	Residuals Variance	Mean
US Equity							
lag 1	-0.008059506	0.071475813	0.346	-0.1139	0.4889	0.002961	0.000466996
lag 2	-0.004050033	0.074122486	0.2817	-0.918	0.2955		
lag 3	-0.009414431	0.071723591	-0.0575	0.0152	0		
UK Equity							
lag 1	-0.01566462	0.089364691	0.4484	-0.1423	0.299		
lag 2	-0.028584323	0.089782349	0.4671	-0.152	0.337	0.005599	4.08603E-05
lag 3	-0.008372955	0.051777963	-0.1527	0.0442	0.08		
JPN Equity							
lag 1	-0.032871424	0.08874209	0.1694	-0.0467	0.0635	0.007375	9.60305E-05
lag 2	-0.02053557	0.091968716	0.0608	-0.0188	0.0095		
lag 3	-0.023069067	0.092978531	-0.1301	0.0247	0.0162		
GER Equity							
lag 1	-0.003929792	0.060827994	-0.0019	-0.0006	0.0002	0.003623	-0.000123067
lag 2	-0.004137307	0.060351908	0.0022	-0.002	0.0028		
lag 3	-0.000313041	0.061393217	-0.0004	0.00005	0		

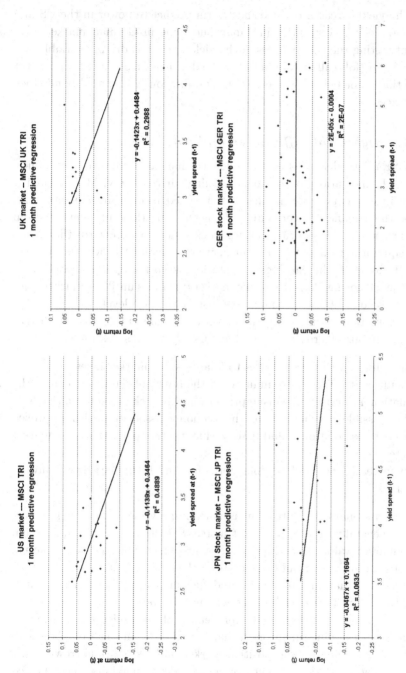

Figure 6.1: One-month Predictive Regressions of the BSEYD for Various Equity Markets, Jan 1985 to Dec 2005.

The yield spread has some short term predictive power in the US and UK markets but very little in Japan and none in German markets. We are not testing the effectiveness of the yield spread as driving variable of a strategic portfolio allocation but only the dependence of short term market corrections (not beyond three months) on previously observed bond-stock yield excesses.

6.3.1. *High yield differences and corrections*

The BSEYD model relies on the evidence that, at current market values, improved expectations on company earnings drive price yields up, making equity investments more attractive than fixed income investments. This pushes the demand for stocks up and triggers a portfolio re-balancing from bonds to stocks. This in turn pushes stock yields down towards their long-term equilibrium value: typically inclusive of a small ERP over the risk free rate. If, however, the earnings expectations keep rising, stock prices may continue increasing. This drives the market dynamics until the market price yield does not stabilise around a consensus long-term level.

A condition of instability in this setting may emerge if the 10-year interest rate also increases. Several factors explain this possibility:

1. The selling of 10 year T-Notes to finance stock market investments.
2. A shift of the yield curve induced by the policy of the Fed, to offset the inflationary impact on consumption from the stock market wealth effect.
3. The possible overheating of the economy associated with improved earning expectations, and partly due to the persistence of market increases.
4. An increased demand for long term funding to finance equity investments.

This latter scenario, in spite of an assumed improvement of earnings expectations, generally induces a modest increase of the theoretical equilibrium stock market value, thus supporting a growing deviation of the actual market capitalisation from the long term theoretical value.

Such a deviation will persist and fuel increasing forward instability until the interest rate tightening will not be perceived by the market sufficient to reduce the expected improvement of companies' earnings. From a different viewpoint, investors initially start rebalancing from bonds to equity, then relying on the positive market outlook, start borrowing and move further up on the efficient frontier in order to maximise the expected return. The subsequent market adjustment will be large due to the sudden and substantial inversion of relative values. Under these circumstances, foreign investors will play a specific role: in the presence of an increasing foreign-domestic interest rate gap they will be attracted to foreign equity markets to attempt to obtain superior returns and also gain from the exchange rate differential. Inflows from foreign markets will further expand the departure of the market from its theoretical value. In this sequence of events, the 10-year Treasury rate will deviate correspondingly from the stock market yield. The 1987 crisis and the comparatively smaller 1997 crisis are consistent with this. On October 17, 1987 the 10 year rate was 10.22%. It was 7.5% in March 1987. As shown in Table 6.1, the BSEYD moved over the same period from 1.49 to 4.32 in September. A prolonged decrease of equity yields and increase of interest rates in a rapidly expanding economy may lead to a market overvaluation and a subsequent market collapse, when the BSEYD reaches a level unsustainable by the market.

6.3.2. High yield difference without corrections

Can the BSEYD remain high on historical terms (above the value of 2.03, the average between Jan 1, 1985 and Dec 31, 2004) for an extended period of time with the market relatively stable? Or, can we have the yield ratio increasing and high, the ratio between actual and theoretical prices increasing, the equity market increasing and no speculative bubble?

Thus, with stable earnings expectations and price yields, a reduction of market interest rates (due for instance to a loose monetary policy by the Federal Reserve, motivated by exogenous factors) below the equity yield decrease will drive the ratio up but there would not be a bubble. Low interest rates will also limit the inflows from foreign equity markets and the currency revaluation. This was the situation, in the US market in 1991–1992 and in 1999. Consider the 1999 period in which no corrections occurred but the BSEYD ratio remained above 3 for a long period. The reason appears to be related to the fact that the market had had a correction during the fall of 1998, was already regaining pace and it took few months before realizing that the theoretical market value was stable and interest rates were low and indeed slightly decreasing. The bond-stock ratio increased during a period of low interest rates (below 6%) in the US and increasing corporate earnings. If the equity yield is decreasing because of a sharply rising equity market and interest rates remain low or decreasing, a relatively high BSEYD can be associated with stable market expectations.

Then a BSEYD in the *danger zone* are not sufficient to lead to a market correction. Inflationary expectations play an additional role in the market sentiment. Decreasing interest rates convey a positive sentiment on the market.

6.3.3. Low yield difference and corrections

Finally, are sufficiently high BSEYD necessary to observe a correction? Not in general: market corrections have been observed even if the bond-stock differential was low and stable; see Table 6.4. Also events like September 11, 2001 can cause market corrections; in that case the S&P500 fell −14% in the week following the reopening of US markets after a week's closure.

The case of market instability and low BSEYD is crucial to assess the validity of the indicators as valuation measures. One such example starts in the third quarter of 2002: after a smooth decrease of the BSEYD during July and August, a sequence of large declines followed (−5.98% in the second week of September, followed by −12.75% in the third week and −6.49% in the first week of October). During this period, the BSEYD never reached the danger zone, remaining below the 2.85 level. The 10-year rate was stable and then started decreasing below 5% in October 2002. A common explanation is that the ratio had just been dramatically decreased from a May maximum of 3.5 and the equity yield was on a positive trend at the time, anticipating the following market recovery. No market corrections have been recorded with low BSEYD and an increasing equity market.

Summing up, the following aspects appear key to the ongoing debate on the robustness of the BSEYD as anticipating signals and their economic implications:

• The relative nature of the valuation measure implies that diverging bond-stock yields may lead to market corrections if the equity market has increased rapidly over the preceding months due to bond-equity rebalancing, equity investments funded through borrowing and incoming foreign capital, even with high and increasing interest rates. The degree of market internationalisation may in this case become relevant. High BSEYD are, however, neither sufficient nor necessary on their own to anticipate a market crisis.
• The stock market phase appears crucial: a high yield differential is consistent with either an increasing or decreasing equity market; the market adjustment will in both cases depend on the relative dynamics

of the 10-year rate and the price yield, conditionally on recent market performance.

• Finally, interest rates and inflationary expectations are relevant. Increasing but relatively low interest rates have a positive effect on market expectations and usually accompany a smooth convergence of equity prices to the theoretical values, avoiding market corrections.

Also an instability period may be induced by an exogenous correction or crisis in a different market, i.e., independently of the local current yield ratio.

6.4. United States and Worldwide Results

We review the evidence in Berge and Ziemba (2006) from five equity markets worldwide. In Section 2 and the appendix it is shown that being out of the market when the BSEYD measure indicated to be out dominates buy and hold strategies during 1975–2005 in the US, Japan, Germany, the UK and Canada. Periods in the danger zone are identified by entry and exit signals: the associated time periods can vary and lack of correction occurrence is identified once the market is in danger zone. Other times are the periods outside the danger zone. Table 6.5 shows that 34 corrections occurred while the yield differential was not in danger zone; while only 13 were correctly called by the BSYED danger zone.

Consider the first row. In the first column a sequence of market corrections is observed as correctly anticipated by the yield differential. In the second column the corrections occurred when the BSEYD was not in the danger zone. In the UK, out of 11 market corrections only one was anticipated by the BSEYD measure yield ratio during the 25-year history. Some of the recent corrections started in a foreign market as part of a domino effect (see the appendix). Tables 6.6 and 6.7 report the series of

Table 6.5: Evaluation of Forecasting Signals for the Best Performing BSEYD Strategy (6) in the US, Germany, Canada, UK, Japan 1980–2005.

	BSEYD Was in Danger Zone (US, GER, CAN, UK, JPN)	BSEYD Was Not in Danger Zone (US, GER, CAN, UK, JPN)
Correction Occurred	3, 4, 3, 1, 2 = 13	4, 8, 7, 10, 5 = 34
Correction Did Not Occur	2, 3, 1, 3, 0 = 9	3, 5, 2, 1, 1 = 12

Source: Berge and Ziemba (2006).

110   *Klaus Berge, Giorgio Consigli and William T. Ziemba*

Table 6.6:   Forecasting Signals and Corrections in the US 1980–2005.

Correction Number	Start Date	Duration (Months)	Decline (%)
1	April 1981	6	−11.6
2	December 1981	8	−11.1
3	**September 1987**	3	−29.4
4	**June 1990**	5	−14.1
5	July 1998	2	−14.7
6	**April 2000**	18	−31.2
7	**April 2002**	6	−29.1

Although the duration of the correction starting in April 2000 is longer than one year, it is considered a correction since the stock market dropped 23.9% within the following twelve months.

Table 6.7:   Forecasting Signals and Corrections in the UK 1980–2005.

Correction Number	Start Date	Duration (Months)	Decline (%)
1	September 1981	1	−16.1
2	**October 1987**	2	−33.4
3	September 1989	2	−10.4
4	January 1990	4	−12.3
5	**July 1990**	3	−16.0
6	June 1992	3	−14.9
7	February 1994	5	−15.1
8	May 1998	5	−14.3
9	January 2000	2	−10.2
10	**September 2000**	13	−17.9
11	**April 2002**	10	−31.6

Although the duration of the correction starting in September 2000 is longer than one year, it is considered a correction since the stock market dropped 14.7% within twelve months between September 2000 and August 2001.

corrections observed in the US and UK markets between 1980 and 2005. In bold are the overlapping corrections sequence, thus only marginally due to internal bond-stock yield differentials. In most of these corrections the BSEYD was previously not in danger zone, after the corrections, monetary authorities intervened, injecting liquidity into the markets or lowering interest rates in an attempt to limit the market fall and its systemic consequences. As a result, the BSEYD was also reduced.

The evidence on the predictive power of the BSEYD in the UK market is partially attributable to a global adjustment of international portfolios which started outside the UK: namely four out of 11 market crises were *imported* from the US market as part of a systemic adjustment. The June

1992 crisis was a side effect of the European currency crisis and as such was imported from a different financial market. The results of the out-of-sample test of the strategies based on the BSEYD are variable across the five countries. Almost all strategies performed better than the stock market; see Section 2 and the appendix. The US and Japan results were the best. In all countries, not all of the corrections were predicted.

The co-movement of the BSEYD and the stock markets demonstrates that some of the corrections were not detectable. The methodology of the strategies recommends moving out of the stock market when the current value of the BSEYD is extremely high compared to its past values. Hence, a rise of the BSEYD prior to the occurrence of corrections is necessary to yield a successful prediction of these corrections. This behavior is observable for some of the corrections in the various countries. However, the stock market did not always fall after a sharp rise in the indicator and other corrections occurred when the indicator was not at historically excessive levels. These corrections did not have their cause in a disequilibrium of the yield on long-term government bonds and the E/P ratio of the stock market. Only one of the corrections which occurred during 1995–2005 was predicted by the strategies. Two strategies for the UK gave correct signals for the correction starting in January 2000.

The results demonstrate a relationship between the yield on long-term government bonds and the E/P ratio of the stock market, at least for the extreme values of the spread between these variables. This relationship was exploitable to outperform the stock market. Since the pattern is observable over a long period of time in several countries and is not limited to a few strategies but rather valid for most of them, it is generally applicable and not data mining.

If the strategies detect negative returns on the stock market for certain periods over a long time, this leads to the conclusion that one could, on average, expect negative returns on the stock market whenever the indicator moves into the danger zone.

The first statement above (trading profits suggest semi-strong EMH violation) can be answered in the affirmative for all countries. Though the net mean returns on the strategies were not always clearly higher than for the stock market, the standard deviation of the returns was always much below the stock market. So risk-adjusted profits net of transaction costs were always positive with higher Sharpe ratios. The second statement (negative expected returns suggest even stronger market inefficiency) cannot be generally supported. Negative stock market returns for out-of-the-market periods are only observable for the US and Japan and partly for Germany and the UK. These returns are not significantly negative due to the high volatility of returns in these periods.

6.5. Endogenous Instability, Risk Premiums and the Nominal Versus Real Variable Issue

Bond-stock yield differentials provide reliable forecasting signals in conjunction with other financial variables such as the level of interest rates, interest rate differentials and equity market cycles. Campbell and Vuolteenaho (2004) criticise the FED model but admit that it has been "remarkably successful as a behavioural description of stock prices, and its descriptions of equity market equilibrium is superficially attractive." Their criticism is inflation based since the major factor determining the bond yield is the expected long-term rate of inflation. Declining inflation raises bond prices so yields fall because the fixed nominal value coupons are worth less. They then argue, correctly, that there is no reason why stocks should have lower yields because stocks are claims on corporate profits, which are not fixed in nominal terms so profits might move in line with inflation. Campbell and Vuolteenaho reject the following two potential explanations:

(1) inflation is bad for the real economy and corporate profits so increasing inflation lowers expected future profits and stock prices; and
(2) inflation increases uncertainty therefore stock prices decline.

However, econometric studies since the 1920s show that corporate dividends are not inversely related to inflation and bond yields. Also, for (2), as in (1), the evidence does not support this.

But Campbell and Vuolteenaho are swayed by the Modiglianni and Cohn (1979) argument that inflation confuses investors, who use nominal based yields to discount real corporate profits. Then stocks are underpriced during high inflation periods and declining inflation eliminates this confusion. Campbell and Vuolteenaho observe that measures of the equity risk premium, based on the cross-sectional pricing of riskier stocks relative to safer stocks or on the relative volatility of stocks and bonds are essentially unrelated to past inflation and bond yields. We agree with the Campbell and Vuolteenaho criticism and their attempt to argue why the bond-stock measures might work. Supporting this is the observation that it is very easy for investors to get confused and rely on few, sometime changing, key factors ignoring other relevant economic factors.

At the heart of the FED model Campbell and Vuolteenaho (2004) criticise the comparability of the Treasury rate with the S&P earnings yield, the first being a nominal return strictly related to the expected rate of inflation and the second an aggregate claim to corporate profits. Bond investors are aware that bond prices will vary in order to compensate inflation expectations and lead to nominal yields in line with the prevailing term structure of interest rates. On the contrary, corporate earnings are not expected to be constant in nominal terms. The idea that investors compare the 10 year (nominal) Treasury rate with the S&P (real) price yield is thus ill founded and not sustainable according to this explanation. Consigli, MacLean, Zhao and Ziemba (2006) test the hypothesis that over the 1970–2005 period market corrections are consistent in the US market with the postulated FED model. They find evidence of a structural positive risk premium, thus rejecting the claimed convergence of equity and bond returns after a sequence of corrections. This suggests the inclusion of the premium in a stochastic model of equity returns. The inclusion of a risk premium addresses the inflation expectations issue indirectly, focusing on the possible deviation of the equity yield from a theoretically sound market yield that *ceteris paribus* should determine the current stock market values. The comparison is thus only on the appropriate discount factor of future earnings, for the current risk free rate. The presence of a risk premium in the market can in this framework be directly implied from market data. Over the 1985–2005 period, the S&P500 index and its theoretical value [equation (1)] performed as shown in Figure 6.2.

The departure of the 10-year rate from the equity yield is captured by the valuation measure, which measures the percentage difference between the actual and the theoretical benchmark value (right Y axis on Figure 6.2). Consider the correction periods in Table 6.5. The 1987 crisis, the 1997 limited correction and the 2000 and 2002 market corrections were associated with an increasing stock market prices and a decreasing theoretical S&P500 fair value as anticipated by the BSEYD. Other corrections, such as the July 1998 and the May–June 2006 crises, occurred while the indicator was not in danger zone.

Following this statistical evidence, the amplitude and frequency of the corrections generated by the market can thus be studied as a function of the yield differential and other variables, driving the mis-valuation process. Consigli *et al.* (2006) suggest a model extension of the basic FED

114   Klaus Berge, Giorgio Consigli and William T. Ziemba

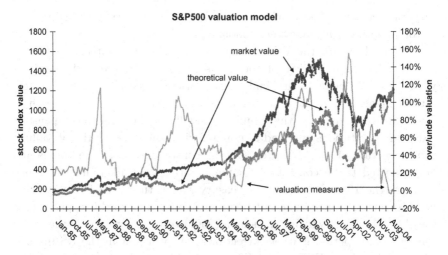

Figure 6.2:   Actual and Theoretical S&P500 and BSYR Process Minus 1.
Source: Consigli et al. (2006).

assumptions able to accommodate the various exceptions discussed above.
They propose an asset pricing model for equity returns in which market
instability phenomena are modelled as a Cox process whose intensity and
market impact depend endogenously on the BSYR and a market specific
risk premium. The economic rationale of this approach is that even if the
BSYR cannot, on its own, be taken as a statistically robust leading indicator
of prolonged market instability, the ratio provides an appropriate over-
under valuation measure as an endogenous state variable of an asset price
model with discontinuous returns. The random dependence of the correction
process from the yield differential is also supported by the evidence in
Figure 6.2. This displays the estimated linear relationship between the
BSEYD and the set of market corrections, adjustments beyond a predefined
−2.5% threshold, during 1985–2005 in the US. The relationship is negative
and statistically significant. The definition of an endogenous source of
instability in the asset return model generalizes previous attempts to model
equity returns as a Gauss Poisson processes with constant jump intensity
(Consigli, 2002). This yields a model whose parameters can be estimated
via maximum likelihood and fitted to market data as shown in Figures 6.2
and 6.3.

   The theoretical market price is generated by a discount rate that
depends on the risk free rate and a risk premium. The risk premium

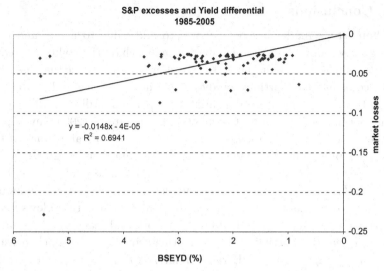

Figure 6.3:   Bond-Stock Earning Yield Differential and Market Corrections (Below −2.5%) in the US Market in the 1985–2005 Period.

depends on factors unaccounted for in the original FED model and, jointly with the BSEYD, will determine the amplitude of forthcoming market adjustments. Investors will modify the strategic portfolio allocation from bonds to equity and vice versa analysing the sustainability of the current deviation of equity prices from their theoretical value and then choosing how much to invest in bonds and equities. Expectations are updated depending on the joint movements of the 10-year rate plus a risk premium and aggregate earnings, assumed to be fully incorporated in prices. The bond-stock-cash strategic portfolio selection problem can, then be formulated and solved as a stochastic control problem. Once an excessive deviation of the current stock market value from its theoretical value is observed, the ratio between actual and theoretical stock price will depart from 1 and the following adjustment can be assumed to be a random function of the BSYR. The suggested approach is consistent with the dynamic version of the Fed model proposed by Koivu *et al.* (2005) and extends the evidence of a cointegration relationship between bond and equity yields in the US, Japan and Germany. See also Durré and Giot (2005) for more on the co-integration of the FED model in various countries.

6.6. Conclusions

The bond-stock model has been shown to add value to a buy and hold strategy in various US and foreign markets and to have the ability to predict corrections to some extent. Thus the model provides evidence that the ERP is not constant and partially predictable. The predictive ability was the best in the US and Japan and in earlier time periods. Still from 1980–2005, the model had good results. Campbell and Thompson (2005) investigate whether or not certain strategies out-predict the historical average of the equity risk premium. The evidence from Berge and Ziemba (2006) is that the bond-stock measures predict better than these historical buy and hold averages. The Consigli *et al.* (2006) model incorporates the bond-stock measure in a stochastic asset pricing model valuation and this allows direct market back testing in a simulation framework and leads to a stochastic control problem for portfolio selection (tilting using the bond-stock measure adds value). High current PE ratios relative to the historical PE ratios have been shown to predict corrections, see Aron (1981), Bleiberg (1989), Campbell and Ammer (1993), Campbell and Shiller (1998, 2005), Fama (1970, 1991, 1998), French and Poterba (1991), Polk *et al.* (2006), Shiller (2000), Siegel (2002), and Ziemba and Schwartz (1991). However, the bond-stock model that compares PE ratios to interest rates seems to have better prediction ability (Ziemba and Schwartz 1991, Rolph and Shen, 1999, Wong and Chew, 1999, Yardeni, 2003, Ziemba, 2003 and Berge and Ziemba 2006). The criticisms of the model by Campbell and Vuolteenaho (2004) and others are valid. The Modigliani and Cohn (1979) inflation confusion argument is one way to theoretically justify the model.

The research on the bond-stock model surveyed here, contributes to the research on the role it plays in portfolio strategies and clarifies its potential as a market crisis signal. The analysis also confirms the partial predictability of equity returns and the need to take agents' risk aversion into account when assessing market mean-reverting behaviour. Furthermore, it provides a basis to a statistical models of equity returns with an endogenous source of instability leading to an approach to strategic asset allocation over time.

References

Aron, P. (1981). Are Japanese P/E Multiples Too High?. Daiwa Securities of America, New York.

Asness, C. (2000). Stocks versus bonds: Explaining the equity risk premium. *Financial Analysts Journal*, March/April, 96–113.

Asness, C. (2003). Fight the fed model: The relationship between future returns and stock and bond market yields. *Journal of Portfolio Management* (Fall), 11–24.

Berge, K., Ziemba, W. T. (2006). The predictive ability of the bond stock earnings yield differential in US and foreign markets, 1970–2005. Working paper, University of British Columbia.

Bleiberg, S. (1989). How little we know ... about P/Es, but also perhaps more than we think. *Journal of Portfolio Management*, 15, 26–31.

Campbell, J. Y. (1987). Stock returns and the term structure. *Journal of Financial Economics* 18, 373-399.

Campbell, J. Y. (1990). Measuring the persistence of expected returns. *American Economic Review Papers and Proceedings*, 80, 43–47.

Campbell, J. Y. (1993). Intemporal asset pricing without consumption data. *American Economic Review*, 83, 487–512.

Campbell, J. Y. and Ammer, J. (1993). What moves the stock and bond markets? A variance decomposition for long-term asset returns. *Journal of Finance*, 48, 3–37.

Campbell, J. Y. and Shiller, R. J. (1988). Stock prices, earnings, and expected dividends. *Journal of Finance*, 43, 661–676.

Campbell, J. Y. and Shiller, R. J. (1998). Valuation ratios and the long-run stock market outlook. *Journal of Portfolio Management*, 24(2), 11–26.

Campbell, J. Y. and Shiller, R. J. (2005). Valuation ratios and the long-run stock market outlook: an update, in R.H. Thaler (ed), *Advances in Behavioral Finance, Volume II.* pp. 173–201. Princeton, NJ: Princeton University Press.

Campbell, J. Y. and Thompson, S. B. (2005). Predicting the equity premium out of sample: can anything beat the historical average? *Review of Financial Studies* (forthcoming).

Campbell, J. Y. and Vuolteenaho, T. (2004). Inflation illusion and stock prices. *American Economic Review, Papers and Proceedings 94* (May), 19–23 and abstracted in *Arrowstreet Journal*, 5(2), 1.

Campbell, J. Y. and Yogo, M. (2006). Efficient tests of stock return predictability, *Journal of Financial Economics*, 81, 27–60.

Consigli, G. (2002). Tail estimation and mean-variance portfolio selection in markets subject to financial instability. *Journal of Banking and Finance*, 26(7), 1355–1382

Consigli, G., MacLean, L. M., Zhao, Y., and Ziemba, W. T. (2006). Speculative bubbles: Asset prices with yield dependent market corrections. Working paper, University of Bergamo.

Constantinides, G. M. (1990). Habit formation: A resolution of the equity premium puzzle. *Journal of Political Economy*, 98, 519–543.

De Long, J. B., Sheifer, A., Summers, L. H., Waldmann, R. J. (1990). Noise trader risk in financial markets. *Journal of Political Economy*, 98(4), 703–738.

Dimson, E., Marsh, P. R., and Staunton, M. (2006a). *Global Investment Returns Yearbook,* ABN Amro, London School of Business School.

Durré, A., Giot, P., 2005, An international analysis of earnings, stock prices and bond yields, Working Paper, European Central Bank, Frankfurt (May).

Fama, E. F. (1970). Efficient capital markets: a review of theory and empirical work. *Journal of Finance*, 25, 383–417.

Fama, E. F. (1991). Efficient capital markets: II. *Journal of Finance*, 46, 1575–1617.

Fama, E. F. (1998). Market efficiency, long-term returns, and behavioral finance. *Journal of Financial Economics*, 49, 283–306.

Fama, E. F. and French, K. R. (1988a). Dividend yields and expected stock returns. *Journal of Financial Economics*, 22, 3–25.

Fama, E. F. and French, K. R. (1988b). Permanent and temporary components of stock prices. *Journal of Political Economy*, 96, 246–273.

Fama, E. F. and French, K. R. (1989). Business conditions and expected returns on stocks and bonds. *Journal of Financial Economics*, 25, 23–49.

French, K. R. and Poterba, J. M. (1991). Were Japanese stock prices too high?. *Journal of Financial Economics*, 29, 337–363.

Goetzmann, W. N. and Ibbotson, R. G. (2006). *The Equity Risk Premium*. Oxford, UK: Oxford University Press.

Jacobs, B. I. and Levy, K. N. (1988). Disentangling equity return regularities: New insights and investment opportunities. *Financial Analysts Journal*, 44, 18–43.

Koivu, M., Pennanen, T., and Ziemba, W. T. (2005). Cointegration of the Fed model. *Finance Research Letters*, 2, 248–259.

Lakonishok, J., Shleifer, A., and Vishny, R. W. (1994). Contrarian investment, extrapolation, and risk. *Journal of Finance*, 49, 1541–1578.

Modigliani, F. and Cohn, R. (1979). Inflation, rational valuation, and the market. *Financial Analysts Journal*, 35, 24–44.

Polk, C., Thompson, S., and Vuolteenaho, T. (2006). Cross-sectional forecasts of the equity premium. *Journal of Financial Economics*, 81, 101–141.

Poterba, J. M. and Summers, L. H. (1988). Mean reversion in stock prices: Evidence and implications. *Journal of Financial Economics*, 22, 27–59.

Ritter, J. R. and Warr, R. S. (2002). The decline of inflation and the bull market of 1982–1999. *Journal of Financial and Quantitative Analysis*, 37, 29–61.

Rolph, D. and Shen, P. (1999). Do the spreads between the E/P ratio and interest rates contain information on future equity market movements? Working paper, Federal Reserve Bank of Kansas City.

Schwartz, S. L. and Ziemba, W. T. (2000). Predicting returns on the Tokyo Stock Exchange. In Keim, D.B., Ziemba, W.T., (Eds.), *Security Market Imperfections in World Wide Equity Markets*, pp. 492–511. Cambridge, UK: Cambridge University Press.

Shiller, R. J. (2000). *Irrational Exuberance*, Princeton, NJ: Princeton University Press.

Siegel, J. J. (2002). *Stocks for the Long Run*. New York, NJ: McGraw-Hill.

Yardeni, E. (2003). Stock valuation models: Topical study 58, Prudential Financial Research.

Wong, W.-K. and Chew, B.-K. (1999). Can the forecasts generated from E/P ratio and bond yield be used to beat stock markets? Working paper, National University of Singapore.

Ziemba, W. T. (2003). *The Stochastic Programming Approach to Asset Liability and Wealth Management*, Charlottesville, VA: AIMR.

Ziemba, W. T. and Schwartz, S. L. (1991). *Invest Japan: The Structure, Performance and Opportunities of Japan's Stock, Bond and Fund Markets*. Chicago, IL: Probus.

APPENDIX A.

All tables are from Berge and Ziemba (2006).

Table A1:   Stock Market Corrections (10% plus) in the US, 1975–2005.

Although the duration of the correction starting in January 1977 is longer than one year, it is considered a correction since the stock market dropped 11% within ten months between January and October 1977. The same is true for the correction starting in April 2000 — the stock market dropped 23.9% within the following twelve months.

Correction Number	Start Date	Duration (Months)	Decline (%)
1	July 1975	3	−11.8
2	January 1977	14	−15.2
3	April 1981	6	−11.6
4	December 1981	8	−11.1
5	September 1987	3	−29.4
6	June 1990	5	−14.1
7	July 1998	2	−14.7
8	April 2000	18	−31.2
9	April 2002	6	−29.1

Table A2:   Evaluation of the Performance of the Strategies for the US.

The mean excess return is the average monthly excess return of the strategy over the stock market. Terminal values refer to the gross performance of $ 100 invested using the strategy signals.

Strategy	Number of Months in the Stock Market	Overall Performance of the Strategies/ the Stock Market				
		Mean Log Return	Standard Deviation	Sharpe Ratio	Mean Excess Return	Terminal Value
1	319 (85,75%)	0.01194	0.03933	0.17814	0.00162	8,480.41
2	300 (80,65%)	0.01255	0.03737	0.20378	0.00222	10,635.11
3	325 (87,37%)	0.01222	0.03936	0.18517	0.00190	9,420.42
4	314 (84,41%)	0.01246	0.03835	0.19632	0.00214	10,299.03
Stock Market (1975–2005)	372 (100%)	0.01032	0.04347	0.12401		4,649.75
5	273 (87,5%)	0.01254	0.03887	0.19773	0.00224	5,009.00
6	266 (85,26%)	0.01300	0.03835	0.21236	0.00270	5,781.16
7	260 (83,33%)	0.01215	0.03831	0.19039	0.00185	4,432.10
8	254 (81,41%)	0.01225	0.03785	0.19529	0.00195	4,569.44
Stock Market (1980–2005)	312 (100%)	0.01030	0.04389	0.12405		2,490.17

Table A3:   Stock Market Corrections (10% plus) in Germany, 1975–2005.

Although the duration of the correction starting in October 1978 is longer than one year, it is considered a correction since the stock market dropped 12.5% within nine months between October 1978 and June 1979. The same is true for the correction starting in March 2000 – the stock market dropped 20.7% within the following twelve months.

Correction Number	Start Date	Duration (Months)	Decline (%)
1	April 1976	7	−13.7
2	October 1978	18	−15.9
3	February 1984	6	−11.2
4	May 1986	3	−16.1
5	December 1986	3	−17.9
6	September 1987	5	−40.7
7	August 1990	2	−31.0
8	June 1992	4	−18.7
9	May 1994	11	−13.6
10	August 1997	3	−15.4
11	August 1998	2	−22.4
12	March 2000	19	−44.0
13	April 2002	12	−53.9

Table A4:   Evaluation of the Overall Performance of the Strategies for Germany.

The mean excess return is the average monthly excess return of the strategy over the stock market. Terminal values refer to the gross performance of €100 invested using the strategy signals.

Strategy	Number of Months in the Stock Market	Overall Performance of the Strategies/ the Stock Market				
		Mean Log Return	Standard Deviation	Sharpe Ratio	Mean Excess Return	Terminal Value
1	302 (81.18%)	0.00881	0.05150	0.09157	0.00068	2,652.80
2	265 (71.24%)	0.00789	0.04986	0.07613	−0.00024	1,884.15
3	322 (86.56%)	0.00934	0.05455	0.09614	0.00121	3,228.95
4	312 (83.87%)	0.00922	0.05425	0.09446	0.00109	3,088.99
Stock Market (1975–2005)	372 (100%)	0.00813	0.05864	0.06886		2,061.27
5	279 (89.42%)	0.00963	0.05836	0.09405	0.00123	2,014.62
6	241 (77.24%)	0.00910	0.05651	0.08787	0.00071	1,711.54
7	259 (83.01%)	0.01032	0.05736	0.10785	0.00193	2,504.27
8	253 (81.09%)	0.01010	0.05719	0.10431	0.00170	2,337.64
Stock Market (1980–2005)	312 (100%)	0.00840	0.06201	0.06870		1,373.26

Table A5:   Stock Market Corrections (10% plus) in Canada, 1975–2005.

Although the duration of the correction starting in September 2000 is longer than one year, it is considered a correction since the stock market dropped 36.4% within twelve months between September 2000 and August 2001.

Correction Number	Start Date	Duration (Months)	Decline (%)
1	July 1975	4	−11.0
2	June 1976	6	−14.6
3	March 1980	1	−18.7
4	July 1981	12	−39.4
5	December 1983	8	−13.8
6	September 1987	3	−25.6
7	January 1990	4	−14.5
8	August 1990	3	−10.9
9	February 1994	5	−11.1
10	June 1998	3	−25.0
11	September 2000	13	−41.2
12	April 2002	6	−21.3

Table A6:   Evaluation of the Overall Performance of the Strategies for Canada.

The mean excess return is the average monthly excess return of the strategy over the stock market. Terminal values refer to the gross performance of $Can 100 invested using the strategy signals.

Strategy	Number of Months in the Stock Market	Overall Performance of the Strategies/ the Stock Market				
		Mean Log Return	Standard Deviation	Sharpe Ratio	Mean Excess Return	Terminal Value
1	295 (79.3%)	0.00954	0.04243	0.08053	−0.00020	3,479.37
2	276 (74.19%)	0.00937	0.04110	0.07906	−0.00036	3,269.07
3	313 (84.14%)	0.00963	0.04384	0.07986	−0.00011	3,590.86
4	304 (81.72%)	0.00997	0.04301	0.08933	0.00023	4,075.27
Stock Market (1975–2005)	372 (100%)	0.00974	0.04925	0.07337		3,743.49
5	273 (87.5%)	0.00937	0.04336	0.07839	0.00094	1,859.80
6	256 (82.05%)	0.00951	0.04146	0.08535	0.00108	1,942.95
7	265 (84.94%)	0.00900	0.04235	0.07149	0.00057	1,656.33
8	254 (81.41%)	0.00890	0.04188	0.06997	0.00047	1,607.12
Stock Market (1980–2005)	312 (100%)	0.00843	0.04941	0.04977		1,387.23

Table A7:   Stock Market Corrections (10% plus) in the UK, 1975–2005.

Although the duration of the correction starting in September 2000 is longer than one year, it is considered a correction since the stock market dropped 14.7% within twelve months between September 2000 and August 2001.

Correction Number	Start Date	Duration (Months)	Decline (%)
1	June 1975	2	−13.0
2	February 1976	9	−25.6
3	October 1977	5	−14.0
4	May 1979	3	−14.6
5	September 1981	1	−16.1
6	October 1987	2	−33.4
7	September 1989	2	−10.4
8	January 1990	4	−12.3
9	July 1990	3	−16.0
10	June 1992	3	−14.9
11	February 1994	5	−15.1
12	May 1998	5	−14.3
13	January 2000	2	−10.2
14	September 2000	13	−17.9
15	April 2002	10	−31.6

Table A8:   Evaluation of the Overall Performance of the Strategies for the UK.

The mean excess return is the average monthly excess return of the strategy over the stock market. Terminal values refer to the gross performance of £ 100 invested using the strategy signals.

Strategy	Number of Months in the Stock Market	Overall Performance of the Strategies/ the Stock Market				
		Mean Log Return	Standard Deviation	Sharpe Ratio	Mean Excess Return	Terminal Value
1	329 (88.44%)	0.01426	0.05020	0.14825	0.00102	20,163.11
2	314 (84.41%)	0.01363	0.04947	0.13757	0.00039	15,911.90
3	362 (97.31%)	0.01346	0.05309	0.12504	0.00022	14,948.86
4	354 (95.16%)	0.01323	0.05279	0.12136	−0.00001	13,714.36
Stock Market (1975–2005)	372 (100%)	0.01324	0.05598	0.11470		13,787.40
5	297 (95.19%)	0.01204	0.04420	0.12277	0.00101	4,275.28
6	289 (92.63%)	0.01163	0.04363	0.11495	0.00060	3,760.35
7	300 (96.15%)	0.01218	0.04419	0.12616	0.00116	4,477.37
8	293 (93.91%)	0.01196	0.04358	0.12266	0.00093	4,168.13
Stock Market (1980–2005)	312 (100%)	0.01103	0.04814	0.09179		3,121.47

Table A9:   Stock Market Corrections (10% plus) in Japan, May 1985–December 2005.

Although the duration of the correction starting in January 1990 is longer than one year, it is considered a correction since the stock market dropped 40% within twelve months between January and December 1990. The same is true for Corrections 4 (23.5% decline between June 1994 and May 1995), 6 (15.3% decline between August 1997 and July 1998) and 7 (20.1% decline between April 2000 and March 2001).

Correction Number	Start Date	Duration (Months)	Decline (%)
1	June 1987	7	−20.3
2	January 1990	31	−56.2
3	September 1993	3	−17.6
4	June 1994	13	−27.0
5	July 1996	7	−17.5
6	August 1997	15	−31.1
7	April 2000	37	−51.8

Table A10:   Evaluation of the Overall Performance of the Strategies for Japan.

The mean excess return is the average monthly excess return of the strategy over the stock market. Terminal values refer to the gross performance of ¥ 100 invested using the strategy signals.

Strategy	Number of Months in the Stock Market	Overall Performance of the Strategies/ the Stock Market				
		Mean Log Return	Standard Deviation	Sharpe Ratio	Mean Excess Return	Terminal Value
1	222 (89.52%)	0.00612	0.05049	0.08427	0.00305	455.72
2	214 (86.29%)	0.00627	0.04942	0.08921	0.00320	473.45
3	229 (92.34%)	0.00648	0.05097	0.09059	0.00341	498.62
4	226 (91.13%)	0.00640	0.05077	0.08942	0.00334	489.16
Stock Market (5/85–12/05)	248 (100%)	0.00307	0.05778	0.02085		213.88
5	172 (91.49%)	0.00120	0.05050	−0.00157	0.00168	125.35
6	169 (89.89%)	0.00128	0.04994	−0.00008	0.00176	127.13
7	174 (92.55%)	0.00177	0.05130	0.00960	0.00225	139.56
8	172 (91.49%)	0.00120	0.05050	−0.00157	0.00168	125.35
Stock Market (5/90–12/05)	188 (100%)	−0.00048	0.05745	−0.03062		91.39

Chapter 7

Do Seasonal Anomalies Still Work?

Constantine Dzhabarov

Alpha Lake Financial Analytics Corp, Vancouver, BC, Canada

William T. Ziemba

Professor Emeritus, University of British Columbia, Vancouver, BC,
Visiting Professor, Mathematical Institute, Oxford University, UK
ICMA Centre, University of Reading, UK
University of Bergamo, Italy

September 17, 2009

We investigate whether or not traditional seasonal anomalies such as the January and monthly effects, the January barometer, sell-in-May-and-go-away, holiday and turn-of-the-month effects still exist in the turbulent markets of the early part of the 21st century. The evidence using futures data from 1993–2009 and 2004–2009 for small cap stocks measured by the Russell2000 index and large cap stocks measured by the S&P500 is that there is still value in these anomalies. The effects tend to be stronger for the small cap stocks. The results are useful for investors to tilt portfolios and speculators to trade the effects.

Seasonality of stock markets has a long history despite the academic research being dominated by efficient market theory as surveyed by Fama (1970, 1991). Small firm effects were popularized by University of Chicago students Banz (1981), Reinganum (1981), and Ritter (1988) among others.

Early surveys are in Lakonishok and Smidt (1988), Thaler (1992) and Ziemba (1994). The latter referencing considerable regularity of various seasonal anomalies in Japan as well as in the US. Jacobs and Levy (1988abc) have used seasonal and fundamental factor model derived anomalies to create a multibillion dollar investment firm. Dimson (1988), Keim and

Ziemba (2000) and Ziemba (2012) present whole books with studies across the world. *The Stock Traders Almanac* discusses some such anomalies in yearly updates; see Hirsh and Hirsh (2009).

In this paper we update and contrast with the past script using 1993–2009 and 2004–2009 futures data research on the following seasonal anomalies: the January and monthly effects, the January barometer, sell-in-May-and-go-away, holiday and turn-of-the-month. These anomalies are discussed in turn and then the paper concludes.

January and Monthly Effects

We refer to the January effect as the tendency of small cap stocks to outperform large cap stocks in the month of January. Rozeff and Kinney (1976) showed that equally weighted indices of all the stocks on the NYSE had significantly higher returns in January than in the other eleven months during 1904–1974. Keim (1983) documented the magnitude of the size effect by month. He found that half the annual size premium was in January. Blume and Stambaugh (1983) showed that, after correcting for an upward bias in mean returns for small stocks that was common to earlier size effect studies, the size effect was only in January. Exhibit 1 shows the historical evidence from January 1926 to December 1995 of the difference in January

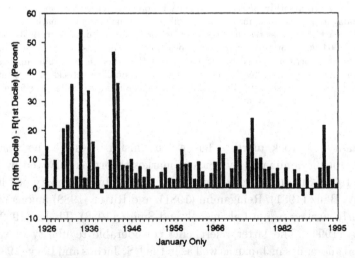

EXHIBIT 1: January Effect, 1926–1995. January Size Premium = R(10th) − R(1st).
Source: Booth and Keim, 2000.

between the lowest decile and the highest decile by market capitalization of the NYSE index plus AMEX and Nasdaq stocks of similar size. Only five years out of 70 did small caps underperform in January and in most years, the small cap outperformance is considerable. The $R_{10th} - R_{1st}$ decile returns averaged 4.48% with a $t = 2.83$ from January 1982 to December 1995.

To update, we calculated the Russell2000/S&P500 futures spread by month from 1993 to 2009. As argued by Rendon and Ziemba (2007), the January turn-of-the-year effect still exists but has moved to December. Indeed, Exhibit 2ab shows that the small cap/large cap spread is positive in December and negative in January; the data is in Exhibit A.1 in Dzhabarov and Ziemba (2009).

The January monthly effect for small and large cap stocks measured by the Russell2000 and S&P500 futures has been negative during February 1993–July 2009 and January 2004–July 2009. Exhibits 3ab and 4ab show the results with the data in Exhibit 5. See Dzhabarov and Ziemba (2009) for the short term data. The results show the historically expected very negative October in the recent S&P500 data and in both sets of Russell2000 data. Surprisingly, the historically strong months of November, January and February were negative for both

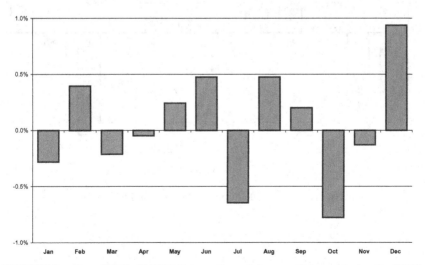

EXHIBIT 2: Russell2000- S&P500 Futures Spread Average Returns during the MOY, 1993–2009.

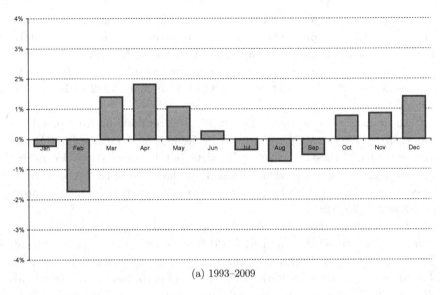

(a) 1993–2009

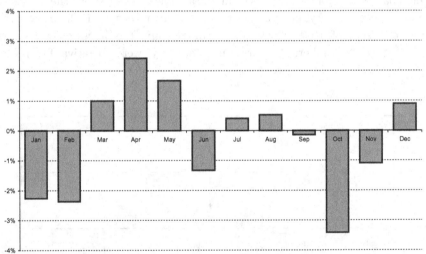

(b) 2004–2009

EXHIBIT 3: S&P500 Futures Average Monthly Returns.

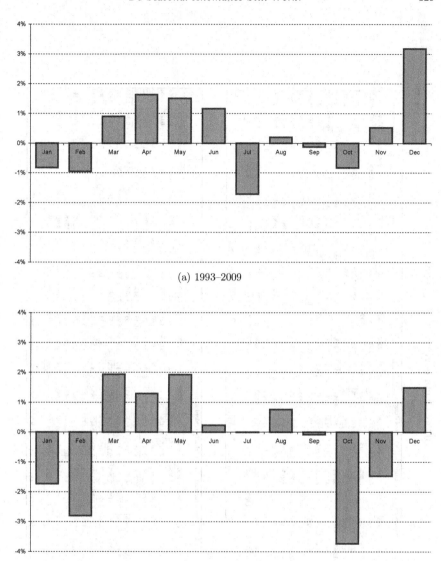

(a) 1993–2009

(b) 2004–2009

EXHIBIT 4:   Russell2000 Futures Average Monthly Returns.

EXHIBIT 5: Futures Average Monthly Returns.

(a) S&P500

MOY Trading in S&P 500 futures contract. Geometrically Linked Returns.

	1993	1994	1995	1996	1997	1998	1999	2000	2001	2002	2003	2004	2005	2006	2007	2008	2009	Average	StDev	t
Jan	3.14%	2.33%	3.07%	5.69%	0.73%	2.71%	-5.91%	2.97%	-1.76%	-2.98%	1.82%	-2.67%	2.25%	1.00%		-6.82%	-9.14%	-0.22%	0.042	-0.212
Feb	-1.28%	-3.29%	2.73%	-0.02%	0.28%	6.30%	-3.76%	-2.20%	-9.94%	-2.22%	-1.73%	1.28%	1.85%	-0.13%	-2.46%	-3.63%	-11.13%	-1.73%	0.042	-1.692
Mar	1.83%	-4.22%	3.92%	1.94%	-4.24%	5.65%	4.49%	10.07%	-5.89%	3.73%	0.44%	-1.82%	-1.72%	1.61%	1.49%	-0.85%	7.28%	1.39%	0.043	1.345
Apr	-3.13%	0.74%	2.43%	0.49%	5.69%	0.70%	3.19%	-2.36%	6.83%	-6.38%	8.00%	-1.73%	-2.23%	0.94%	3.97%	4.55%	9.07%	1.81%	0.042	1.757
May	2.56%	1.26%	3.15%	1.78%	5.84%	-2.60%	-3.08%	-4.54%	-0.04%	-1.10%	5.05%	1.34%	2.88%	-3.41%	2.96%	0.96%	5.27%	1.08%	0.031	1.410
Jun	0.17%	-2.50%	2.54%	1.45%	4.52%	4.61%	6.41%	3.12%	-1.44%	-7.45%	0.95%	1.64%	0.24%	0.47%	-1.22%	-8.69%	-0.44%	0.26%	0.039	0.272
Jul	-0.69%	3.09%	2.88%	-5.22%	7.47%	-1.86%	-2.99%	-2.10%	-1.98%	-8.64%	1.54%	-3.50%	3.43%	0.12%	-3.65%	-1.30%	7.34%	-0.36%	0.043	-0.345
Aug	3.39%	3.28%	-0.07%	1.32%	-5.91%	-15.59%	-1.73%	5.73%	-6.72%	0.05%	1.80%	0.21%	-1.28%	1.84%	0.79%	1.07%		-0.74%	0.051	-0.584
Sep	-0.87%	-2.17%	4.48%	6.09%	5.51%	6.86%	-1.79%	-4.58%	-8.38%	-11.31%	-1.43%	0.94%	1.03%	3.02%	4.07%	-9.79%		-0.52%	0.057	-0.366
Oct	1.87%	2.59%	-0.77%	-3.78%	7.38%	5.73%	-1.15%	1.46%	7.96%	5.51%	1.32%	-2.08%	2.79%	1.00%	-4.85%	-20.11%		0.77%	0.065	0.476
Nov	1.35%	-4.78%	3.98%	6.80%	3.21%	5.06%	1.04%	-8.46%	7.35%	5.49%	0.75%	3.83%	3.39%	1.39%	-4.85%	-9.22%		0.85%	0.052	0.655
Dec	1.09%	1.59%	1.80%	-1.93%	2.40%	6.92%	6.60%	0.30%	0.71%	-6.25%	4.82%	3.34%	0.27%	1.80%	-0.56%	-0.40%		1.41%	0.032	1.755
Average	0.33%	-0.11%	2.45%	1.53%	2.22%	2.01%	1.40%	-1.01%	-1.26%	-2.32%	1.89%	0.72%	0.26%	1.06%	0.21%	-4.52%	1.18%	0.34%		
StDev	0.020	0.031	0.016	0.032	0.046	0.066	0.039	0.052	0.056	0.060	0.033	0.021	0.023	0.017	0.029	0.067	0.083		0.046	
t	0.546	-0.120	5.466	1.652	1.687	1.063	1.229	-0.672	-0.774	-1.352	1.977	1.172	0.394	2.135	0.257	-2.321	0.375			
Geom r	3.46%	-1.78%	33.54%	19.34%	28.75%	23.93%	17.18%	-12.73%	-15.61%	-26.10%	24.53%	8.76%	2.85%	13.29%	2.11%	-44.22%				

(b) Russell2000

MOY Trading in Russell 2000 futures contract. Geometrically Linked Returns.

	1993	1994	1995	1996	1997	1998	1999	2000	2001	2002	2003	2004	2005	2006	2007	2008	2009	Average	StDev	t
Jan	2.95%	-1.60%	4.17%	-0.32%	2.04%	-2.48%	0.32%	-3.17%	3.91%	-1.37%	-3.03%	4.16%	-4.50%	8.54%	1.12%	-7.74%	-11.93%	-0.82%	0.049	-0.668
Feb	-3.16%	-1.43%	1.38%	1.58%	-2.87%	7.31%	-8.02%	16.64%	-7.33%	-3.05%	-3.21%	0.67%	1.39%	-0.70%	1.51%	-4.18%	-12.63%	-0.95%	0.065	-0.604
Mar	2.59%	-4.43%	3.48%	4.20%	-1.16%	5.20%	1.15%	-6.53%	-3.92%	8.00%	9.29%	0.62%	-2.69%	5.34%	1.51%	-0.01%	6.83%	0.90%	0.042	0.883
Apr	-3.05%	-0.55%	2.39%	4.59%	-0.10%	-0.13%	8.47%	-7.92%	6.33%	0.56%	10.49%	-5.36%	-6.16%	-0.48%	1.29%	3.79%	14.65%	1.62%	0.059	1.142
May	4.00%	-1.16%	2.21%	3.17%	10.25%	-6.34%	1.64%	-7.30%	1.83%	-4.81%	1.34%	4.10%	6.16%	-6.26%	3.54%	4.26%	2.51%	1.50%	0.053	1.170
Jun	1.51%	-3.49%	4.64%	-3.66%	4.75%	1.13%	4.66%	9.34%	3.00%	-5.14%	1.53%	4.10%	4.11%	0.94%	-0.86%	-7.82%	0.93%	1.16%	0.043	1.114
Jul	0.55%	2.00%	5.28%	-9.32%	4.13%	-9.34%	-3.88%	-3.52%	-5.04%	-15.86%	5.96%	-7.03%	5.96%	-3.90%	-7.41%	3.05%	9.29%	-1.71%	0.069	-1.020
Aug	3.95%	5.42%	1.44%	5.01%	1.98%	-20.31%	-3.99%	6.04%	-3.70%	-0.82%	4.35%	-0.81%	-2.30%	2.30%	1.42%	3.18%		0.20%	0.063	0.126
Sep	2.47%	-0.58%	1.82%	4.17%	7.70%	8.02%	0.36%	-1.99%	-13.82%	-7.55%	-2.13%	4.64%	0.66%	1.34%	2.15%	-9.21%		-0.12%	0.059	-0.083
Oct	2.96%	-0.40%	-5.11%	-1.50%	-5.13%	3.75%	0.44%	-5.48%	5.24%	2.48%	8.11%	1.71%	-3.62%	5.21%	2.15%	-24.11%		-0.83%	0.074	-0.449
Nov	-4.28%	-4.75%	4.42%	3.89%	-1.16%	4.24%	4.69%	-10.54%	7.38%	8.50%	3.30%	8.42%	4.38%	2.04%	-7.96%	-14.20%		0.52%	0.069	0.301
Dec	4.12%	2.84%	3.13%	2.01%	2.05%	6.76%	12.58%	8.02%	5.94%	-5.87%	1.78%	3.06%	-0.03%	0.88%	0.10%	3.42%		3.17%	0.040	3.144
Average	1.06%	-0.30%	2.02%	1.09%	1.62%	-0.18%	1.53%	-0.54%	-0.02%	-2.08%	3.11%	1.29%	0.28%	1.27%	-0.36%	-4.13%	1.38%	0.39%		
StDev	0.031	0.031	0.029	0.042	0.047	0.084	0.056	0.085	0.066	0.067	0.047	0.043	0.042	0.040	0.037	0.089	0.104		0.058	
t	1.124	-0.329	2.388	0.896	1.205	-0.076	0.948	-0.219	-0.009	-1.072	2.302	1.049	0.231	1.098	-0.338	-1.614	0.353			
Geom r	11.76%	-4.03%	26.46%	12.78%	19.88%	-6.17%	18.06%	-9.77%	-2.67%	-24.27%	42.85%	15.50%	2.43%	15.38%	-4.95%	-42.69%	6.58%			

the small and large cap data. While most of the other effects we study
in this paper have still produced valuable reliable anomalies, the monthly
effect does not look to be of much use for traders and investors.

The January Barometer

Historically, returns in January have been a valuable signal for the returns
in the following eleven months that year. If stocks have positive returns in
January, then it is likely that the market as a whole will rise in that year.
Hirsch (1986) has called this the January barometer. The supposition is
that:

> if the market rises in January, then it will rise for the year as a whole;
> but if it falls in January, then there will be a decline or a flat market
> that year.

Exhibit 6 updates Hensel and Ziemba (1993) and Ziemba (1994) which
had the results for the 54 years 1940–93. There are 70 years in the total
sample with a 16 year update to the current 2009 year to the end of August.

For the 70 years, when the return in January was positive, the rest of
the year was up 86.4% of the time. This compares with 71% of all years
that the whole the year was up.

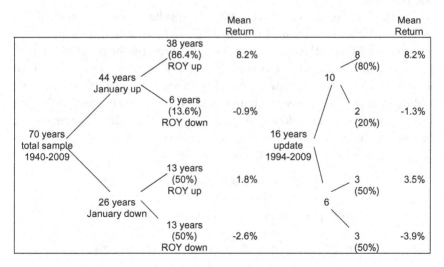

EXHIBIT 6:   January Barometer Results, 1940–2009 and 1994–2009.

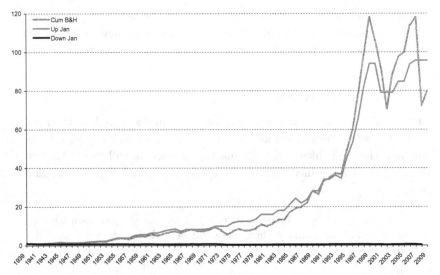

EXHIBIT 7: Rest of Year after Positive and Negative January and B&H Cumulative Returns. S&P500 Index (Cash), 1940–2009.

When the return in January was negative which was 26 of the 70 years, the whole year was down 50% of the time. Thus even in years when January is down, the whole year is equally likely to be up or down. This 50% is significantly less than the 71% proportion of all the years that the whole the year went up.

In the 16 year update (1994–2009), the results as seen in Exhibit 6 are similar with the January up ROY up 80% (8 of 10) of the time.

Exhibit 7 shows the cumulative rest of year returns for positive January, negative January and buy and hold. Positive January has the highest final wealth with negative January producing almost no gains at all. Buy and Hold had returns that were high except the recent drop in the S&P500 led to the positive January dominating. Exhibits 8 and 9 show the regression of rest of the year returns versus January returns, January positive and January negative with t's in (). The equations are:

$$ROY = 0.0549 \quad +0.932 Jan \qquad R^2 = 9.3\%$$
$$(3.20) \qquad (2.65)$$
$$ROY_+ = 0.135 \quad -0.384 Jan_+ \qquad R^2 = 1.0\%$$
$$(4.59) \qquad (-0.66)$$
$$ROY_- = -0.0764 \quad -1.41 Jan_- \qquad R^2 = 4.7\%$$
$$(-1.31) \qquad (-1.09)$$

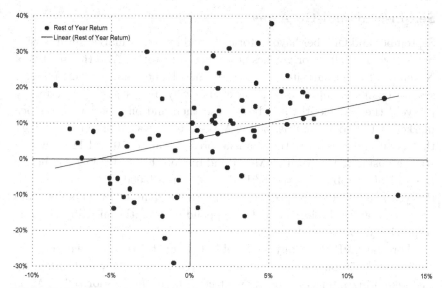

EXHIBIT 8: January Return (x-axis) vs. Rest of Year Return (y-axis). S&P500 Index (Cash), 1940–2009.

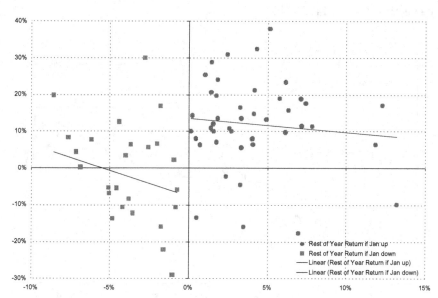

EXHIBIT 9: January Return (x-axis) (Up and Down Cases) vs. Rest of Year Return (y-axis). S&P500 Index (Cash), 1940–2009.

Sell-in-May-and-Go-Away

September and October have historically had low stock market returns with many serious declines or crashes occurring in October. Also the months of November to February have historically had higher than average returns; see, for example, Gultekin and Gultekin (1983). This suggests the strategy to avoid the bad months and be in cash then and only be long the stock market in the good months. Sell-in-May-and-go-away is one such strategy that is often discussed in the financial press. Exhibits 10 and 11 show this strategy using the rule sell on May 1 and buy on the 6th trading day before the end of October, for the S&P500 and Russell2000 futures indices for the years 1993–2009, respectively. This rule did indeed beat a buy and hold strategy. Exhibits 5 and the Appendix show the monthly returns, respectively, for those 16 years.

For the S&P500 a buy and hold strategy turns $1 on February 4, 1993, into $1.56 on August 17, 2009; whereas, sell in May and move into cash, counting interest (Fed funds effective monthly rate for sell in May) and dividends for the buy and hold, had a final wealth of $3.18, some 103.8% higher. For the Russell2000, the final wealths were $1.49 and $3.69, respectively, some 147.7% higher.

EXHIBIT 10: S&P500 Futures Sell in May (SIM) and B&H Cumulative Returns Comparison. 1993–2009. (Entry at Close on 6th Day before End of October. Exit 1st Day of May.)

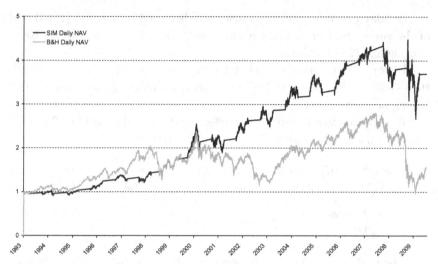

EXHIBIT 11:   Russell2000 Futures Sell in May (SIM) and B&H Cumulative Returns Comparison. 1993–2009. (Entry at Close on 6th Day before End of October. Exit 1st Day of May.)

Holiday Effects

There has been a very strong holiday effect in U.S. markets throughout the twentieth century. Ariel (1990), Zweig (1986), Lakonishok and Smidt (1988) have documented this. For example, for the ninety years from 1897 to 1986, Lakonishok and Smidt found that fully 51.5% of the non-dividend returns on the Dow Jones industrials were made on the approximately eight preholidays. Ariel using data from 1963–1982 found a very strong effect with the average preholiday having returns that were about 23 times an average day for large capitalized stocks measured by a value weighted index of all NYSE stocks. Small capitalized stocks (equally weighted NYSE stocks) had returns 14 times larger but since this period was one of extremely high small stock returns, the actual returns exceeded the large capitalized securities. Lakonishok and Smidt also found that preholidays were associated with higher mean returns on all days of the week compared to average returns those days. Investigation of the holiday effect in Japan by Ziemba (1991) yielded very similar results. Using daily data on the Nikkei stock average from May 1949 when the market opened up after World War II to 1988, he found that the typical preholiday had returns of about five times the average non preholiday trading day, namely 0.246% versus 0.0489%.

Holiday effects in other countries are discussed by Ziemba (1994) and in the survey by Cervera and Keim (2000) and other papers in the Keim and Ziemba (2000) volume.

Historically it was the preholiday that had the highest returns with the -3 day having the next highest returns, with the day after the holiday having negative returns.

A regression to separate out the effects on trading days -3 to $+2$ around a holiday using $0, 1$ variables led to the daily return

$$R = 0.0352 \ +0.0799 Day_{-3} \ +0.0222 Day_{-2} \ +0.1894 Day_{-1} \ -0.0663 Day_{+1}$$
$$(3.745) \quad (1.491) \quad\quad (0.424) \quad\quad (3.709) \quad\quad (-1.334)$$

$$+0.00114 Day_{+2}$$
$$(0.023)$$

The evidence we have to update this is from the futures markets from 1993–2009 and it is that the effect seems to have moved to the -3 day before the holiday and is much weaker than in the past. The pre-holiday is marginally positive for both the S&P500 and Russell2000. Labor day for the Russell2000 is the most reliable with a mean gain of 0.88% with a $t = 4.81$ and 15 of 16 positive. Presidents' day was also reliable 82.4% of the time with a $t = 2.11$. Since none of the holidays were highly significantly positive for the S&P500 and, except for these two, the Russell2000 results were marginal, we conclude that the holiday effect exists to some extent on the -3 day but has diminished greatly in the 1990s and 2000s. The mean gain for the S&P500 was 0.19% ($t = 1.74$) and the Russell2000 was 0.26% ($t = 2.14$).

Exhibit 12 documents the overall results for these two indices on days -3 to +2 plus other days and all the days.

Turn-of-the-Month Effects

Historically there have been high returns for both large and small cap stocks around the turn-of-the-month (TOM). Market advisors such as Merrill (1966), Fosback (1976) and Hisrch (1986) have argued that stocks advance at the TOM. Ariel (1987) documented this for the US using equally and value weighted indices of all NYSE stocks from 1963–1981; see Exhibit 13a,b.

The five days -1 to $+4$ historically were the TOM and had a large amount of the monthly gains. Indeed that period and the second week

EXHIBIT 12:   Futures holiday average returns by day, 1993–2009*.

S&P500

Count	4168	132	132	132	132	3405
St Dev	0.0126	0.0125	0.0095	0.0106	0.0131	0.0143	0.0127
Average	0.02%	0.19%	−0.08%	0.03%	0.08%	0.02%	0.01%
z	0.9206	1.7357	−0.9675	0.3138	0.6726	0.1927	0.5231
Positive	52.7%	56.1%	51.5%	49.2%	53.8%	56.1%	52.5%
	All Days	Pre H −3	Pre H −2	Pre H −1	After H 1	After H 2	Others

Russell2000

Count	4174	133	133	133	133	133	3405
St Dev	0.0147	0.0141	0.0132	0.0109	0.0146	0.0190	0.0148
Average	0.02%	0.26%	−0.01%	0.12%	−0.01%	0.06%	0.00%
z	0.8566	2.1370	−0.0600	1.3133	−0.0647	0.3572	0.0735
Positive	53.2%	64.7%	51.9%	53.4%	48.9%	57.1%	52.9%
	All Days	Pre H −3	Pre H −2	Pre H −1	After H 1	After H 2	Others

*For some years Xmas 2 AH = New Year −3PH.

actually had all the monthly gains as Ariel (1987) found the following portfolio gains

	Equally weighted	Value weighted
First half of trading month	2552.40%	565.40%
Last half of trading month	−0.25%	−33.80%
Nineteen years	2545.90%	339.90%

Lakonishok and Smidt (1988) found that during the ninety year period, 1897–1986, the large capitalized Dow Jones industrials rose 0.475% during the four day period −1 to +3 each month whereas the average gain for a four day period was 0.061%. There was an increase in prices over 56% of the time. The average gain per month over these 90 years was 0.349%. Hence aside from these four days at the turn of the month, the DJIA actually fell.

The effect has continued in recent years even in the presence of index futures contracts which began trading in the US in 1982. Hensel, Sick and Ziemba (1994) found for the period May 1982 to April 1992 using the S&P500 large cap and Value Line small cap indices, consistent with the previous evidence that about two thirds of the months gains occur on trading days −1 to +4, the turn of the month, and the rest of the months gains occur on trading days +5 to +9 so that all or more than all of the gains occurs in the first half of the month. The second half was at best

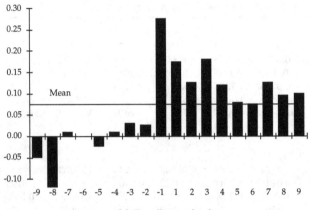

(a) Equally weighted

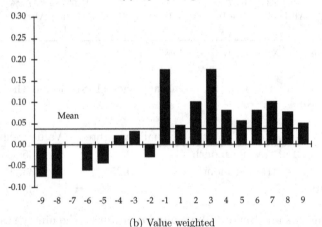

(b) Value weighted

EXHIBIT 13: The US Turn of the Month Effect, Mean Daily Percent Returns on Trading Days −9 to +9, 1963–81.

Source: Ariel, 1987.

noise. The effect was monthly dependent with the largest gains in January and size dependent with the small capitalized value line index of about 1650 stocks having higher means and lower standard deviations than the large capitalized S&P500 index. There was partial anticipation in the futures market as shown in Exhibit 14. For the small capitalized value line index, the cash effect on day −1 was partially anticipated on days −4 to −2. Then the effect in the cash market on days +2 and +3 was partially anticipated on day +1. Hence the cash market effect on days −1 to +4 was as Ariel found for the 1963 to 1981 data with small gains on days −4 to −2. For the

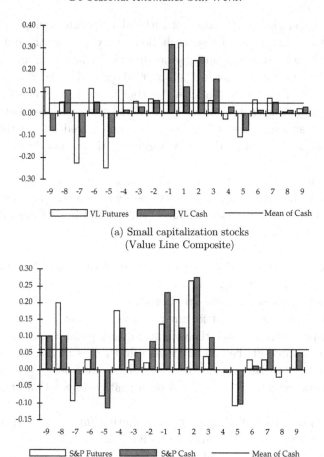

(a) Small capitalization stocks
(Value Line Composite)

(b) Large capitalized stocks (S&P500)

EXHIBIT 14: Mean Percentage Daily Returns in the Cash and Futures Market for Small and Large Capitalized Stocks by Trading Day of the Month, May 1982–April 1992.

Source: Hensel, Sick and Ziemba, 1994.

large capitalized S&P500 index, the results were similar except that there are higher returns in the cash market in the anticipation period (-4 to -2) and lower returns in the -1 to $+4$ period.

The reasons for the turn of the month effect are several but they are largely cash flow and institutionally based. The US economy uses a system where much money is paid on the -1 day such as salaries and bills and debt payments. In addition to some of this money being invested in the stock market, there are institutional corporate and pension fund purchases at that time. These cash flows vary by month and lead to higher average returns in January which has the highest cash inflow. Ogden (1990) presents some empirical support of this hypothesis and related monetary actions for U.S. markets. Another factor in this effect seems to be behavioral. One manifestation is that bad news such as that relating to earnings announcements is delayed and announced late in the month while good news is released at the beginning of the month; see Penman (1987).

The turn of the month was similar in Japan except that the dates change with the turn being days −5 to +2, with +3 to +7 being the rest of the first half of the month. Ziemba (1989, 1991) investigated this. The reasons for the effect in Japan seem to be:

- Most salaries were paid during the period of the 20th–25th day of the month, with the 25th being especially popular.
- There was portfolio window dressing on day −1.
- Security firms could invest for their own accounts on amounts based on their capitalization. Since their capitalization usually rises each month and is computed at the end of the month, there is buying on day −3 to account for this. Buying was done as soon as possible.
- Large brokerage firms had a sales push that on day −3 and lasted 7 to 10 days.
- Employment stock holding plans and mutual funds received money in this period to invest, starting around day −3.
- Individual investors bought mutual funds with their pay, which they received on calendar days 15 to 25 of the month; the funds then invested in stocks with a lag, so most of the buying occurred on days −5 to +2.
- For low liquidity stocks, buying occurred over several days by dealing in accounts to minimize price pressure effects.

Using data on the NSA from 1949 to 1988 Ziemba (1991) found that all of the days −5 to +2 had significantly positive returns. As in the U.S. all the gains occurred in the first half of the month and the second half had zero or negative returns.

Ziemba (1989) investigated the futures market trading outside Japan on the Simex in Singapore on the turn of the month and other anomalous effects in Japanese security markets during the period September 1986 to September 1988 before there was futures trading on the NSA or Topix

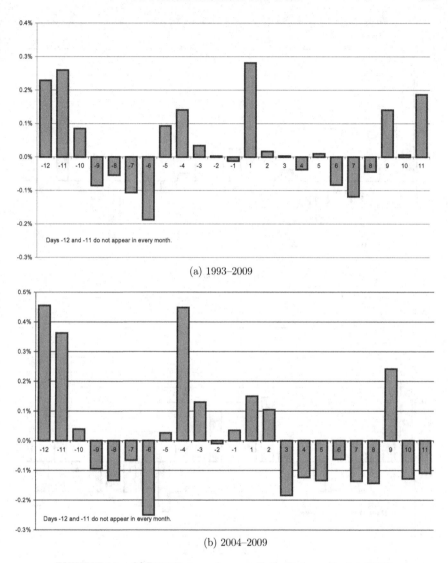

(a) 1993–2009

(b) 2004–2009

EXHIBIT 15:   S&P500 Futures Average Daily Returns During TOM.

in Japan. He found that the spot effect was consistent with past data so the futures market did not alter the effect. However, the futures market in Singapore totally anticipated the effect on days −8 to −5 with a total average rise on 2.8%. Then when the effect occurred on days −5 to +2 and the spot market gained 1.7%, the futures market was flat.

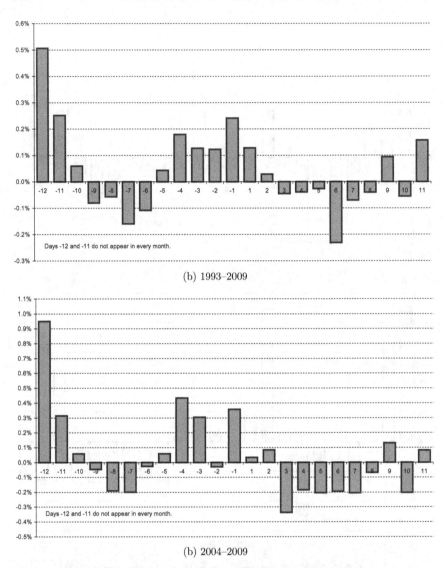

(b) 1993–2009

(b) 2004–2009

EXHIBIT 16:   Russell2000 Futures Average Daily Returns in Respect to TOM.

In our update using S&P500 and Russell2000 futures data from 1993–2009 and 2004–2009, we found that the TOM effect still exists with a bit of anticipation. Exhibits 15ab and 16ab and Exhibits A.4 and A.5 in Dzhabrov and Ziemba (2009) document the results. For example, for the S&P500, for the longer sample and also for the shorter more recent data, the days

−5 to +2 all have positive returns except −1 (which has a small mean loss). For the Russell2000 the same days all have positive mean returns for the longer sample and for the more recent data with −2 having a slightly negative mean.

Conclusions and Final Remarks

In the main, the anomalies are still there with some moving around. In the past, some of the anomalies such as the turn-of-the-month and January effect had very high prediction accuracy. Currently the January barometer and sell in May and go away which deal with longer range predictions have similar reliability. Other anomalies such as the January and holiday effects still exist and ad value. The monthly effect has become noise and has no predictive value.

I have been running a futures fund which is registered and audited since July 2013 using some of these ideas concerning calendar anomalies as well as mispriced options based on behavorial biases and institutional practices as well as mean reversion. The results have been good as shown in Exhibit 17.

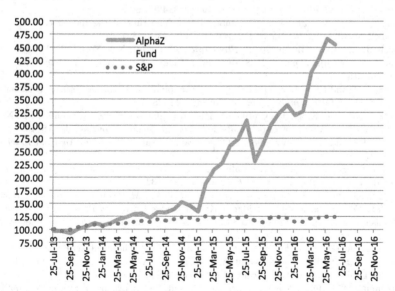

EXHIBIT 17: Gross returns before fees of the alpha z futures fund versus the S&P 500 July 25 2013 to June 30 2016.

References

Ariel, R. A. (1987). A monthly effect in stock returns. *Journal of Financial Economics*, 18, 161–174.

Ariel, R. A. (1990). High stock returns before holidays: Existence and evidence on possible causes. *Journal of Finance*, 45, 1611–1626.

Banz, R. (1981). The relationship between return and market value of common stock. *Journal of Financial Economics*, 9, 3–18.

Blume, M. E. and R. R. Stambaugh (1983). Biases in computed returns: An application to the size effect. *Journal of Financial Economics*, 12, 387–404.

Booth, D. G. and D. Keim (2000). Is thee still a january effect? In D. B. Keim and W. T. Ziemba (Eds.), *Security Market Imperfections in World Wide Equity Markets*, pp. 169–178. Cambridge, UK: Cambridge University Press.

Cervera, A. and D. B. Keim (2000). High stock returns before holidays: International evidence and additional tests. In D. B. Keim and W. T. Ziemba (Eds.), *Security Market Imperfections in World Wide Equity Markets*, pp. 512–531. Cambridge, UK: Cambridge University Press.

Dimson, E. (Ed.) (1988). *Stock Market Anomalies*. Cambridge, UK: Cambridge University Press.

Dzhabarov, C. and W. T. Ziemba (2009). Do seasonal anomalies still work? Working Paper, www.williamtziemba.com/wtzpublications.

Fama, E. F. (1970). Efficient capital markets: A review of theory and empirical work. *Journal of Finance*, 25, 383–417.

Fama, E. F. (1991). Efficient capital markets II. *Journal of Finance*, 46(5), 1575–1617.

Fosback, N. G. (1976). Stock market logic. The Institute for Economic Research, Fort Lauderdale.

Gultekin, M. N. and N. B. Gultekin (1983). Stock market seasonality: International evidence. *Journal of Financial Economics*, 12, 469–482.

Hensel, C., G. Sick, and W. T. Ziemba (1994). The turn of the month effect in the S&P500, 1926–92. *Review of Futures Markets*, 13(3), 827–856.

Hirsch, J. A. and Y. Hirsch (2009). *Stock traders almanac*. New York, NY: Wiley.

Hirsch, Y. (1986). *Don't Sell Stocks on Monday*. New York, NY: Facts on File Publications.

Jacobs, B. I. and K. N. Levy (1988a). Calendar anomalies: Abnormal returns at calendar turning points. *Financial Analysts Journal*, 44, 28–39.

Jacobs, B. I. and K. N. Levy (1988b). Disentangling equity return regularities: New insights and investment opportunities. *Financial Analysts Journal*, 44, 18–43.

Jacobs, B. I. and K. N. Levy (1988c). On the value of value. *Financial Analysts Journal*, 44, 47–62.

Keim, D. (1983). Size related anomalies and stock return seasonality: Further empirical evidence. *Journal of Financial Economics*, 12, 3–32.

Keim, D. B. and W. T. Ziemba (Eds.) (2000). *Security Market Imperfections in World Wide Equity Markets*. Cambridge, UK: Cambridge University Press.

Lakonishok, J. and S. Smidt (1988). Are seasonal anomalies real? A ninety-year perspective. *Review of Financial Studies*, 1, 403–425.

Merrill, A. A. (1966). *Behavior of prices on Wall Street*. The Analysis Press.

Penman, S. H. (1987). The distribution of earnings news over time and seasonalities in aggregate stock returns. *Journal of Financial Economics*, 18, 199–228.

Reinganum, M. (1981). A misspecification of capital asset pricing: Empirical anomalies based on earnings yields and market values. *Journal of Financial Economics*, 9, 19–46.

Rendon, J. and W. T. Ziemba (2007). Is the January effect still alive in the futures markets? *Financial Markets Portfolio Management*, 381–396.

Ritter, J. (1988). The buying and selling behavior of individual investors at the turn of the year. *Journal of Finance*, 43, 701–717.

Roll, R. (1983). Vas ist dat: The turn of the year effect and the return premia of small firms. *Journal of Portfolio Management*, 9 (Winter), 18–28.

Rozeff and Kinney (1976). Capital market seasonality: The case of stock returns. *Journal of Financial Economics*, 3, 379–402.

Thaler, R. H. (1992). *The Winners Curse*. New York, NY: The Free Press.

Wachtel, S. (1942). Certain observations on seasonal movements in stock prices. *Journal of Business* (April), 184–193.

Ziemba, W. T. (1989). Seasonality effects in japanese futures markets? In Rhee and Chang (Eds.), *Research on Pacific Basin Security Markets*. Amsterdam: North Holland.

Ziemba, W. T. (1991). Japanese security market regularities: Monthly, turn of the month and year, holiday and Golden Week effects. *Japan and the World Economy*, 3, 119–146.

Ziemba, W. T. (1994). Worldwide security market regularities. *European Journal of Operational Research*, 74, 198–229.

Ziemba, W. T. (2012). *Calendar Anomalies and Arbitrage*. Singapore: World Scientific.

Zweig, M. (1986). *Winning on Wall Street*. New York, NY: Warner Books.

Chapter 8

How Does the *Fortune's Formula*-Kelly Capital Growth Model Perform?*

Leonard C. MacLean

Herbert Lamb Chair, School of Business Administration,
Dalhousie University, Halifax, Canada B3H 3J5
l.c.maclean@dal.ca

Edward O. Thorp

Edward O. Thorp and Associates, 610 Newport Center Dr,
Suite 1240, Newport Beach, CA, Professor Emeritus,
University of California , Irvine, CA
EOThorp@ix.netcom.com

Yonggan Zhao

Canada Research Chair, School of Business Administration,
Dalhousie University, Halifax, Canada B3H 3J5
yonggan.zhao@dal.ca

William T. Ziemba

Alumni Professor of Financial Modeling and Stochastic
Optimization (Emeritus), University of British Columbia,
Vanvouver, Canada, Visiting Professor, Mathematical Institute,
Oxford University, UK, ICMA Centre, University of Reading,
UK, and University of Bergamo,
Italy wtzimi@mac.com

William Poundstone's book, *Fortune's Formula*, brought the Kelly capital growth criterion to the attention of investors. But how do full and fractional Kelly strategies preform in practice? We study three simple investment

---

*A preliminary version of some of the topics discussed here is in MacLean, Thorp, Zhao and Ziemba (2010). Thanks to the referee, Jarrod Wilcox, for helpful comments on an earlier version of this paper.

situations and simulate the behavior of these strategies over medium term horizons using a large number of scenarios. The results show:

1. the great superiority of full Kelly and close to full Kelly strategies over longer horizons with very large gains a large fraction of the time;
2. that the short term performance of Kelly and high fractional Kelly strategies is very risky;
3. that there is a consistent tradeoff of growth versus security as a function of the bet size determined by the various strategies; and
4. that no matter how favorable the investment opportunities are or how long the finite horizon is, a sequence of bad scenarios can lead to very poor final wealth outcomes, with a loss of most of the investor's initial capital.

Hence, in practice, financial engineering is important to deal with the short term volatility and long run situations with a sequence of bad scenarios. But properly used, the strategy has much to commend it, especially in trading with many repeated investments.

Introduction

In 1738 Daniel Bernoulli postulated that the marginal utility of an extra amount of money was proportional to the person's wealth. So $u'(w) = \frac{1}{w}$ where u is the investor's utility function, primes denote derivatives and w is wealth. Integrating gives $u(w) = \log w$. So log is the suggested utility function. Kelly (1956) and Latané (1959) argued that maximizing the expected utility with a log utility function is equivalent to the maximization of the long run growth rate. A derivation of this appears below. Breiman (1961) showed that the Kelly capital growth criterion had two long run properties. First, it maximizes the asymptotic long run growth rate. Secondly, it minimizes the time to achieve asymptotically large investment goals.

The literature provides discussion of various aspects of expected log maximization Kelly strategies and fractional Kelly strategies where one blends the Kelly strategy with cash.[1] Ziemba (2005) discusses the use of Kelly strategies by great investors such as Keynes, Buffett, Soros and others. Use of the Kelly strategies by Morningstar and Motley Fool are discussed by Fuller (2006) and Lee (2006). These follow Poundstone (2005). These references fail to understand the multivariate aspects of multiple assets,

---

[1]See, for example, Browne (1998), Hakansson and Ziemba (1995), MacLean, Ziemba and Blazenko (1992), MacLean, Ziemba and Li (2005), McEnally (1986), Merton and Samuelson (1979), Mulvey, Pauling and Madey (2003), Rubinstein (1976, 1991), Samuelson (1969, 1971, 1979), Stutzer (2000, 2004), Thorp (2006, 2010), Wilcox (2003ab, 2005) and Ziemba (2010ab).

short-term risk, transaction costs and other features of these strategies. MacLean, Thorp and Ziemba (2010) provides a fuller analysis of the advantages and disadvantages, theory and practice of these strategies and additional references.

The Simplest Case

The asymptotic rate of asset growth is

$$G = \lim_{N \to \infty} \log\left(\frac{w_N}{w_0}\right)^{\frac{1}{N}},$$

where w_0 is initial wealth and w_N is period N's wealth. Consider Bernoulli trials that win $+1$ with probability p and lose -1 with probability $1 - p$. If we win M out of N of these independent trials, then the wealth after period N is

$$w_N = w_0(1+f)^M(1-f)^{N-M}$$

where f is the fraction of our wealth bet in each period. Then

$$G(f) = \lim_{N \to \infty} \left[\frac{M}{N}\log(1+f) + \frac{N-M}{N}\log(1-f)\right]$$

which by the strong law of large numbers is

$$G(f) = p\log(1+f) + q\log(1-f) = E\log(w).$$

Hence, the criterion of maximizing the long run exponential rate of asset growth is equivalent to maximizing the one period expected logarithm of wealth. So, to maximize long run (asymptotic) wealth maximizing expected log is the way to do it period by period. See MacLean, Thorp and Ziemba (2010a) for papers that generalize these simple Bernoulli trial asset return assumptions.

The optimal fractional bet, obtained by setting the derivative of $G(f)$ to zero, is $f^* = p - q$ which is simply the investor's edge or the expected gain on the bet.[2] If the bets are win $O + 1$ or lose 1, that is the odds are O

---

[2] If there are two independent wagers and the size of the bets does not influence the odds, then an analytic expression can be derived, see Thorp (2006). In general, to solve for the optimal wagers in cases where the bets influence the odds, there is dependence, or for cases with three or more wagers, one must solve a non-convex nonlinear program, see Ziemba and Hausch (1987) for techniques. This gives the optimal wager taking into account the effect of our bets on the odds (prices).

to 1 to win, then the edge is $pO - q$ and the optimal Kelly bet is $f^* = \frac{pO-q}{O}$
or the $\frac{edge}{odds}$. Since the edge $pO - q$ is the measure of the mean and the
odds is a risk concept, you wager more with higher mean and less with
higher risk.

Observe that the bets can be very large. For example, if $p = 0.99$ and
$q = 0.01$, the optimal bet is 98% of one's fortune! A real example of this
by Mohnish Pabrai (2007), who won the bidding for the 2008 lunch with
Warren Buffett paying more than \$600,000, had the following investment in
Stewart Enterprises as discussed by Thorp (2010). Over a 24-month period,
with probability 0.80 the investment at least doubles, with 0.19 probability
the investment breaks even and with 0.01 probability all the investment is
lost. The optimal Kelly bet is 97.5% of wealth, half Kelly is 38.75%. Pabrai
invested 10%. While this seems rather low, other investment opportunities,
miscalculation of probabilities, risk tolerance, possible short run losses, bad
scenario Black Swan events, price pressures, buying in and exiting suggest
that a bet a lot lower than 97.5% is appropriate.

In general, Kelly bets are large and risky short term. One sees that
from the Arrow-Pratt absolute risk aversion of the log utility criterion

$$R_A(w) = \frac{-u''(w)}{u'(w)} = 1/w$$

which is essentially zero for non-bankrupt investors. Hence, log can be an
exceedingly risky utility function with wide swings in wealth values because
the optimal bets can be so large.

Chopra and Ziemba (1993) investigated the effect of errors in mean,
variance and covariance estimates in portfolio problems and show that the
relative error impact is risk aversion dependent. For example, for typical
problems there is a 20:2:1 ratio implying that errors in estimating the
mean are ten times variance errors and twenty times co-variance errors
in certainty equivalent value. But for log utility with extremely low risk
aversion, this is more like 100:3:1. What's clear is that getting means
correctly estimated is crucial for portfolio success.

Log utility is related to negative power utility, since with αw^α for $\alpha < 0$
since negative power converges to log when $\alpha \to 0$. So we can think of
log as being the most risky and extreme negative power utility function.
MacLean, Ziemba and Li (2005) have shown that the handy formula for the
fraction $f = \frac{1}{1-\alpha}$ is optimal when the asset returns are lognormal. Here k is
the Kelly strategy and fxk is the fractional Kelly strategy. But, as Thorp

(2010) has shown, this approximation can be poor if the assets are far from lognormal. Betting more than the Kelly amount leads to lower growth and more risk. That is linked to positive power utility which is to be avoided as it will invariably lead to disaster. See Ziemba and Ziemba (2007) for a discussion of some of these overbet disasters including LTCM, Niederhoffer and Amarath.

In continuous time, the long term optimal growth rate is

$$G^* = \frac{1}{2} \left(\frac{\mu - r}{\sigma} \right)^2 + r = \frac{1}{2}(\text{Sharpe Ratio})^2 + \text{ risk free asset},$$

where μ is the mean portfolio return, r is the risk free return and σ^2 is the portfolio return variance. So the ordinary Sharpe ratio determines the optimal growth rate.

A very important question is how much of an investor's wealth should be allocated to investments including cash and other assets using the Kelly or fractional Kelly criterions. The capital growth literature has optimal dynamic consumption-investment models such as Phelps (1962), Samuelson (1969), Hakansson (1970), etc. Ziemba-Vickson (1975, 2006) and MacLean, Thorp and Ziemba (2010a) discuss many of these models.

One way to look at this is to assume that there is consumption (c) and discretionary wealth $(w - c)$. Wilcox (2003) has studied this and notes that discretionary wealth can be written in terms of an implicit leverage ratio $L = \frac{w}{w-c}$. The returns on risky assets are weighted or rescaled to reflect leveraging. The weighted return on a unit of capital invested is $1 + xLR$ where x and $1 - x$ are the fractions in risky assets and risk free assets, respectively, and R is the random rate of return on the risky asset portfolio. The standard Kelly problem is $\max E_R \log(1 + xR)$ with Kelly optimal strategy weighting x^*. Wilcox's modification is $\max E \log(1 + xLR)$. So if x_w is a solution to this model — how does it relate to the Kelly weighting x^*? It is clear that $x_w = \frac{1}{L}x^*$ so the Wilcox discretionary portfolio is a fractional Kelly strategy.

This is not surprising since fractional Kelly strategies are a blend of the Kelly weighting and cash. The higher $L = \frac{w}{w-c}$ is the lower is the optimal Kelly fraction. Wilcox discusses some implications of the impact of leverage. Higher leverage investors are sensitive to fat tails in the returns distribution and will reduce the Kelly fraction strategy. In this paper we analyze the returns at the end of 40 periods and other horizons and show wealth trajectories and how the Kelly fraction affects those trajectories.

Motivation for this Paper

The Kelly optimal capital growth investment strategy has many attractive long run theoretical properties. MacLean, Thorp and Ziemba (2010b) discuss the good and bad properties. It has been dubbed "fortunes formula" by Thorp (see Poundstone, 2005). However, the attractive long run properties are countered by negative short to medium term behavior based on conservative utility functions because of the almost zero Arrow-Pratt risk aversion of log utility. In this paper, the empirical performance of various Kelly and fractional Kelly strategies is considered in realistic investment situations. Three experiments from the literature (Ziemba and Hausch, 1986 and Bicksler and Thorp, 1973) are more fully examined with many more scenarios and strategies. The class of investment strategies generated by varying the fraction of investment capital allocated to the Kelly portfolio are applied to simulated returns from the models, and the distribution of final wealth is described.

Fractional Kelly Strategies: The Ziemba and Hausch Experiment

Consider an investment situation with five possible independent investments where one wagers \$1 and either loses it with probability $1 - p$ or wins $\$(O + 1)$ with probability p, with odds 0 to 1. The five wagers with odds of $O = 1, 2, 3, 4$ *and* 5 to one all have the same expected value of 1.14. The optimal Kelly wagers in the one dimensional case are the expected value edge of 14% over the odds. Hence the wagers are from 14%, down to 2.8% of initial and current wealth at each decision point for the five investments. Exhibit 1 describes these investments. The value 1.14 was chosen as it is the recommended cutoff for profitable place and show racing bets using the system described in Ziemba and Hausch (1986).

Ziemba and Hausch (1986) used 700 decision points and 1000 scenarios and compared full with half Kelly strategies. We use the same 700

EXHIBIT 1:   The Investment Opportunities.

Win Probability	Odds	Prob of Selection in Simulation	Kelly Bets
0.570	1-1	0.1	0.140
0.380	2-1	0.3	0.070
0.285	3-1	0.3	0.047
0.228	4-1	0.2	0.035
0.190	5-1	0.1	0.028

EXHIBIT 2:   Final Wealth Statistics by Kelly Fraction for the
Ziemba and Hausch Model.

	Kelly Fraction				
Statistic	1.0k	0.75k	0.50k	0.25k	0.125k
Max	318854673	4370619	1117424	27067	6330
Mean	524195	70991	19005	4339	2072
Min	4	56	111	513	587
St. Dev.	8033178	242313	41289	2951	650
Skewness	35	11	13	2	1
Kurtosis	1299	155	278	9	2
$>5 \times 10$	1981	2000	2000	2000	2000
10^2	1965	1996	2000	2000	2000
$>5 \times 10^2$	1854	1936	1985	2000	2000
$>10^3$	1752	1855	1930	1957	1978
$>10^4$	1175	1185	912	104	0
$>10^5$	479	284	50	0	0
$>10^6$	111	17	1	0	0

decision points and 2000 scenarios and calculate more attributes of the various strategies. We use full, 3/4, 1/2, 1/4, and 1/8 Kelly strategies and compute the maximum, mean, minimum, standard deviation, skewness, excess kurtosis and the number out of the 2000 scenarios for which the final wealth starting from an initial wealth of $1000 is more than $50, $100, $500 (lose less than half), $1000 (breakeven), $10,000 (more than 10-fold), $100,000 (more than 100-fold), and $1 million (more than a thousand-fold). Exhibit 2 shows these results and illustrates the conclusions listed in the abstract. The final wealth levels are much higher on average, the higher the Kelly fraction. With 1/8 Kelly, the average final wealth is $2072, starting with $1000. It is $4339 with 1/4 Kelly, $19,005 with half Kelly, $70,991 with 3/4 Kelly and $524,195 with full Kelly. So as you approach full Kelly, the typical final wealth escalates dramatically. This is shown also in the maximum wealth levels which for full Kelly is $318,854,673 versus $6330 for 1/8 Kelly.

Exhibit 3 shows the wealth paths of these maximum final wealth levels. Most of the gain is in the final 100 of the 700 decision points. Even with these maximum graphs, there is much volatility in the final wealth with the amount of volatility generally higher with higher Kelly fractions. Indeed with 3/4 Kelly, there were losses from about decision points 610 to 670.

Considering the chance of losses (final wealth is less than the initial $1000) in all cases, even with 1/8 Kelly with 1.1% and 1/4 Kelly with 2.15%, there are losses with 700 independent bets each with an edge of

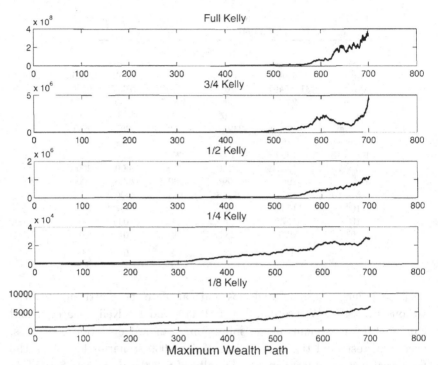

EXHIBIT 3:   Highest Final Wealth Trajectory for the Ziemba and Hausch Model.

14%. For full Kelly, it is fully 12.4% losses, and it is 7.25% with 3/4 Kelly
and 3.5% with half Kelly. These are just the percent of losses. But the size
of the losses can be large as shown in the >50, >100, and >500 rows of
Exhibit 2. The minimum final wealth levels were 587 for 1/8 and 513 for 1/4
Kelly so you never lose more than half your initial wealth with these lower
risk betting strategies. But with 1/2, 3/4 and full Kelly, the minimums
were 111, 56, and only \$4. Exhibit 4 shows these minimum wealth paths.
With full Kelly, and by inference 1/8, 1/4, 1/2, and 3/4 Kelly, the investor
can actually never go fully bankrupt because of the proportional nature of
Kelly betting.

If capital is infinitely divisible and there is no leveraging, then the
Kelly bettor cannot go bankrupt since one never bets everything (unless the
probability of losing anything at all is zero and the probability of winning
is positive). If capital is discrete, then presumably Kelly bets are rounded
down to avoid overbetting, in which case, at least one unit is never bet.
Hence, the worst case with Kelly is to be reduced to one unit, at which

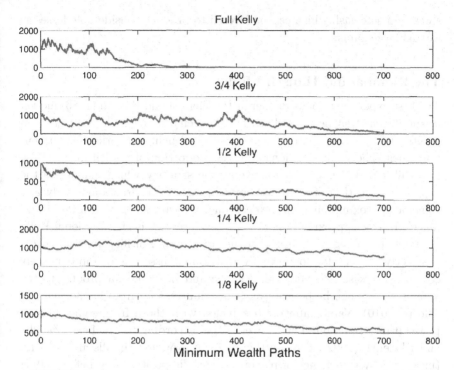

EXHIBIT 4:   Lowest Final Wealth Trajectory for the Ziemba and Hausch Model.

point betting stops. Since fractional Kelly bets less, the result follows for all such strategies. For levered wagers, that is, betting more than one's wealth with borrowed money, the investor can lose more than their initial wealth and become bankrupt.

Proportional Investment Strategies: Alternative Experiments

The growth and risk characteristics for proportional investment strategies such as the Kelly depend upon the returns on risky investments. We now consider two other investment experiments where the return distributions are quite different. The mean returns are similar: 14% for Ziemba-Hausch, 12.5% for Bicksler-Thorp Example I, and 10.2% for Bicksler-Thorp Example II. However, the variation around the mean is not similar and this produces much different Kelly strategies and corresponding wealth trajectories for scenarios. The third experiment involves two assets: risky stock and safe cash which can be levered to produce considerable losses as well as large gains.

The Ziemba and Hausch Model

The first experiment looks further at the Ziemba and Hausch (1986) model. A simulation was performed with 3000 scenarios over $T = 40$ decision points with the five types of independent investments for various investment strategies. The Kelly fractions and the proportion of wealth invested are in Exhibit 5. Here, $1.0k$ is full Kelly, the strategy which maximizes the expected logarithm of wealth. Values below 1.0 are fractional Kelly and coincide approximately with the decision from using a negative power utility function. The approximation $f = \frac{1}{1-\alpha}$, where fxk is the fractional Kelly strategy and $\alpha < 0$ is from the negative power utility function αw^α, is exactly correct for lognormally distributed assets and approximately correct otherwise, see MacLean, Ziemba and Li (2005) for proof. But the approximation can be poor for asset distributions far from log normal; see Thorp (2010). Values above 1.0 coincide with those from some positive power utility function. This is overbetting according to MacLean, Ziemba and Blazenko (1992), because the long run growth rate falls and security (measured by the chance of reaching a specific positive goal before falling to a negative growth level) also falls. This is very important and not fully understood by many hedge fund and other investors. Long Term Capital's 1998 demise from overbetting is a prime example. Examples of other similar blowouts are discussed in Ziemba and Ziemba (2007). They argue that the recipe for hedge fund disaster is almost always the same: the portfolio is overbet and not well diversified in some scenarios and then a bad scenario occurs in a non-diversified part of the portfolio and disaster quickly follows.

EXHIBIT 5: The Investment Proportions (λ) and Kelly Fractions. The Investment Proportions λ's are Full Kelly as in the 5th Column; see Exhibit 1. The Other Proportions are Scaled from the Kelly Fractions f in this Column.

	Kelly Fraction: f						
Opportunity	1.75k	1.5k	1.25k	1.0k	0.75k	0.50k	0.25k
A	0.245	0.210	0.175	0.140	0.105	0.070	0.035
B	0.1225	0.105	0.0875	0.070	0.0525	0.035	0.0175
C	0.08225	0.0705	0.05875	0.047	0.03525	0.0235	0.01175
D	0.06125	0.0525	0.04375	0.035	0.02625	0.0175	0.00875
E	0.049	0.042	0.035	0.028	0.021	0.014	0.007

EXHIBIT 6:   Wealth Statistics by Kelly Fraction for the Ziemba and Hausch Model.

Statistic				Fraction			
	1.75k	1.5k	1.25k	1.0k	0.75k	0.50k	0.25k
Max	50364.73	25093.12	21730.90	8256.97	6632.08	3044.34	1854.53
Mean	1738.11	1625.63	1527.20	1386.80	1279.32	1172.74	1085.07
Min	42.77	80.79	83.55	193.07	281.25	456.29	664.31
St. Dev.	2360.73	1851.10	1296.72	849.73	587.16	359.94	160.76
Skewness	6.42	4.72	3.49	1.94	1.61	1.12	0.49
Kurtosis	85.30	38.22	27.94	6.66	5.17	2.17	0.47
$>5 \times 10$	2998	3000	3000	3000	3000	3000	3000
10^2	2980	2995	2998	3000	3000	3000	3000
$>5 \times 10^2$	2338	2454	2634	2815	2939	2994	3000
$>10^3$	1556	11606	1762	1836	1899	1938	2055
$>10^4$	43	24	4	0	0	0	0
$>10^5$	0	0	0	0	0	0	0
$>10^6$	0	0	0	0	0	0	0

The trouble is that the penalty for losses, especially with large portfolios in the billions is way too low. Fees are kept and fired traders either retire or get rehired by other funds. Examples include John Merriwether, Victor Niederhoffer and Brian Hunter.

The initial wealth for investment was 1000. Exhibit 6 reports final wealth statistics on the for $T = 40$ periods with the various strategies.

Since the Kelly bets are small, the proportion of current wealth invested is not high for any of the fractions. The upside and down side are not dramatic in this example, although there is a substantial gap between the maximum and minimum wealth with the highest fraction. Exhibit 7 shows the trajectories which have the highest and lowest final wealth for a selection of fractions. The log-wealth is displayed to show the rate of growth at each decision point. The lowest trajectories are almost a reflection of the highest ones.

The skewness and kurtosis indicate that final wealth is not normally distributed. This is expected since the geometric growth process suggests a log-normal wealth. Exhibit 8 displays the simulated log-wealth for selected fractions at the horizon $T = 40$. The normal probability plot will be linear if terminal wealth is distributed log-normally. The slope of the plot captures the shape of the log-wealth distribution. For this example the final wealth distribution is close to log-normal. As the Kelly fraction increases the slope increases, showing the longer right tail but also the increase in downside risk in the wealth distribution.

158　　　　　　　　*Leonard C. MacLean, et al.*

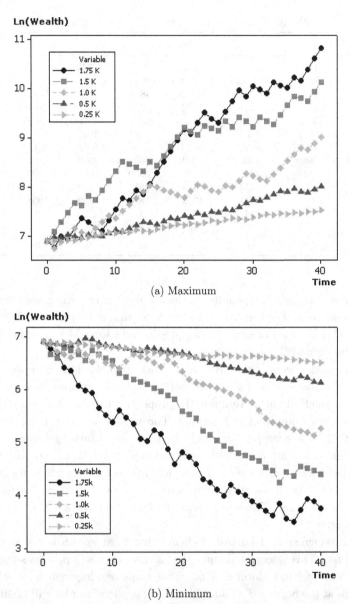

(a) Maximum

(b) Minimum

EXHIBIT 7: Trajectories with Final Wealth Extremes for the Ziemba and Hausch Model.

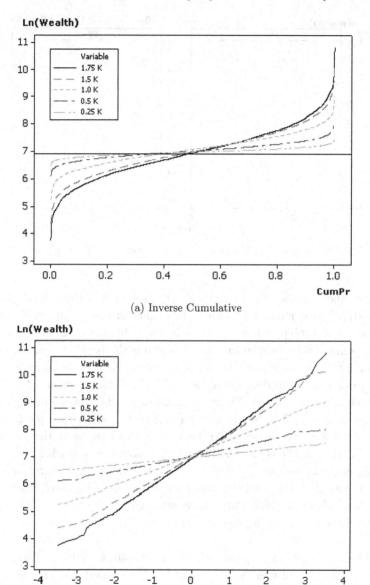

(a) Inverse Cumulative

(b) Normal Plot

EXHIBIT 8:   Final Ln(Wealth) Distributions by Fraction for the Ziemba and Hausch Model.

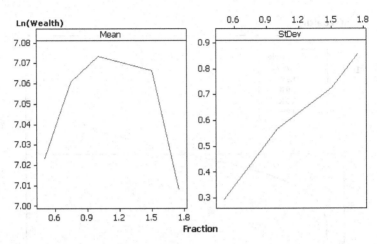

EXHIBIT 9:   Mean-Std Tradeoff for the Ziemba and Hausch Model.

On the inverse cumulative distribution plot, the initial wealth $\ln(1000) = 6.91$ is indicated to show the chance of losses. And indeed there can be considerable losses as shown in the left side of Exhibit 8a. The inverse cumulative distribution of log-wealth is the basis of comparisons of accumulated wealth at the horizon. In particular, if the plots intersect then first order stochastic dominance by a wealth distribution does not exist (Hanoch and Levy, 1969). The mean and standard deviation of log-wealth are considered in Exhibit 9, where the growth versus security trade-off by Kelly fraction is shown. The mean log-wealth peaks at the full Kelly strategy whereas the standard deviation is monotone increasing. Fractional strategies greater than full Kelly are inefficient in log-wealth, since the growth rate decreases and the standard deviation of log-wealth increases. It is these where the hedge fund disasters occur.

We have the following conclusions:

1. The statistics describing end of horizon $(T = 40)$ wealth are all monotone in the fraction of wealth invested in the Kelly portfolio. The maximum terminal wealth and the mean terminal wealth increase in the Kelly fraction. In contrast the minimum wealth decreases as the fraction increases and the standard deviation grows as the fraction increases. There is a trade-off between wealth growth and risk. The cumulative distributions in Exhibit 8 supports the theory for fractional strategies, as there is no dominance, and the distribution plots all intersect.

2. The maximum and minimum final wealth trajectories show the wealth growth — risk trade-off of the strategies. The worst scenario is the same for all Kelly fractions so that the wealth decay is greater with higher fractions. The best scenario differs for the low fraction strategies, but the growth path is almost monotone in the fraction. The mean-standard deviation trade-off demonstrates the inefficiency of levered strategies (greater than full Kelly) which, as shown, are growth-security dominated and to be avoided in practice by responsible traders.

Bicksler and Thorp Example I — Uniform Returns

There is one risky asset R with mean return of $+12.5\%$, that is uniformly distributed between -25% and $+50\%$ for each dollar invested. Assume we can lend or borrow capital at a risk free rate $r = 0.0$. Let λ be the proportion of capital invested in the risky asset, where λ ranges from 0.4 to 2.4. So $\lambda = 2.4$ means \$1.4 is borrowed for each \$1 of current wealth and \$2.40 is invested in the risky asset. The Kelly optimal growth investment in the risky asset is $x = 2.8655$. The Kelly fractions for the different values of λ are shown in Exhibit 10.[3] Bicksler and Thorp used 10 and 20 yearly decision

EXHIBIT 10: The Investment Proportions and Kelly Fractions for the Bicksler and Thorp Example I.

Proportion: λ	0.4	0.8	1.2	1.6	2.0	2.4
Fraction: f	0.140	0.279	0.419	0.558	0.698	0.838

---

[3]The formula relating λ and f for this experiment is as follows. For the problem

$$Max_x\{E(ln(1 + r + x(R - r))\},$$

where R is uniform on $[a, b]$ and $r =$ the risk free rate. The first order condition

$$\int_a^b \frac{R - r}{1 + r + x(R - r)} \times \frac{1}{b - a} dR = 0,$$

reduces to

$$x(b - a) = (1 + r)ln\left(\frac{1 + r + x(b - r)}{1 + r + x(a - r)}\right) \Longleftrightarrow \left[\frac{1 + r + x(b - r)}{1 + r + x(a - r)}\right]^{\frac{1}{x}} = e^{\frac{b-a}{1+r}}.$$

For $a = -0.25, b = 0.5, r = 0$. The equation becomes

$$\left[\frac{1 + 0.5x}{1 - 0.25x}\right]^{\frac{1}{x}} = e^{0.75},$$

with a solution $x = 2.8655$.

EXHIBIT 11:   Final Wealth Statistics by Kelly Fraction for the Bicksler and Thorp
Example I.

			Fraction			
Statistic	0.14k	0.28k	0.42k	0.56k	0.70k	0.84k
Max	34435.74	743361.14	11155417.33	124068469.50	1070576212.0	7399787898
Mean	7045.27	45675.75	275262.93	1538429.88	7877534.72	36387516.18
Min	728.45	425.57	197.43	70.97	18.91	3.46
St. Dev.	4016.18	60890.61	674415.54	6047844.60	44547205.57	272356844.8
Skewness	1.90	4.57	7.78	10.80	13.39	15.63
Kurtosis	6.00	31.54	83.19	150.51	223.70	301.38
$>5 \times 10$	3000	3000	3000	3000	2999	2998
10^2	3000	3000	3000	2999	2999	2998
$>5 \times 10^2$	3000	2999	2999	2997	2991	2976
$>10^3$	2998	2997	2995	2991	2980	2965
$>10^4$	529	2524	2808	2851	2847	2803
$>10^5$	0	293	1414	2025	2243	2290
$>10^6$	0	0	161	696	1165	1407

periods, and 50 simulated scenarios. We use 40 yearly decision periods, with
3000 scenarios.

The numerical results from the simulation with $T = 40$ are in
Exhibits 11–14. Although the Kelly investment is levered, the fractions
in this case are less than 1.

In this experiment the Kelly proportion is high, based on the attrac-
tiveness of the investment in stock. The largest fraction (0.838k) has
high returns, although in the worst scenario most of the wealth is lost.
The trajectories for the highest and lowest terminal wealth scenarios are
displayed in Exhibit 12. The highest rate of growth is for the highest
fraction, and correspondingly it has the largest wealth fallback.

The distribution of terminal wealth in Exhibit 13 illustrates the growth
of the $f = 0.838k$ strategy. It intersects the normal probability plot for other
strategies very early and increases its advantage. The linearity of the plots
for all strategies is evidence of the log-normality of final wealth. The inverse
cumulative distribution plot indicates that the chance of losses is small —
the horizontal line indicates the log of initial wealth.

As further evidence of the superiority of the $f = 0.838k$ strategy
consider the mean and standard deviation of log-wealth in Exhibit 14. The
growth rate (mean ln(Wealth)) continues to increase since the fractional
strategies are less then full Kelly. So there is no more than full Kelly over
betting in this strategy.

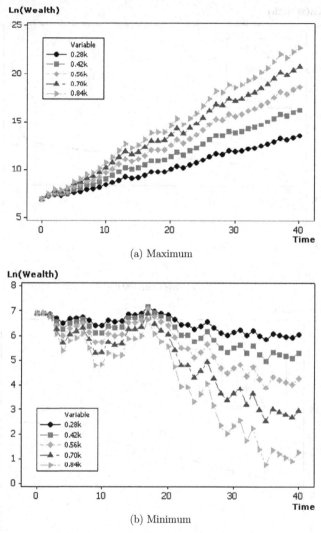

(a) Maximum

(b) Minimum

EXHIBIT 12:   Trajectories with Final Wealth Extremes for the Bicksler and Thorp Example I.

We have the following conclusions:

1. The statistics describing end of horizon ($T = 40$) wealth are again monotone in the fraction of wealth invested in the Kelly portfolio. Specifically the maximum terminal wealth and the mean terminal wealth increase in the Kelly fraction. In contrast the minimum wealth decreases

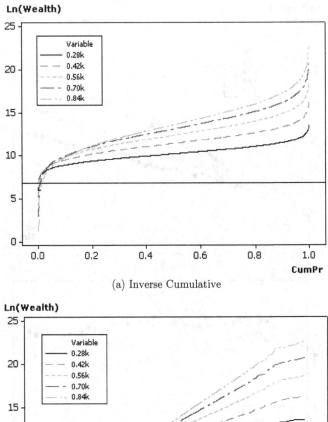

(a) Inverse Cumulative

(b) Normal Plot

EXHIBIT 13:   Final Ln(Wealth) Distributions by Fraction: Bicksler-Thorp Example I.

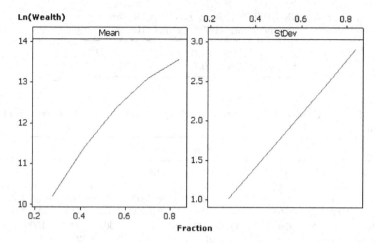

EXHIBIT 14:   Mean-Std Trade-off for the Bicksler and Thorp Example I.

as the fraction increases and the standard deviation grows as the fraction increases. The growth and decay are much more pronounced then was the case in experiment 1. The minimum still remains above 0 since the fraction of Kelly is less than 1. There is a trade-off between wealth growth and risk, but the advantage of leveraged investment is clear. As illustrated with the cumulative distributions in Exhibit 13, the log-normality holds and the upside growth is more pronounced than the downside loss. Of course, the fractions are less than 1 so improved growth is expected.

2. The maximum and minimum final wealth trajectories clearly show the wealth growth — risk of various strategies. The mean-standard deviation trade-off favors the largest fraction, even though it is highly levered.

Bicksler — Thorp Example II — Equity versus Cash

In the third experiment there are two assets: US equities and US T-bills. According to Siegel (2002), during 1926–2001 US equities returned 10.2% with a yearly standard deviation of 20.3%, and the mean return was 3.9% for short term government T-bills with zero standard deviation. We assume the choice is between these two assets in each period. The Kelly strategy is to invest a proportion of wealth $x = 1.5288$ in equities and sell short the T-bill at $1 - x = -0.5228$ of current wealth. With the short selling and levered

EXHIBIT 15:   Kelly Fractions for the Bicksler and Thorp (1973) Example II.

λ	0.4	0.8	1.2	1.6	2.0	2.4
f	0.26	0.52	0.78	1.05	1.31	1.57

EXHIBIT 16:   Final Wealth Statistics by Kelly Fraction for the Bicksler and Thorp
Example II.

	Fraction					
Statistic	0.26k	0.52k	0.78k	1.05k	1.31k	1.57k
Max	65842.09	673058.45	5283234.28	33314627.67	174061071.4	769753090
Mean	12110.34	30937.03	76573.69	182645.07	416382.80	895952.14
Min	2367.92	701.28	−4969.78	−133456.35	−6862762.81	−102513723.8
St. Dev.	6147.30	35980.17	174683.09	815091.13	3634459.82	15004915.61
Skewness	1.54	4.88	13.01	25.92	38.22	45.45
Kurtosis	4.90	51.85	305.66	950.96	1755.18	2303.38
>5 × 10	3000	3000	2998	2970	2713	2184
10^2	3000	3000	2998	2955	2671	2129
>5 × 10^2	3000	3000	2986	2866	2520	1960
>10^3	3000	2996	2954	2779	2409	1875
>10^4	1698	2276	2273	2112	1794	1375
>10^5	0	132	575	838	877	751
>10^6	0	0	9	116	216	270

strategies, there is a chance of substantial losses. For the simulations, the
proportion: λ of wealth invested in equities[4] and the corresponding Kelly
fraction f are provided in Exhibit 15. Bicksler and Thorp used 10 and
20 yearly decision periods, and 50 simulated scenarios. We use 40 yearly
decision periods, with 3000 scenarios.

The results from the simulations with experiment 3 appear in
Exhibits 16–19. The striking aspects of the statistics in Exhibit 16 are
the sizable gains and losses. For the most aggressive strategy ($1.57k$), it

---

[4]The formula relating λ and f for this example is as follows. For the problem

$$Max_x\{E(ln(1 + r + x(R - r))\},$$

where R is assumed to be Gaussian with mean μ_R and standard deviation σ_R, and
r =the risk free rate. The solution is given by Merton (1990) as

$$x = \frac{\mu_R - r}{\sigma_R}.$$

Since $\mu_R = 0.102, \sigma_R = 0.203, r = 0.039$, the Kelly strategy is $x = 1.5288$.

is possible to lose 10,000 times the initial wealth. This assumes that the shortselling is permissable through to the decision period at the horizon $T = 40$.

The highest and lowest final wealth trajectories are presented in Exhibit 17. In the worst case, the trajectory is terminated to indicate the

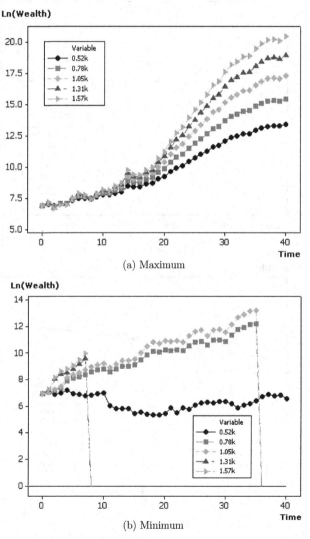

(a) Maximum

(b) Minimum

EXHIBIT 17:   Trajectories with Final Wealth Extremes for the Bicksler and Thorp Example II.

timing of vanishing wealth. There is quick bankruptcy for the aggressive strategies.

The substantial downside is further illustrated in the distribution of final wealth plot in Exhibit 18. The normal probability plots are almost

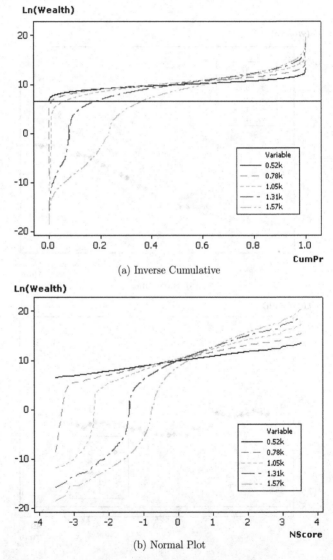

(a) Inverse Cumulative

(b) Normal Plot

EXHIBIT 18: Final Ln(Wealth) Distributions by Fraction for the Bicksler and Thorp Example II.

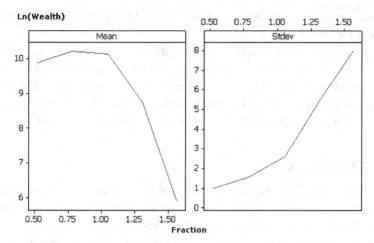

EXHIBIT 19:   Mean-Std Tradeoff: Bicksler and Thorp Example II.

linear on the upside (log-normality), but the downside is much more
extreme than log-normal for all strategies except for $0.52k$. Even the full
Kelly is very risky in this example largely because the basic position
is levered. The inverse cumulative distribution shows a high probability
of large losses with the most aggressive strategies. In constructing these
plots the negative growth was incorporated with the formula $growth =
[signW_T] \, ln(|W_T|)$.

The mean-standard deviation trade-off in Exhibit 19 provides more
evidence concerning the riskyness of the high proportion strategies. When
the fraction exceeds the full Kelly, the drop-off in growth rate is sharp, and
that is matched by a sharp increase in standard deviation.

The results in experiment 3 lead to the following conclusions.

1. The statistics describing the end of the horizon $(T = 40)$ wealth are
   again monotone in the fraction of wealth invested in the Kelly portfolio.
   Specifically (i) the maximum terminal wealth and the mean terminal
   wealth increase in the Kelly fraction; and (ii) the minimum wealth
   decreases as the fraction increases and the standard deviation grows as
   the fraction increases. The growth and decay are pronounced and it is
   possible to have extremely large losses. The fraction of the Kelly optimal
   growth strategy exceeds 1 in the most levered strategies and this is very
   risky. There is a trade-off between return and risk, but the mean for the
   levered strategies is growing far less than the standard deviation. The
   disadvantage of leveraged investment is illustrated with the cumulative

distributions in Exhibit 18. The log-normality of final wealth does not
hold for the levered strategies.
2. The maximum and minimum final wealth trajectories show the return —
risk of levered strategies. The worst and best scenarios are not same for
all Kelly fractions. The worst scenario for the most levered strategy
shows the rapid decline in wealth. The mean-standard deviation trade-
off confirms the extreme riskyness of the aggressive strategies.

Final Comments

The Kelly optimal capital growth investment strategy is an attractive
approach to wealth creation. In addition to maximizing the asymptotic
rate of long term growth of capital, it avoids bankruptcy and overwhelms
any essentially different investment strategy in the long run. See MacLean,
Thorp and Ziemba (2010b) for a discussion of the good and bad properties
of these strategies. However, automatic use of the Kelly strategy in any
investment situation is risky and can be dangerous. It requires some
adaptation to the investment environment: rates of return, volatilities,
correlation of alternative assets, estimation error, risk aversion preferences,
and planning horizon are all important aspects of the investment process.
Poundstone's (2005) book, while a very good read, does not explain these
important investment aspects and the use of Kelly strategies by advisory
firms such as *Morningstar* and *Motley Fools* is flawed. The experiments in
this paper represent some of the diversity in the investment environment.
By considering the Kelly and its variants we get a concrete look at the
plusses and minusses of the capital growth model. The main points from
the Bicksler and Thorp (1973) and Ziemba and Hausch (1986) studies are
confirmed.

- The wealth accumulated from the full Kelly strategy does not stochasti-
  cally dominate fractional Kelly wealth. The downside is often much more
  favorable with a fraction less than one.
- There is a tradeoff of risk and return with the fraction invested in
  the Kelly portfolio. In cases of large uncertainty, either from intrinsic
  volatility or estimation error, security is gained by reducing the Kelly
  investment fraction.
- The full Kelly strategy can be highly levered. While the use of borrowing
  can be effective in generating large returns on investment, increased
  leveraging beyond the full Kelly is not warranted as it is growth-security

dominated. The returns from over-levered investment are offset by a growing probability of bankruptcy.

- The Kelly strategy is not merely a long term approach. Proper use in the short and medium run can achieve wealth goals while protecting against drawdowns. MacLean, Sanegre, Zhao and Ziemba (2004) and MacLean, Zhao and Ziemba (2009) discuss a strategy to reduce the Kelly fraction to stay above a prespecified wealth path with high probability.

The great economist Paul Samuelson was a long time critic of the Kelly strategy which maximizes the expected logarithm of final wealth, see, for example, Samuelson (1969, 1971, 1979) and Merton and Samuelson (1974). His criticisms are well dealt with in this simulation paper and we see no disagreement with his various analytic points:

1. the Kelly strategy maximizes the asymptotic long run growth of the investor's wealth, and we agree;
2. the Kelly strategy maximizes expected utility of only logarithmic utility and not necessarily any other utility function, and we agree; and
3. the Kelly strategy always leads to more wealth than any essentially different strategy; this we know from this paper is not true since it is possible to have a large number of very good investments and still lose most of one's fortune.

Samuelson seemed to imply that Kelly proponents thought that the Kelly strategy maximizes for other utility functions but this was neither argued nor implied.

It is true that the expected value of wealth is higher with the Kelly strategy but bad outcomes are very possible.

In correspondence with Ziemba (private correspondence, 2006, 2007, 2008) he seems to feel that half Kelly or $u(w) = -\frac{1}{w}$ explains the data better. We agree that in practice, half Kelly is a toned down version of full Kelly that provides a lot more security to compensate for its loss in long term growth. Samuelson proposes an analysis of three investors $-\frac{1}{w}$, $\log w$ and $w^{\frac{1}{2}}$. In Ziemba (2015) these are explored adding two tail investors αw^α, $\alpha \to -\infty$ the safest investor and w, namely $\alpha = 1$, the riskiest investor which span the range of absolute Arrow-Pratt risk aversion from 0 to ∞.

References

Bernoulli, D. (1954). Exposition of a new theory on the measurement of risk (translated by Louise Sommer). *Econometrica*, 22, 23–36.

Bicksler, J. L. and E. O. Thorp (1973). The capital growth model: An empirical investigation. *Journal of Financial and Quantitative Analysis*, 8(2), 273–287.

Breiman, L. (1961). Optimal gambling system for favorable games. *Proceedings of the 4th Berkeley Symposium on Mathematical Statistics and Probability*, 1, 63–8.

Browne, S. (1999). The risk and rewards of minimizing shortfall probability. *Journal of Portfolio Management*, 25(4), 76–85.

Chopra, V. K. and W. T. Ziemba (1993). The effect of errors in mean, variance and co-variance estimates on optimal portfolio choice. *Journal of Portfolio Management*, 19, 6–11.

Fuller, J. (2006). Optimize your portfolio with the Kelly formula. morningstar.com, October 6.

Hakansson, N. (1970). Optimal investment and consumption strategies under risk for a class of utility functions. *Econometrica*, 38, 587–607.

Hakansson, N. H. and W. T. Ziemba (1995). Capital growth theory. In R. A. Jarrow, V. Maksimovic, and W. T. Ziemba (Eds.), *Finance*, pp. 65–86. Amsterdam: North Holland.

Hanoch, G. and H. Levy (1969). The efficiency analysis of choices involving risk. *The Review of Economic Studies*, 36, 335–346.

Kelly, Jr., J. R. (1956). A new interpretation of the information rate. *Bell System Technical Journal*, 35, 917–926.

Latané, H. (1959). Criteria for choice among risky ventures. *Journal of Political Economy*, 67, 144–155.

Lee, E. (2006). How to calculate the Kelly formula. fool.com, October 31.

MacLean, L. C., R. Sanegre, Y. Zhao, and W. T. Ziemba (2004). Capital growth with security. *Journal of Economic Dynamics and Control*, 28(4), 937–954.

MacLean, L. C., E. O. Thorp, Y. Zhao, and W. T. Ziemba (2010). Medium term simulations of the full Kelly and fractional Kelly investment strategies. In L. C. MacLean, E. O. Thorp, and W. T. Ziemba (Eds.), *The Kelly Capital Growth Investment Criterion: Theory and Practice*. World Scientific Press, Singapore.

MacLean, L. C., E. O. Thorp, and W. T. Ziemba (Eds.) (2010a). *The Kelly Capital Growth Investment Criterion: Theory and Practice*. World Scientific Press, Singapore.

MacLean, L. C., E. O. Thorp, and W. T. Ziemba (2010b). Long term capital growth: the good and bad properties of the Kelly criterion criterion. *Quantitative Finance* (September).

MacLean, L. C., Y. Zhao, and W. T. Ziemba (2009). Optimal capital growth with convex loss penalties. Working paper, Dalhousie University.

MacLean, L. C., W. T. Ziemba, and G. Blazenko (1992). Growth versus security in dynamic investment analysis. *Management Science*, 38, 1562–85.

MacLean, L. C., W. T. Ziemba, and Y. Li (2005). Time to wealth goals in capital accumulation and the optimal trade-off of growth versus security. *Quantitative Finance*, 5(4), 343–357.

McEnally, R. W. (1986). Latané's bequest: The best of portfolio strategies. *Journal of Portfolio Management*, 12(2), 21–30.

Merton, R. C. (1990). *Continuous-Time Finance*. Blackwell Publishers, Cambridge, MA.

Merton, R. C. and P. A. Samuelson (1974). Fallacy of the log-normal approximation to optimal portfolio decision-making over many periods. *Journal of Financial Economics*, 1, 67–94.

Mulvey, J. M., B. Pauling, and R. E. Madey (2003). Advantages of multiperiod portfolio models. *Journal of Portfolio Management*, 29, 35–45.

Pabrai, M. (2007). *The Dhandho Investor.*

Phelps, E. S. (1962). The accumulation of risky capital: A sequential utility analysis. *Econometrica,* 30, 729–743.

Poundstone, W. (2005). *Fortune's Formula: The Untold Story of the Scientific System that Beat the Casinos and Wall Street.* Hill and Wang, NY.

Rubinstein, M. (1976). The strong case for the generalized logarithmic utility model as the premier model of financial markets. *Journal of Finance,* 31(2), 551–571.

Rubinstein, M. (1991). Continuously rebalanced investment strategies. *Journal of Portfolio Management,* 18(1), 78–81.

Samuelson, P. A. (1969). Lifetime portfolio selection by dynamic stochastic programming. *Review of Economics and Statistics,* 51, 239–246.

Samuelson, P. A. (1971). The fallacy of maximizing the geometric mean in long sequences of investing or gambling. *Proceedings National Academy of Science,* 68, 2493–2496.

Samuelson, P. A. (1979). Why we should not make mean log of wealth big though years to act are long. *Journal of Banking and Finance,* 3, 305–307.

Samuelson, P. A. (various). Letters to William T. Ziemba. Private Correspondence, December 13, 2006, May 7, 2007, May 12, 2008.

Siegel, J. J. (2002). *Stocks for the Long Run.* New York, NY: Wiley.

Stutzer, M. (2000). A portfolio performance index. *Financial Analysts Journal,* 56(3), 52–61.

Stutzer, M. (2004). Asset allocation without unobservable parameters. *Financial Analysts Journal,* 60(5), 38–51.

Thorp, E. O. (2006). The Kelly criterion in blackjack, sports betting and the stock market. In S. A. Zenios and W. T. Ziemba (Eds.), *Handbook of Asset and Liability Management, Volume 1,* pp. 387–428. Amsterdam: North Holland.

Thorp, E. O. (2010). Understanding the kelly criterion. In L. C. MacLean, E. O. Thorp, and W. T. Ziemba (Eds.), *The Kelly Capital Growth Investment Criterion: Theory and Practice.* Singapore: World Scientific.

Wilcox, J. (2003a). Harry Markowitz and the discretionary wealth hypothesis. *Journal of Portfolio Management,* 29 (Spring), 58–65.

Wilcox, J. (2003b). Risk management: Survival of the fittest. Wilcox Investment Inc.

Wilcox, J. (2005). A better paradigm for finance. *Finance Letters,* 3(1), 5–11.

Ziemba, R. E. S. and W. T. Ziemba (2007). *Scenarios for Risk Management and Global Investment Strategies.* New York, NY: Wiley.

Ziemba, W. T. (2005). The symmetric downside risk Sharpe ratio and the evaluation of great investors and speculators. *Journal of Portfolio Management, Fall,* 108–122.

Ziemba, W. T. (2015). A response to Professor Paul A Samuelson's objections to Kelly capital growth investing. *Journal of Portfolio Management.*

Ziemba, W. T. and D. B. Hausch (1986). *Betting at the Racetrack.* Dr Z Investments, San Luis Obispo, CA.

Ziemba, W. T. and D. B. Hausch (1987). *Dr Z's Beat the Racetrack.* William Morrow.

Ziemba, W. T. and R. G. Vickson (Eds.) (1975). *Stochastic Optimization Models in Finance.* New York, NY: Academic Press.

Ziemba, W. T. and R. G. Vickson (Eds.) (2006). *Stochastic Optimization Models in Finance* (2 ed.). Singapore: World Scientific.

Chapter 9

Great Investors: Their Methods, Results and Evaluation*

Olivier Gergaud and William T. Ziemba[†]

We discuss the records of some great investors and hedge fund managers. Their graphs of wealth over time leads us to a search for smooth monotone paths and how we might fairly evaluate superior as opposed to average investors. Some investors prefer high long run growth and accept bumps, rather than smooth wealth paths and lower growth. These include some Kelly criterion investors such as Buffett, Keynes and Soros who have concentrated portfolios with few asset positions. Earlier, Ziemba (2005), following an idea in Ziemba and Schwartz (1991), proposed a modification of the ordinary normal distribution based Sharpe ratio to evaluate right skewed great investor portfolios. This measure only counts losses and is useful in evaluating superior investors such as the Renaissance Medallion hedge fund which has a high rating by the modified downside symmetric Sharpe ratio as opposed to a modest rating with the ordinary Sharpe ratio. Using the University of Massachusetts hedge fund database, we show some funds with superior records and from this evaluation learn more about the properties of the DSSR and the modified downside symmetric information ratio (DISR).

*Many thanks to Professor Thomas Schneeweis for making available the University of Massachusetts Center for International Securities and Derivative Markets hedge fund database.
[†]Olivier Gergaud is professor at the Bordeaux Management School and the University of Reims, France, olivier.gergaud@bem.edu and William T Ziemba is the alumni professor of financial modeling and stochastic optimization (emeritus) at the University of British Columbia in Vancouver, BC, Canada and professor at the ICMA Centre at the University of Reading in the UK, wtzimi@mac.com. The research leading to these results has received funding from the European Unions Seventh Framework Programme (FP7/2007-2013) under the grant agreement n 230589 (ERC Long Term Risks Christian Gollier University of Toulouse.

Some Wealth Paths of Outstanding Investors and their Evaluation

We begin by observing some wealth paths and then using the University of Massachusetts derivative hedge fund (UMass DHF) database, we show some funds with superior records and from this evaluation learn more about the properties of the DSSR and the modified downside symmetric information ratio (DISR). Exhibit 1 shows the Yale endowment net asset value from 1999 to 2010 and the comparison with a broad universe of colleges and universities and inflation.[1] Exhibit 2 presents some highlights relating to the endowment from 2005 to 2010. Exhibit 3 shows the university revenue by source from 1905–2010. Exhibit 4 shows the endowment market value wealth path from 1950 to 2010. Observe the contribution of Swensen's strategies on the endowment income since 1985, yet much of the university budget comes from sources other than the endowment and student tuition. Recent results have been strong with a 21.9% return for the year ending June 30, 2011. That puts the endowment at $19.4 billion based on investment gains of $3.6 billion with $1.0 billion going to the operating budget.

David Swensen, who took over management of the endowment in 1985, pioneered a new multistrategy approach in which equities, broadly defined,

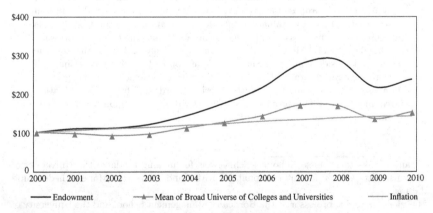

EXHIBIT 1: Yale's Performance Exceeds Peer Results, 1999 to 2010, 1999 = $1,000.
Source: YER, 2010.

---

[1]For more on the Yale endowment, see Ziemba's March 2007 and January 2011 columns in *Wilmott* magazine.

EXHIBIT 2:   Yale Endowment Highlights.

	2010	2009	2008	2007	2006	2005
Market Value (in mils)	$16.7	$16,326.6	$22,869.7	$22,530.2	$18,030.6	$15,224.9
Return	8.9%	−24.6%	4.5%	28.0%	22.9%	22.3%
Spending (in mils)	$1,119.0	$ 1,175.2	$ 849.9	$ 684.0	$ 616.0	$ 567.0
Operating Budget Revenues (in mils)	2,664.3	2,559.8	2,280.2	2,075.0	1,932.0	1,768.0
Endowment Percentage	42%	45.9%	37.3%	33.0%	31.9%	32.2%
Asset Allocation (as of June 30)						
Absolute Return	19%	24.3%	25.1%	23.3%	23.3%	25.7%
Domestic Equity	7.5	7.5	10.1	11.0	11.6	14.1
Fixed Income	4.0	4.0	4.0	3.8	4.9	4.9
Foreign Equity	8.5	9.8	15.2	14.1	14.6	13.7
Private Equity	33%	24.3	20.2	18.7	16.4	14.8
Real Assets	28%	32.0	29.3	27.1	27.8	25.0
Cash		−1.9	−3.9	1.9	2.5	1.9

Source: YER, 2010.

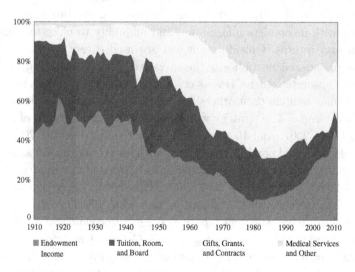

EXHIBIT 3:   University Revenue by Source 1905–2010.
Source: YEC, 2010.

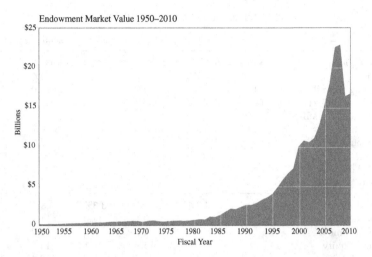

EXHIBIT 4:   Yale Endowment Market Values, 1950–2010.
Source: YER, 2010.

were emphasized. He holds a diversified portfolio and avoids market timing and fine tunes allocations at extreme valuations. He invests in private markets with incomplete information and illiquidity to increase long-term incremental returns. Outside managers are used except for all the most routine or indexed portfolios. A mean-variance not fat-tailed approach is used and absolute returns, real assets, private equity are emphasized along with smaller weights than others have in domestic exchange listed equity and fixed income. The strategy worked well with a mean return of 16% net from 1986 to 2007. And 10.1% over ten years ending June 30, 2011 versus US stocks 3.9% and bonds 5.1%. Most years have produced profits, however, fiscal 2009, which included the difficult fall of 2008 and first quarter of 2009, had a −24.6% loss. Still the 1992–2011 record is 14.2% per year versus an endowment average of 9.42% according to Conroy (2011).

Exhibit 5 shows the wealth path of the great economist John Maynard Keynes running the endowment of King's College, Cambridge University from 1927 until his death in 1945. Keynes was a very aggressive investor and had a violent wealth path. Ziemba (2003) estimated that his overall strategy is about 80% full Kelly maximum expected log strategy plus 20% cash or a utility function of the concave risk averse negative power utility function wealth of $u(w) = -w^{-0.25}$. See MacLean, Thorp, and Ziemba (2010) for the good and bad properties of this strategy and MacLean, Thorp, Zhao and

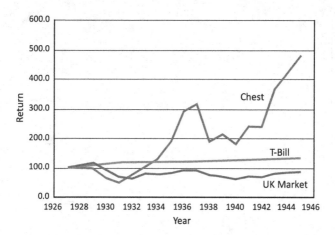

EXHIBIT 5:   Graph of the Performance of the Chest Fund, 1927–1945.
Source: Ziemba (2005).

Ziemba (2011) for simulations of the typical behavior. Keynes actually lost more than half the portfolio which was even more than the market index in the first two years. Over the 19 years which included the depression of the 1930s and its recovery and World War II, he had a geometric mean of 9.12% versus the market index of −0.89%. So he was a great investor but his wealth path was not smooth.

Two full Kelly investors who hold very few concentrated positions are Warren Buffett and George Soros. Their wealth paths from December 1985 to April 2000 plus the Windsor fund of George Neff, the Ford Foundation, the Tiger Fund of Julian Robertson, the S&P500 total return index plus T-bills and US inflation are shown in Exhibit 6. Exhibit 7 shows the concentration of their equity portfolios on September 30, 2008. Soros had a 50.53% position in Petroleo Brasileiro, plus 11.58% in the Potash Corporation of Saskatchewan, 5.95% in Walmart, 4.49% in Hess Corporation and 3.28% in Conoco Phillips. Buffett has many close to 10% positions such as 8.17% in Conoco Phillips, 8.00% in Proctor and Gamble, 5.62% in Kraft Foods and 3.55% in Wells Fargo. Both of them, especially Soros, trade futures, options and other derivative positions as well.

While both of these famous billionaire investors have had many gains, these also have many monthly losses. For example, Berkshire Hathaway had 58 and Quantum 53 losing months out of 172 total months in the data

EXHIBIT 6:   Growth of Assets, Log Scale, Various High Performing Funds, 1985–2000.
Source: Ziemba (2005) using data from Siegel, Kroner and Clifford (2001).

sample. Also the gains of these two investors were very high as shown in the right side of Exhibit 9 which ranks all the monthly returns, but losses were high too as shown on the left side. In both tails these two investors are more extreme than the others.

The Downside Symmetric Sharpe Ratio

The DSSR as it is called was discussed in Ziemba (2005) following its use in Japan in Ziemba and Schwartz (1991). The idea is simple. If great investors are to be evaluated as those who do not lose much and have many gains, then do not penalize them for these gains. The Sharpe ratio, namely

$$S = \frac{\mu_p - R_F}{\sigma_p}$$

penalizes gains as well as losses through σ_p so if gains are large, S is reduced. Here μ_p is the portfolio mean returns, R_F, the risk free asset, and σ_p is the standard deviation. So the DSSR only uses

$$\sigma_{x_-}^2 = \frac{\sum_{i=1}^{n}(x_i - \bar{x})_-^2}{n - 1} = (\sigma_{x_-})^2.$$

EXHIBIT 7: Top Ten Equity Holdings of Soros Fund Management and Berkshire Hathaway, September 30, 2008.

Company	Current Value × 1000	Shares	% Portfolio
Soros Fund Management			
Petroleo Brasileiro SA	$1,673,048	43,854,474	50.53
Potash Corp Sask Inc	378,020	3,341,027	11.58
Wal Mart Stores Inc	195,320	3,791,890	5.95
Hess Corp	115,001	2,085,988	4.49
Conoco Phillips	96,855	1,707,900	3.28
Research in Motion Ltd	85,840	1,610,810	2.88
Arch Coal Inc	75,851	2,877,486	2.48
iShares TR	67,236	1,300,000	2.11
Powershares QQQ Trust	93,100	2,000,000	2.04
Schlumberger Ltd	33,801	545,000	1.12
Berkshire Hathaway			
ConocoPhillips	$4,413,390	77,955,80	8.17
Procter & Gamble Co	4,789,440	80,252,000	8.00
Kraft Fods Inc	3,633,985	120,012,700	5.62
Wells Fargo & Co	1,819,970	66,132,620	3.55
Wesco Finl Corp	1,927,643	5,703,087	2.91
US Bancorp	1,1366,385	49,461,826	2.55
Johnson & Johnson	1,468,689	24,588,800	2.44
Moody's	1,121,760	48,000,000	2.34
Wal Mart Stores, Inc	1,026,334	19,944,300	1.71
Anheuser Busch Cos, Inc	725,201	13,845,000	1.29

Source: SEC Filings.

So we replace σ_p with σ_{x_-} where $\bar{x} = 0$, ( )$_-$ means take only minus values. The total variance is twice the downside variance. Pictorially, one erases the actual gains and takes as fictitious gains the mirror image of the losses. So the risk is symmetric. Hence the name, downside symmetric Sharpe ratio. The corresponding downside symmetric information ratio is

$$DSIR = \frac{\mu_p}{\sigma_{x_-}}.$$

Observe that the higher the DSSR is the better is the fund with the range of the measure from zero, when $\mu_p \leq R_F$, to ∞, when there are no losses.

We cannot use this measure to evaluate the Yale endowment as monthly data is unavailable.[2] But we can use it to evaluate the funds in Exhibit 6.

---

[2]There are other great trading records that we cannot analyze because of lack of availability of monthly data including two billionaires who the second author has worked with. Both are futures traders. Data bases cannot include all funds such as the very best

EXHIBIT 8: Comparison of Ordinary and Symmetric
Downside Sharpe Yearly Performance Measures, Monthly
Data and Arithmetic Means.

	Ordinary	Downside
Ford Foundation	0.970	0.920
Tiger Fund	0.879	0.865
S&P500	0.797	0.696
Berkshire Hathaway	0.773	0.917
Quantum	0.622	0.458
Windsor	0.543	0.495

Source: Ziemba (2005).

Exhibit 8 shows that Warren Buffett's Berkshire Hathaway is the only one
that improves when you switch from S to DSSR but he still does not beat
the Ford Foundation and the Harvard endowment is also slightly better
than Berkshire Hathaway using quarterly data.

Why is this? Exhibit 9 shows that Buffett and Soros had many more
large gains than the other funds but also more losses when we rank the
worst to best monthly returns. As noted above, Berkshire Hathaway and
Quantum had losses in about a third of the 172 months in the sample
period. Observe that in the tails, Berkshire and Quantum (George Soros's
fund) are asymptotically equivalent. It is clear that Buffett and Soros do
not care about monthly losses but aim to maximize long run wealth. This
and the high concentration of positions leads to the conclusion that they
are full Kelly investors.

Smoother wealth paths are those in Exhibit 10 of Bill Benter of the
Hong Kong racing syndicate and Ed Thorp of the Princeton Newport hedge

who are closed and the very worst who are secretive. One other extremely successful
trading outfit that John Mulvey has pointed out to us is the Commodity Corporation
(CC) formed by Professors Paul Samuelson and Paul Cootner and others such as
Amos Hostetter. The CC was the training ground for great traders such as Paul Tudor
Jones, founder of Tudor Investment Corporation, Louis Bacon, founder of Moore Capital
Management, Grenville Craig, founder of Tiverton Trading, Bruce Kovner, founder of
Caxton Associates, Christian Levett, founder of Clive Capital LLP, Michael Marcus, a
leading commodities and currency trader, Jack D. Schwager, an author on financial topics
and hedge fund manager, Ed Seykota, a computer scientist, technical trader and pioneer
in System Trading and Willem Kooyker, founder of Blenheim Capital. Their performance
was 89% per year after fees for their first ten years. Lintner (1983) did analyze CC and
other commodity funds and futures account managers for 42 months from July 1979 to
December 1982. CC had a net mean of 8.42% per month with a standard deviation of
21.709. Lintner's unpublished paper is highly recommended but it uses a mean-variance
approach rather than what we do here.

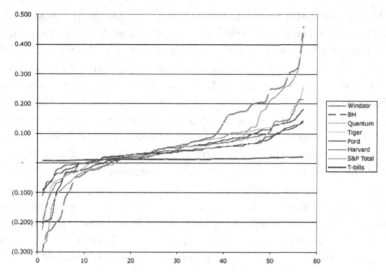

EXHIBIT 9: Return Distributions of All the Funds, Quarterly Returns Distribution, December 1985 to March 2000.

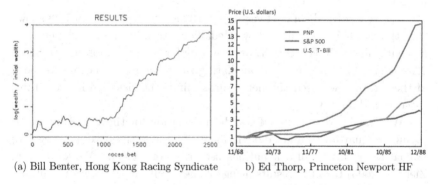

(a) Bill Benter, Hong Kong Racing Syndicate   b) Ed Thorp, Princeton Newport HF

EXHIBIT 10: Smoother Wealth Paths.

fund. Thorp had the amazing record of just three monthly losses in twenty years of trading from 1968 to 1988. This DSSR = 13.8.

Renaissance Medallion: Arguably the Greatest Hedge Fund

The Medallion Fund uses mathematical ideas such as the Kelly criterion to run a superior hedge fund. The staff of technical researchers and traders, working under mathematician James Simons, is constantly devising edges that they use to generate successful trades of various durations focussing on many short term trades that enter and exit in seconds. They pioneered this type of short algorithmic trading and remain successful doing it despise the competition. The second author told Simons about the advantages of Kelly investing in the early stage of this fund and since their trades approximate an infinite sequence, it is the natural investment criterion to use. The fund, whose size is in the $5 billion area, has very large fees (5% management and 44% incentive). Despite these fees and the large size of the fund, the net returns have been consistently outstanding, with a few small monthly losses and high positive monthly returns; see the histogram in Exhibit 14. Exhibit 12 shows the monthly net returns from January 1993 to April 2005, along with quarterly and yearly returns. There were only 17 monthly losses in 148 months and 3 losses in 49 quarters and no yearly losses in these 12+ years of trading in our data sample. Exhibit 13 lists the US T-bill interest rates in percent, January 1993 to April 2005, yearly, quarterly and monthly. These numbers were compiled from http://treasurydirect.gov. This section updates an earlier discussion in Ziemba and Ziemba (2007).

The yearly DSSR of 26.4 versus an ordinary Sharpe ratio of 1.68 shows that the DSSR is needed to show Medallion's true brilliance. The effect is less with quarterly DSSR's 11.6 versus 1.09 for S, and a monthly DSSR of 2.20 versus 0.76 for the S. In calculating the standard deviations for both of these ratios, we used the net returns minus the risk free interest rates listed in Exhibit 13.

We calculated the annual standard deviation for the DSSR by multiplying the quarterly standard deviation by 2 because there were no negative annual net returns. All calculations use arithmetic means. We know from Ziemba (2005) that the results using geometric means will have essentially the same conclusions.

Exhibit 14a shows the percent monthly returns sorted in increasing order. Exhibit 14b shows the accumulation of wealth over time assuming that the fund had an initial wealth of 100 dollars on Dec 31, 1992.

Medallion's outstanding yearly DSSR of 26.4 is even higher than Princeton Newport's 13.8 during 1969–1988. Jim Simon's Medallion fund is near or at the top of the worlds hedge funds. Indeed, the amount that Simons earned, $1.4 billion in 2005, was the highest in the world for hedge fund managers, and his $1.6 billion in 2006 was the second best and 2007–2011 were similar. The fund was closed to all but about six outside investors

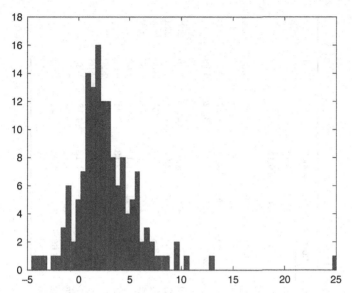

EXHIBIT 11:   Histogram of Monthly % Returns of the Medallion Fund, January 1993 to April 2005.

plus employees. But in recent years even those six are out or reduced in their percent in the fund. Monthly data since 2005 is unavailable to us, however the 2006–2009 estimated yearly net returns, according to Insider Monkey (2010), were 44.3%(2006), 73.0% (2007), 80.0% (2008), and 39.0% (2009).

Outstanding Funds in the UMASS DHF Universe

We have found some funds with even higher DSSRs then Renaissance Medallion. For example, Logos Trading Inc, a commodity trading advisor, had a mean return of 8.5% per month from its inception in June 1984 to its closing 157 months later in June 1997. Its Sharpe ratio was 2.77 and its DSSR was 64.4. Exhibit 15 show the wealth graph, assets under management, net asset value and monthly losses and gains.

Exhibit 16 shows the results for the GJ Investment Fund of Flemington, New Jersey managed by Jeeva Ramaswamy whose DSSR is 491.8! There were very high mean returns of 15.5% per month and only one monthly loss yield this huge DSSR. The stated objective of the Fund is to, over the long term, outperform all three major U.S. stock market indices and

EXHIBIT 12:   Net Returns in Percent of the Medallion Fund, January 1993 to April 2005, Yearly, Quarterly and Monthly.

	1993	1994	1995	1996	1997	1998	1999	2000	2001	2002	2003	2004	2005
Yearly	39.06	70.69	38.33	31.49	21.21	41.50	24.54	98.53	31.12	29.14	25.28	27.77	
Quarterly													
Q1	7.81	14.69	22.06	7.88	3.51	7.30	(0.25)	25.44	12.62	5.90	4.29	9.03	8.30
Q2	25.06	35.48	4.84	1.40	6.60	7.60	6.70	20.51	5.64	7.20	6.59	3.88	
Q3	4.04	11.19	3.62	10.82	8.37	9.69	6.88	8.58	7.60	8.91	8.77	5.71	
Q4	(0.86)	(1.20)	4.31	8.44	1.41	11.73	9.48	20.93	2.42	4.44	3.62	6.72	
Monthly													
January	1.27	4.68	7.4	3.25	1.16	5.02	3.79	10.5	4.67	1.65	2.07	3.76	2.26
February	3.08	5.16	7.54	1.67	2.03	1.96	(2.44)	9.37	2.13	3.03	2.53	1.97	2.86
March	3.28	4.19	5.68	2.77	0.29	0.21	(1.49)	3.8	5.36	1.12	(0.35)	3.05	2.96
April	6.89	2.42	4.10	0.44	1.01	0.61	3.22	9.78	2.97	3.81	1.78	0.86	0.95
May	3.74	5.66	5.53	0.22	4.08	4.56	1.64	7.24	2.44	1.11	3.44	2.61	
June	12.78	25.19	(4.57)	0.73	1.36	2.28	1.71	2.37	0.15	2.13	1.24	0.37	
July	3.15	6.59	(1.28)	4.24	5.45	(1.10)	4.39	5.97	1.00	5.92	1.98	2.20	
August	(0.67)	7.96	5.91	2.97	1.9	4.31	1.22	3.52	3.05	1.68	2.38	2.08	
September	1.54	(3.38)	(0.89)	3.25	0.85	6.33	1.15	(1.02)	3.38	1.13	4.18	1.33	
October	1.88	(2.05)	0.3	6.37	(1.11)	5.33	2.76	6.71	1.89	1.15	0.35	2.39	
November	(1.51)	(0.74)	2.45	5.93	(0.22)	2.26	5.42	8.66	0.17	1.42	1.42	3.03	
December	(1.20)	1.62	1.52	(3.74)	2.77	3.73	1.06	4.30	0.35	1.81	1.81	1.16	

EXHIBIT 13: Annualized T-bill Interest Rates in Percent, January 1993 to April 2005, Yearly, Quarterly and Monthly.

	1993	1994	1995	1996	1997	1998	1999	2000	2001	2002	2003	2004	2005
Yearly	3.33	4.98	5.69	5.23	5.36	4.85	4.76	5.86	3.36	1.68	1.05	1.56	3.39
Quarterly													
Q1	2.99	3.27	5.77	4.94	5.06	5.07	4.41	5.53	4.85	1.71	1.14	0.90	2.56
Q2	2.98	4.05	5.61	5.04	5.08	5.00	4.43	5.75	3.70	1.71	1.05	1.06	
Q3	3.02	4.52	5.38	5.13	5.06	4.89	4.67	6.00	3.25	1.63	0.92	1.48	
Q4	3.08	5.31	5.28	4.97	5.08	2.30	5.05	6.03	1.93	1.36	0.91	2.01	
Monthly													
January	2.99	3.14	5.46	5.16	5.00	5.07	4.33	5.21	5.63	1.85	1.28	0.91	2.18
February	2.99	3.21	5.62	5.05	5.03	5.07	4.37	5.37	5.24	1.78	1.21	0.91	2.36
March	2.99	3.27	5.77	4.94	5.06	5.07	4.41	5.53	4.85	1.71	1.14	0.90	2.54
April	2.99	3.53	5.72	4.97	5.07	5.05	4.41	5.61	4.45	1.71	1.11	0.95	2.65
May	2.98	3.79	5.67	5.01	5.07	5.02	4.42	5.68	4.05	1.71	1.08	1.01	
June	2.98	4.05	5.61	5.04	5.08	5.00	4.43	5.75	3.66	1.71	1.05	1.06	
July	2.99	4.21	5.54	5.07	5.07	4.96	4.51	5.83	3.52	1.68	1.00	1.20	
August	3.00	4.36	5.46	5.10	5.07	4.92	4.59	5.92	3.39	1.66	0.96	1.34	
September	3.02	4.52	5.38	5.13	5.06	4.89	4.67	6.00	3.25	1.63	0.92	1.48	
October	3.04	4.78	5.34	5.08	5.07	4.69	4.80	6.01	2.81	1.54	0.92	1.66	
November	3.06	5.05	5.31	5.03	5.07	4.49	4.93	6.02	2.37	1.45	0.91	1.83	
December	3.08	5.31	5.28	4.97	5.08	4.30	5.05	6.03	1.93	1.36	0.91	2.01	

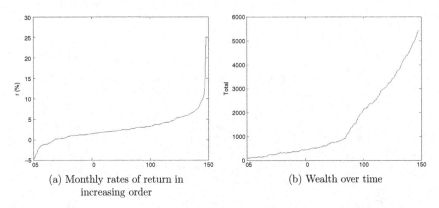

(a) Monthly rates of return in   (b) Wealth over time
increasing order

EXHIBIT 14:   Medallion Fund, January 1993 to April 2005.

over 90% of all U.S. mutual fund and hedge fund managers using a non-levered Warren Buffett style value investing approach. The assumption is that the market over reacts to good and bad news resulting in volatile stock price movements that do not correspond to the company's long-term fundamentals, hence undervalued stocks can be purchased. Special situations investing is also used and there are investments in India and China. Fees are just for performance at 25% above a 6% hurdle rate. To date, the Fund has consistently outperformed the Dow30, the S&P500 and the Nasdaq100.

Exhibit 17 has the wealth graph of the FMG Fund in the Federated MGT Group of funds plus the assets under management and the ordered monthly losses and gains. This CPO reported results from January 1987 to July 2003, some 199 months. It had a geometric mean of +2.3% per month and a Sharpe ratio of 12.35, higher than any other fund in the UMASS DHF database. Apparently there were no monthly losses so the DSSR=DISR=∞! This sounds too good to be true and indeed the CFTC on December 7, 2010 announced that the principals were ordered to pay $26 million for running a Ponzi scheme with 140 participants, see Greenberg (2011). So FMG is suspect and had Madoff madeup elements in its reporting and misuse of funds. See Thorp (2009) for a discussion of his confidential 1991 analysis of the Madoff scheme which was exposed in December 2008. Our point in this paper is to discuss the use of the DSSR measure and an infinity measure is suspect!

To understand more fully the characteristics of the DSSR measure we have plotted in Exhibit 18 the DSSR-Sharpe ratios versus the ranking

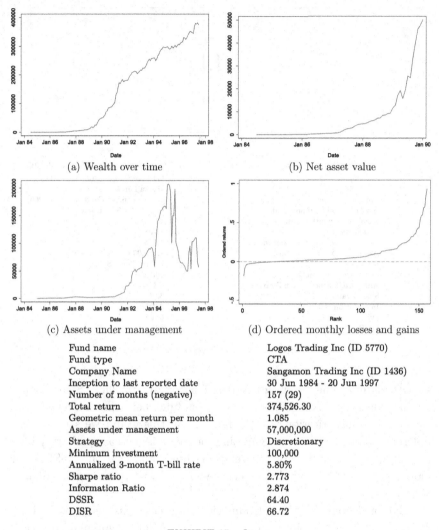

(a) Wealth over time

(b) Net asset value

(c) Assets under management

(d) Ordered monthly losses and gains

Fund name	Logos Trading Inc (ID 5770)
Fund type	CTA
Company Name	Sangamon Trading Inc (ID 1436)
Inception to last reported date	30 Jun 1984 - 20 Jun 1997
Number of months (negative)	157 (29)
Total return	374,526.30
Geometric mean return per month	1.085
Assets under management	57,000,000
Strategy	Discretionary
Minimum investment	100,000
Annualized 3-month T-bill rate	5.80%
Sharpe ratio	2.773
Information Ratio	2.874
DSSR	64.40
DISR	66.72

EXHIBIT 15:   Logos.

based on the Sharpe ratio with the right hand side vertical axis being the proportion of negative months. Exhibit 19 is the same except it estimates a curve for the individual funds shown as dots in Exhibit 18.

Exhibit 18 shows on the left-hand side vertical axis the difference between the DSSR and Sharpe ratios. The second vertical axis plots the proportion of negative months per fund as proxied by a local polynomial

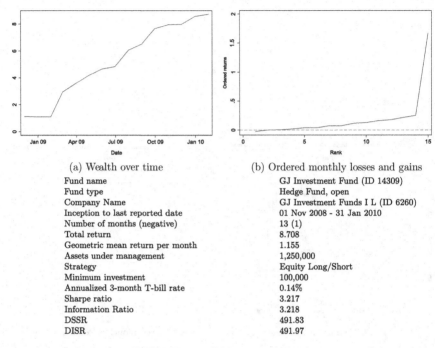

(a) Wealth over time

(b) Ordered monthly losses and gains

Fund name	GJ Investment Fund (ID 14309)
Fund type	Hedge Fund, open
Company Name	GJ Investment Funds I L (ID 6260)
Inception to last reported date	01 Nov 2008 - 31 Jan 2010
Number of months (negative)	13 (1)
Total return	8.708
Geometric mean return per month	1.155
Assets under management	1,250,000
Strategy	Equity Long/Short
Minimum investment	100,000
Annualized 3-month T-bill rate	0.14%
Sharpe ratio	3.217
Information Ratio	3.218
DSSR	491.83
DISR	491.97

EXHIBIT 16:   GJ Investment Fund.

smoothed line. The funds are ordered according to their Sharpe ratio on the horizontal axis (0 being the worst fund here that matched with the constraining criterion we adopted). From this graph we see that the difference between the two competing measures is increasing sharply near the top of the scale, i.e. for the very best funds and that the DSSR is far more sensitive to the number of negative months than the regular Sharpe ratio is.

Exhibit 19 plots on the left-hand side horizontal axis the value for both ratios. Again, each ratio is summarized by a local polynomial smoothed line for ease or interpretation. These two Exhibits tell more or less the same story.

Exhibit 20 is a summary of various types of funds regarding their performance and Exhibits 21–24 list the Commodity Pool Operators (CPO), Commodity Trading Advisors (CTA), Fund of Funds (FOF) and Hedge Funds (HF) ranked by DSSR that have a mean return of at least 1.5% per month and at least 100 months of reported trading.

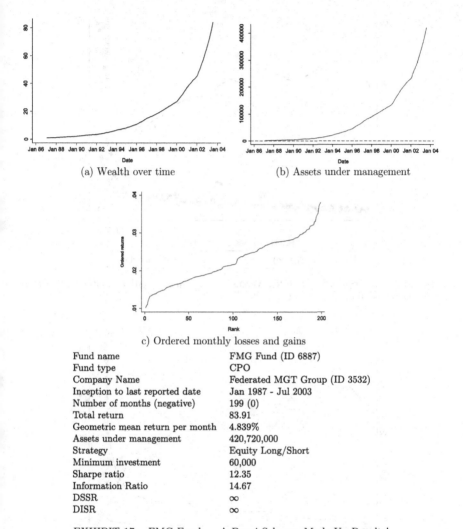

(a) Wealth over time   (b) Assets under management

c) Ordered monthly losses and gains

Fund name	FMG Fund (ID 6887)
Fund type	CPO
Company Name	Federated MGT Group (ID 3532)
Inception to last reported date	Jan 1987 - Jul 2003
Number of months (negative)	199 (0)
Total return	83.91
Geometric mean return per month	4.839%
Assets under management	420,720,000
Strategy	Equity Long/Short
Minimum investment	60,000
Sharpe ratio	12.35
Information Ratio	14.67
DSSR	∞
DISR	∞

EXHIBIT 17: FMG Fund — A Ponzi Scheme, Made Up Results!

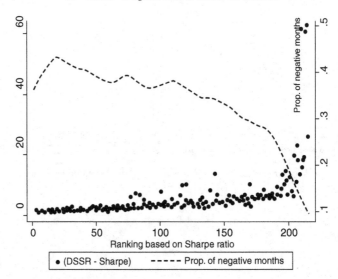

EXHIBIT 18:   DSSR-Sharpe Ratios Versus Proportion of Negative Months for UMASS
DHF Database Individual Funds.

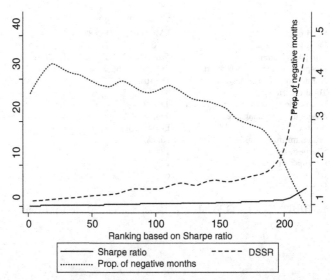

EXHIBIT 19:   DSSR-Sharpe Ratios Versus Proportion of Negative Months for UMASS
DHF Database.

EXHIBIT 20: Some Summary Statistics by Fund Type for the UMASS DHF Database.

Fund type	nbmonths	nbneg	% neg	gmeanreturn	S	I	DSSR	DISR
CPO								
mean	155	53	0.25	1.019	1.463	1.760	4.903	5.949
stdev	42	25		0.004	2.596	3.079	2.948	3.619
CTA								
mean	179	75	0.29	1.022	0.724	0.854	5.436	6.270
stdev	68	34		0.011	0.408	0.435	8.317	8.623
FOF								
mean	128	26	0.17	1.016	2.328	2.759	14.542	17.222
stdev	28	20		0.001	1.030	1.196	7.997	9.345
HF								
mean	135	43	0.24	1.019	1.082	1.272	6.772	7.905
stdev	32	16		0.004	0.669	0.774	8.682	9.870

EXHIBIT 21: Performance and Main Features of Commodity Pool Operators.

Fund name	Fund ID	Total Months	Neg. months	Inception date	Last report date	AUM	Av. Return	S	IR	DSSR	DISR
Trout Trading Fund	6548	131	11	Jan 1988	Nov 1998	2137000	1.018	1.812	2.354	11.808	15.337
Cyril Finance	6661	130	43	Jan 1991	Nov 2001		1.019	1.368	1.662	9.892	12.018
Mjc Aggressive Multi-Sector Fund	6191	103	37	Jul 1995	Jan 2004	411000	1.029	1.228	1.358	7.921	8.762
Crystal Currency Fund	6653	100	31	Jan 1990	Apr 1998		1.02	1.285	1.571	7.238	8.849
High Sierra Partners 1 (Qp)	6291	219	52	Jul 1984	Sep 2002	627000	1.02	1.315	1.636	6.972	8.673
Gamut A	7025	107	35	Jul 1986	May 1995		1.02	1.158	1.454	6.219	7.807
Abba Fund Lp	6152	119	42	Mar 2000	Jan 2010	2266000	1.015	1.041	1.198	5.809	6.687
Tulip Trend Fund Ltd. Class A Eur	8028	186	74	Jan 1994	Jun 2009	11790000	1.024	1.056	1.185	5.501	6.171
Tulip Trend Fund Ltd. Class C Usd	8029	186	75	Jan 1994	Jun 2009	11790000	1.024	1.054	1.183	5.497	6.167
Tulip Trend Fund Ltd. Class G Chf	8030	186	76	Jan 1994	Jun 2009	11790000	1.022	0.957	1.086	4.833	5.488
Quickpool Lp	6117	174	65	Aug 1995	Jan 2010	1039000	1.019	0.879	1.01	4.028	4.63
Sunrise Sierra Intl Currency Fund	6503	183	74	Oct 1985	Dec 2000	435000	1.019	0.562	0.711	2.871	3.634

(Continued)

EXHIBIT 21: (*Continued*)

Fund name	Fund ID	Total Months	Neg. months	Inception date	Last report date	AUM	Av. Return	S	IR	DSSR	DISR
Bright Capital Beach Technical Fund Ltd	6983	128	56	Jan 1996	Aug 2006	2810000	1.015	0.591	0.723	2.731	3.344
Emory Partners	6072	198	42	Sep 1993	Feb 2010		1.016	0.644	0.771	2.462	2.946
Liberty Portfolio Fund	6337	187	86	Jun 1985	Dec 2000	683000	1.016	0.417	0.562	2.303	3.098
Tactical Futures Fund Iii	6510	100	46	Jul 1991	Oct 1999	547000	1.015	0.417	0.539	1.926	2.492
Colorado Commodities Ptnrs. I	6775	118	50	Apr 1987	Jan 1997	30000	1.019	0.414	0.531	1.794	2.297
Waldner Pool	6565	129	56	Jan 1987	Sep 1997	187000	1.017	0.393	0.515	1.704	2.231
Tactical Commodity Fund	6508	219	102	Jul 1981	Sep 1999	191000	1.016	0.325	0.473	1.643	2.394
Fmg Fund	6887	199	0	Jan 1987	Jul 2003	1680000	1.023	12.353	14.672	0	0

EXHIBIT 22:   Performance and Main Features of Commodity Trading Advisors.

Fund name	Fund ID	Duration	Neg months	Inception date	Last report date	AUM	Av. Return	S	IR	DSSR	DISR	Strat.
Logos Trading Inc.	5770	157	29	Jun 1984	Jun 1997		1.085	2.773	2.874	64.395	66.72	DIS
Gollyhott Trading (Discretionary)	5408	112	47	Jan 1993	Apr 2002	1,602,000	1.044	1.037	1.112	14.661	15.709	DIS
Hirst Currency Program	5608	135	68	Jul 1994	Sep 2005		1.019	0.921	1.086	11.081	13.07	DIS
Kenzie Global Asset Mgt.	5863	210	64	Jan 1981	Jun 1998		1.032	1.626	1.906	10.926	12.807	DIS
Hirst Currency Fund Ltd	5609	135	68	Jul 1994	Sep 2005		1.019	0.911	1.077	10.883	12.855	DIS
Michael N. Trading (Financial Futures Trading Program)	5218	119	31	Jan 1997	Nov 2006	1,000,000	1.019	1.522	1.772	8.939	10.408	SYS
Kmj Capital Llc Currency Program	5079	222	105	Sep 1991	Feb 2010	229,000	1.017	0.843	1	8.602	10.208	DIS
Moore Capital Mgt.	5800	121	34	Jul 1990	Jul 2000	210,000,000	1.016	1.404	1.799	8.105	10.383	DIS
Forecast Trading Group	5919	103	40	Dec 1999	Jun 2008	42,000	1.025	1.046	1.148	8.004	8.78	DIS
Golden Mountain Trading Inc.	5406	136	55	Jan 1985	Nov 1996		1.041	0.713	0.785	7.983	8.784	SYS
Oxeye Managed Accounts (Ftse 100)	5535	130	45	Jul 1997	Apr 2008	44,000	1.04	1.145	1.216	7.081	7.524	DIS
Tudor Investment Corp.	5074	249	98	Jul 1984	Mar 2005		1.021	0.963	1.16	6.814	8.202	DIS

(Continued)

EXHIBIT 22: (*Continued*)

Fund name	Fund ID	Duration	Neg months	Inception date	Last report date	AUM	Av. Return	S	IR	DSSR	DISR	Strat.
Capricorn Fxst (Aggressive)	5375	134	46	Jan 1999	Feb 2010		1.015	1.12	1.305	6.297	7.338	DIS
Chescor (High Beta)	5890	125	50	Oct 1989	Feb 2000	36,000	1.03	0.92	1.037	6.092	6.872	DIS
Rosetta Trading Program	13236	119	48	Apr 2000	Feb 2010	50,029	1.034	0.888	0.936	6.037	6.368	DIS
Hollingsworth Trading Co	5987	180	46	Feb 1987	Jan 2002	100,000	1.022	0.787	0.957	6.033	7.335	SYS
Sea Express Futures Fund	12561	105	42	Jun 2001	Feb 2010	1,400,655	1.019	1.001	1.098	5.344	5.864	SYS
Sarkis Ozdemirci	5681	132	57	Jan 1987	Dec 1997		1.022	0.859	1.054	5.313	6.524	SYS
Alpha Program	9601	118	58	May 2000	Feb 2010	2,606,558	1.02	0.89	0.984	5.114	5.653	DIS
Hanseatic (Discretionary)	4997	113	51	Feb 1996	Jun 2005	76,000	1.023	0.805	0.907	4.799	5.404	DIS
Sarkis Ozdemirci	5808	120	45	Jan 1988	Dec 1997	67,000	1.018	0.788	1.011	4.536	5.82	SYS
Hathersage Capital (Accelerated)	5164	135	43	Dec 1991	Feb 2003	1,287,000	1.03	0.968	1.074	4.473	4.964	DIS
Kmj Capital Mgt (Diversified)	5090	109	54	Dec 1989	Dec 1998	616,000	1.023	0.707	0.835	4.417	5.222	SYS
Urkena Mgt (Currency)	5275	129	46	Jan 1990	Dec 2000	1,050,000	1.02	0.889	1.093	4.199	5.162	SYS
Quicksilver Trading Diversified Program	5898	182	66	Dec 1994	Jan 2010	176,000	1.019	0.884	1.02	4.062	4.69	SYS
Ashley Capital Management Fund	5350	221	104	Aug 1991	Dec 2009	86,000	1.015	0.697	0.846	4.009	4.869	SYS

(*Continued*)

EXHIBIT 22: (*Continued*)

Fund name	Fund ID	Duration	Neg months	Inception date	Last report date	AUM	Av. Return	S	IR	DSSR	DISR	Strat.
Trading Solutions (Program #1)	5886	116	55	Jan 1997	Aug 2006	270,000	1.016	0.654	0.78	3.836	4.573	SYS
Lasalle Portfolio (Financial)	5107	175	59	Mar 1984	Sep 1998	59,000	1.018	0.586	0.772	3.594	4.735	DIS
Witter & Lester Stock Index	5191	328	122	Oct 1982	Jan 2010	10,000	1.021	0.577	0.69	3.592	4.289	SYS
Clarke Capital Global Basic	5046	169	87	Feb 1996	Feb 2010	100,000	1.018	0.54	0.624	3.517	4.062	SYS
Blenheim Investments Inc.	5450	157	72	Apr 1985	Apr 1998		1.022	0.655	0.808	3.499	4.314	DIS
Daniel R Meyer & Co	5325	218	91	Sep 1986	Oct 2004	42,000	1.019	0.661	0.805	3.346	4.078	SYS
Azf Commodity Mgt.	5546	185	87	May 1982	Sep 1997		1.017	0.532	0.733	3.336	4.603	SYS
Rabar Diversified Program	5032	302	140	Jan 1985	Feb 2010		1.018	0.44	0.54	3.222	3.954	SYS
Tactical Institutional Commodity Program	5594	203	85	Apr 1993	Feb 2010	1,003,000	1.015	0.64	0.775	3.05	3.694	SYS
Meyer Capital Management	5326	127	61	Jan 1998	Jul 2008	218,000	1.018	0.572	0.667	3.05	3.561	SYS
Eckhardt Trading (Higher Leverage)	5367	221	90	Oct 1991	Feb 2010	470,000	1.017	0.608	0.72	3.004	3.557	SYS
Spackenkill Trading Co Diversified	5386	398	173	May 1973	Jun 2006	11,000	1.025	0.423	0.515	2.829	3.446	SYS
Mc Futures	5791	184	89	Jan 1984	Aug 2000	1,000,000	1.02	0.435	0.549	2.739	3.457	SYS

(*Continued*)

EXHIBIT 22:   (*Continued*)

Fund name	Fund ID	Duration	Neg months	Inception date	Last report date	AUM	Av. Return	S	IR	DSSR	DISR	Strat.
Infinity Futures	5185	178	77	Feb 1984	Nov 1998	70,000	1.018	0.482	0.641	2.666	3.545	SYS
Willowbridge Associates (Mtech)	5426	103	45	Jan 1991	Jul 1999	1,947,000	1.018	0.511	0.628	2.624	3.228	DIS
Abraham Trading	5328	266	117	Jan 1988	Feb 2010	102,000	1.015	0.484	0.605	2.577	3.222	SYS
Jwh Financial & Metals Portfolio	5343	305	145	Oct 1984	Feb 2010	37,000	1.016	0.449	0.567	2.237	2.823	SYS
Timetech Mgt	5260	235	105	Jul 1980	Feb 2000	70,000	1.017	0.367	0.524	2.223	3.174	DIS
Emc Capital Management (Classic)	5047	302	145	Jan 1985	Feb 2010	1,267,000	1.017	0.369	0.455	2.218	2.732	SYS
Willowbridge Associates (Argo)	5182	207	86	Jan 1988	Mar 2005	4,465,000	1.015	0.493	0.635	2.157	2.776	SYS
Mark J Walsh Co (Standard)	5181	294	133	Sep 1985	Feb 2010	98,000	1.016	0.422	0.528	2.04	2.554	SYS
Friedberg Currency Program	5629	262	118	Jan 1986	Oct 2007	281,000	1.021	0.267	0.319	2.011	2.399	DIS
Ace Stock Index Premium Collection (Regular Program)	5330	101	22	Oct 2001	Feb 2010	2,000	1.016	0.595	0.662	1.987	2.211	DIS
Saxon Invest (Aggressive Diversified)	5911	196	83	Nov 1993	Feb 2010	788,000	1.017	0.442	0.522	1.96	2.314	SYS

(*Continued*)

EXHIBIT 22: *(Continued)*

Fund name	Fund ID	Duration	Neg months	Inception date	Last report date	AUM	Av. Return	S	IR	DSSR	DISR	Strat.
Isq Fund	11554	130	57	Jan 1997	Oct 2007		1.023	0.439	0.496	1.958	2.213	SYS
Dunn Capital Mgt (Standard)	5828	264	114	Jan 1979	Dec 2000	2,093,000	1.017	0.424	0.608	1.93	2.767	SYS
Vector Commodity Services	5861	225	114	Jul 1982	Mar 2001	500,000	1.02	0.327	0.422	1.847	2.384	SYS
Hawksbill Capital (Global Diversified)	5340	256	119	Nov 1988	Feb 2010	741,000	1.017	0.36	0.439	1.788	2.181	SYS
Ljm Partners Client Accounts	5728	134	24	Jan 1999	Feb 2010	2,189,688	1.017	0.603	0.691	1.743	1.997	DIS
District Capital Mgt (Select)	5378	183	81	Jan 1990	Mar 2005	125,000	1.015	0.348	0.437	1.676	2.103	SYS
Willowbridge Associates (Xlim)	5016	123	57	Jan 1995	Mar 2005	6,271,000	1.017	0.321	0.389	1.467	1.774	DIS
Mangin Capital Management (Cta Composite)	5978	161	68	Jul 1992	Nov 2005	24,000	1.018	0.281	0.332	1.424	1.684	SYS
John W. Henry & Co. Inc (Kt Diversified)	5169	125	56	Oct 1983	Feb 1994		1.016	0.282	0.403	1.376	1.969	SYS

Note: SYS: Systematic; DIS: Discretionary.

EXHIBIT 23:   Performance and Main Features of Multi-Strategy Funds of Funds.

Fund name	Fund ID	Total Months	Neg months	Inception date	Last report date	AUM	Av. Return	S	IR	DSSR	DISR
Ts Multi-Strategy Fund Ltd Usd	3928	117	12	Jan 1999	Sep 2008	2,600,000	1.016	3.293	3.864	22.575	26.494
Ts Multi-Strategy Fund Ltd Eur	7370	117	12	Jan 1999	Sep 2008	2,600,000	1.016	3.229	3.807	21.703	25.589
Ts Multi-Strategy Fund Lp	9672	117	11	Jan 1999	Sep 2008		1.016	3.069	3.606	18.902	22.209
Tif Offshore Fund (Master Shares)	4745	123	34	Mar 1994	May 2004	1,110,000	1.017	2.014	2.44	13.836	16.761
Fairfax Fund Ltd Class A (Usd)	4148	110	22	Jan 1999	Feb 2008	23,200,000	1.015	1.555	1.867	6.969	8.364
Triad Trading Fund, Lp	6130	184	62	Nov 1994	Feb 2010		1.016	0.807	0.967	3.268	3.913

EXHIBIT 24: Performance and Main Features of Hedge Funds

Fund name	Fund ID	Duration	Neg months	Inception date	Last report date	AUM	Av. Return	S	IR	DSSR	DISR	Strat.
Ajw Offshore Ii, Class A	14103	108	3	Feb 2001	Jan 2010		1.015	3.978	4.5	66.593	75.338	
Ajw Offshore Ii, Class B	14104	108	4	Feb 2001	Jan 2010		1.015	3.942	4.462	64.708	73.243	
Jmg Capital Ptnrs (Hot Income 1/20)	830	140	9	May 1992	Dec 2003		1.016	4.233	5.198	30.325	37.242	CA
Ya Global Investments (U.S.), Lp	717	108	9	Feb 2001	Jan 2010	1,400,000	1.015	2.455	2.774	25.32	28.604	SS
Atlantis Capital Markets Fund	3625	103	9	Jan 1997	Jul 2005	1,500,000	1.025	2.173	2.407	21.743	24.086	RVMS
Finvest Primer Ltd	12180	102	12	Jan 2001	Jun 2009	3,000,000	1.016	2.571	2.909	20.584	23.291	RVMS
Marathon Special Opportunity Fund Lp	2746	112	18	May 1999	Aug 2008		1.016	1.833	2.166	16.312	19.268	DS
Claritas Hedge	13880	126	23	Aug 1999	Jan 2010		1.017	2.634	2.999	16.194	18.436	MS
Marathon Special Opportunity Fund Ltd	7849	112	20	May 1999	Aug 2008		1.016	1.771	2.099	15.162	17.975	DS
Prosperity Quest Fund (Power)	7749	100	30	Jan 2000	Apr 2008	3,990,000	1.049	2.007	2.091	14.816	15.432	SEC
Ultima Partners	1315	105	29	Sep 1994	May 2003	6,241,000	1.016	1.909	2.423	13.366	16.965	ELS
Greenlight Capital, Lp	2556	127	27	May 1996	Nov 2006	1,300,000	1.02	2.178	2.512	13.111	15.122	ELS
Tail Wind Fund	2790	114	26	Oct 1995	Mar 2005		1.021	1.257	1.446	11.54	13.27	ELS

(*Continued*)

EXHIBIT 24: (*Continued*)

Fund name	Fund ID	Duration	Neg months	Inception date	Last report date	AUM	Av. Return	S	IR	DSSR	DISR	Strat.
Manalapan Oracle Eagle Fund L.P.(Domestic Returns)	10924	106	30	May 2001	Feb 2010	1,082,930	1.017	1.687	1.877	10.678	11.879	ELS
Watch Hill Fund	910	108	11	Apr 1994	Mar 2003		1.02	2.044	2.439	9.784	11.674	FI
York Select Unit Trust	3419	120	36	Jan 1996	Dec 2005		1.02	1.007	1.158	9.009	10.363	RVMS
Welch Life Sciences Fund Lp	2227	118	44	May 2000	Feb 2010	2,166,000	1.016	1.003	1.135	8.897	10.076	SEC
Spinnaker Global Emerging Markets	2525	109	16	Dec 2000	Dec 2009	41,000,000	1.018	2.151	2.391	8.736	9.711	EMM
Cobalt Partners	3554	123	24	Jan 1995	Mar 2005	29,500,000	1.017	1.957	2.365	8.731	10.552	ELS
Nevsky Fund Limited Class A (Usd)	97	108	34	Oct 2000	Sep 2009	35,400,000	1.02	1.663	1.834	8.509	9.382	ELS
Chinafund Cayman Ltd.	9567	123	36	Aug 1998	Oct 2008		1.032	1.32	1.419	8.323	8.944	ELS
Turnberry Capital Partners, L.P. (Master Limited Credit)	2827	222	48	May 1989	Oct 2007	34,000,000	1.019	1.6	1.927	8.269	9.958	DS
Parallax Fund, L.P.	3394	170	52	Jan 1996	Feb 2010	8,600,000	1.017	1.329	1.556	8.104	9.489	OA
Moore Global Investment+	1492	121	34	Jul 1990	Jul 2000	210,000,000	1.016	1.404	1.799	8.102	10.379	GM
Teton Capital Partners, L.P.	14295	131	34	Apr 1999	Feb 2010		1.017	1.686	1.923	8.039	9.173	ELS
Tonga Partners	1871	112	34	Jul 1992	Oct 2001	600,000	1.02	1.536	1.854	7.761	9.368	ELS

(*Continued*)

EXHIBIT 24: *(Continued)*

Fund name	Fund ID	Duration	Neg months	Inception date	Last report date	AUM	Av. Return	S	IR	DSSR	DISR	Strat.
Perceptive Life Sciences Fund Lp	1132	128	46	Jul 1999	Feb 2010	2,774,000	1.024	0.903	0.987	7.669	8.378	SEC
Jlh Capital Investment	829	121	38	Jan 1993	Jan 2003	1,400,000	1.016	1.462	1.822	7.613	9.491	ELS
Forum Absolute Return Fund, Ltd.	3000	126	32	Sep 1999	Feb 2010		1.016	1.12	1.28	7.568	8.649	EMM
Spectrum Trading Partners L.P.	1276	112	43	Jan 1985	Apr 1994		1.019	0.732	0.95	7.448	9.666	CA
Rebel Investments	1177	100	30	Jan 1992	Apr 2000		1.028	1.318	1.488	7.392	8.349	EMN
Tonga Partners, Lp	12987	112	32	Jan 1999	Apr 2008		1.017	1.443	1.685	7.333	8.562	ELS
Circle-T Partners, Lp	2182	139	48	Feb 1996	Aug 2007		1.018	1.207	1.433	7.295	8.659	ELS
Maverick Fund	760	105	25	Jan 1993	Sep 2001	21,000,000	1.018	1.397	1.74	7.242	9.026	ELS
Emperor Greater China Fund Ltd	8998	101	27	Feb 2001	Jun 2009	10,000,000	1.028	1.274	1.359	7.239	7.723	ELS
York Select Lp	2638	120	36	Jan 1996	Dec 2005	1,600,000	1.017	1.326	1.58	7.04	8.39	EDMS
Spm Structured Servicing Holdings Fund (Ssh)	12721	145	29	Feb 1998	Feb 2010	4,061,357	1.02	1.596	1.794	6.91	7.771	FI
Orbis Africa Equity (Rand) Fund	9511	132	49	Jul 1998	Jun 2009		1.021	1.356	1.516	6.881	7.692	ELO
Gamut Investments	45	279	86	Jul 1986	Sep 2009		1.016	1.151	1.451	6.671	8.407	GM
Balestra Capital Partners, Lp	562	134	62	Jan 1999	Feb 2010	1,200,000	1.022	0.7	0.774	6.66	7.369	GM
Jlf Offshore Fund Ltd.	10093	106	30	Mar 1999	Dec 2007		1.016	1.298	1.537	6.644	7.869	MS
Steel Partners Ii	2240	136	41	Oct 1993	Jan 2005	3,500,000	1.016	1.249	1.531	6.508	7.979	EDMS

(Continued)

EXHIBIT 24: (*Continued*)

Fund name	Fund ID	Duration	Neg months	Inception date	Last report date	AUM	Av. Return	S	IR	DSSR	DISR	Strat.
Watson Investment Partners	2219	114	38	Oct 1995	Mar 2005	1,000,000	1.018	1.166	1.376	6.491	7.661	ELS
Libra Fund, Lp	2708	239	66	Apr 1990	Feb 2010	5,120,000	1.019	1.22	1.422	6.044	7.046	ELS
Dafna Lifescience Ltd.	3424	134	48	Jan 1999	Feb 2010	300,000	1.018	0.931	1.056	5.86	6.649	SEC
Alpha Max L.P.	2059	153	52	Oct 1982	Jun 1995	2,032,000	1.017	1.138	1.575	5.817	8.054	GM
The Tail Wind Fund Ltd	12906	173	47	Oct 1995	Feb 2010	564,857	1.016	0.962	1.142	5.773	6.853	ELS
Sr Global Fund Inc. Class G (Emerging)	2784	168	62	Mar 1996	Feb 2010	20,000,000	1.018	1.1	1.273	5.773	6.683	EMM
Irvine Capital Partners, Lp	2951	143	41	Apr 1994	Feb 2006	10,000,000	1.015	1.063	1.308	5.764	7.095	ELS
Libra Offshore, Ltd.	2617	145	48	Feb 1998	Feb 2010		1.018	1.195	1.36	5.595	6.369	ELS
Wermuth Greater Europe Fund Ltd.	11998	116	39	Apr 1998	Nov 2007		1.02	1.129	1.293	5.513	6.315	ELS
Prosperity Quest Fund	7752	121	37	Jan 2000	Jan 2010	6,200,000	1.031	1.255	1.336	5.375	5.721	EMM
Puma	1143	132	42	Oct 1986	Sep 1997		1.023	1.169	1.413	5.346	6.466	GM
Needham Emerging Growth Partners	2160	176	64	Jul 1992	Feb 2007	4,000,000	1.015	1.05	1.295	5.27	6.498	ELS

(*Continued*)

EXHIBIT 24: (Continued)

Fund name	Fund ID	Duration	Neg months	Inception date	Last report date	AUM	Av. Return	S	IR	DSSR	DISR	Strat.
Simpson Partners	2686	123	44	Oct 1994	Dec 2004	446,000	1.024	1.001	1.135	5.252	5.954	ELS
Holmes Partners	2654	112	35	Jan 1991	Apr 2000	237,000	1.022	0.926	1.098	5.251	6.224	ELS
Braddock Partners	475	138	44	Oct 1993	Mar 2005	1,351,000	1.017	1.144	1.379	5.248	6.329	ELS
Cima Aconcagua Fund	3116	127	47	Oct 1998	Apr 2009	24,700,000	1.017	0.893	1.036	5.233	6.073	EMM
Belvedere Futures Fund	9967	115	41	Jul 2000	Jan 2010		1.019	0.929	1.033	5.055	5.621	MS
Crestwood Capital Partners	1376	109	39	Jul 1995	Jul 2004	6,543,000	1.016	1.011	1.226	4.927	5.977	ELS
Prism Partners, L.P	2844	131	47	Apr 1999	Feb 2010	1,500,000	1.018	0.957	1.08	4.829	5.453	ELS
Blenheim Global Markets Strategy	2102	108	46	Jan 1987	Dec 1995		1.02	0.895	1.122	4.793	6.009	GM
Cypress Intl Partners (A)	2267	114	45	Oct 1994	Mar 2004	15,000,000	1.017	0.933	1.141	4.77	5.834	ELS
Keefe-Rainbow Partners	1740	108	25	Jul 1995	Jun 2004	2,155,000	1.017	1.242	1.49	4.726	5.668	SEC
Futurewatch I	3463	178	60	May 1995	Feb 2010	1,933	1.023	1.008	1.128	4.662	5.218	EMM
Sterling Equity Partners Lp	120	103	40	Jan 1998	Jul 2006	101,000	1.017	0.835	0.981	4.547	5.339	ELS

(Continued)

EXHIBIT 24:   (*Continued*)

Fund name	Fund ID	Duration	Neg months	Inception date	Last report date	AUM	Av. Return	S	IR	DSSR	DISR	Strat.
China Convergence Fund	10462	116	35	Jul 2000	Feb 2010		1.021	0.89	0.977	4.546	4.987	MS
Lacm Macro Discretionary Share Class F	8659	121	46	Feb 2000	Feb 2010	4,800,000	1.017	0.811	0.918	4.387	4.965	GM
Jro Associates	833	173	35	Aug 1982	Dec 1996	1,000,000	1.016	1.104	1.553	4.371	6.148	ELS
Maverick Fund Usa	761	138	37	Apr 1990	Sep 2001	30,000,000	1.019	0.939	1.155	4.339	5.338	ELS
Caduceus Capital, L.P.	35	170	70	Jan 1993	Feb 2007	739,000	1.017	0.784	0.945	4.337	5.222	SEC
Mindful Partners	530	105	41	May 1993	Jan 2002	1,005,000	1.017	0.846	1.065	4.314	5.433	ELS
Consulta Emerging Markets Debt Fund	2821	140	33	Jan 1995	Aug 2006	18,300,000	1.018	1.267	1.514	4.286	5.12	EMM
Crestwood Capital Intl	1375	105	38	Nov 1995	Jul 2004		1.015	0.919	1.128	4.282	5.257	SEC
Gam Japan Inc.	1063	142	57	Aug 1985	May 1997		1.017	0.876	1.167	4.279	5.698	ELS
Frontier Performance Partnership	3509	114	44	Oct 1994	Mar 2004	2,000,000	1.018	0.941	1.133	4.224	5.086	ELS
Polaris Prime Technology, Lp	3269	156	53	Oct 1996	Sep 2009	6,345,000	1.015	0.881	1.053	4.158	4.971	SEC
Apodaca Investment Partners	2346	105	34	Jan 1992	Sep 2000	5,200,000	1.03	0.808	0.904	4.07	4.556	SEC
Ashmore Emerging Markets Liquid Investment Portfolio	2874	156	43	Nov 1992	Oct 2005	17,832,000	1.016	1.104	1.348	3.996	4.877	EMM

(*Continued*)

EXHIBIT 24: (*Continued*)

Fund name	Fund ID	Duration	Neg months	Inception date	Last report date	AUM	Av. Return	S	IR	DSSR	DISR	Strat.
Global Undervalued Securities Fund	3145	153	53	Feb 1996	Oct 2008	800,000	1.02	0.837	0.964	3.992	4.599	GM
Tradewinds Russia Value Fund, Llc	2454	101	36	Mar 2000	Jul 2008	678,000	1.022	0.958	1.068	3.906	4.353	EMM
Kingdon Offshore (A)	1748	187	53	Mar 1986	Sep 2001	964,000	1.015	1.002	1.373	3.778	5.176	ELS
Rosseau Limited Partnership	11111	134	47	Jan 1999	Feb 2010		1.018	0.829	0.937	3.678	4.16	EDMS
Prosperity Cub Fund	7748	142	52	May 1998	Feb 2010	11,260,000	1.025	0.796	0.87	3.623	3.96	EMM
Quaker Capital Partners I, Lp	133	144	57	Jan 1996	Dec 2007	10,703,000	1.017	0.625	0.747	3.604	4.307	ELS
Mercury International Fund Equities	10582	100	36	Nov 2001	Feb 2010		1.021	0.853	0.926	3.558	3.86	EMM
Media Group Investors	2233	114	47	Oct 1995	Mar 2005	1,000,000	1.015	0.683	0.836	3.556	4.352	ELS
Jaguar Fund Nv+	801	156	52	Jan 1986	Dec 1998	37,000,000	1.017	0.885	1.157	3.544	4.634	GM
Sf Investments (Aggressive)	952	151	44	Jan 1985	Jul 1997	128,000	1.021	0.799	1.003	3.503	4.397	ELS
Appaloosa Investment I	2347	115	32	Jul 1993	Jan 2003	40,239,000	1.02	0.978	1.165	3.453	4.11	DS
Dickstein & Co. L.P.	3484	241	49	Mar 1986	Mar 2006	3,000,000	1.017	0.934	1.175	3.444	4.33	EDMS
Potomac Capital Partners	2523	119	41	Feb 1998	Dec 2007	3,440,000	1.017	0.816	0.963	3.442	4.062	ELS
Value Partners Classic Fund "A"	10460	122	36	Jan 2000	Feb 2010		1.017	0.909	1.028	3.417	3.863	ELS

(*Continued*)

EXHIBIT 24: (Continued)

Fund name	Fund ID	Duration	Neg months	Inception date	Last report date	AUM	Av. Return	S	IR	DSSR	DISR	Strat.
Horizon Growth Fund Nv	2694	122	46	Jan 2000	Feb 2010	3,000,000	1.018	0.716	0.806	3.379	3.802	ELO
Gwi Classic Fia	12003	124	41	Jan 1999	Apr 2009		1.026	0.818	0.895	3.311	3.622	ELO
Polaris Prime Europe Lp	8887	155	65	Feb 1997	Dec 2009		1.019	0.532	0.61	3.299	3.781	ELS
Tradewinds Fund, Lp	2602	185	68	Oct 1994	Feb 2010	1,072,000	1.019	0.78	0.904	3.253	3.77	EMM
Caduceus Capital, Ltd.	3250	120	51	Mar 1997	Feb 2007	6,492,000	1.015	0.601	0.732	3.248	3.956	SEC
Key Colony Fund	3141	114	45	Dec 1998	May 2008	6,172,000	1.017	0.715	0.834	3.191	3.722	EDMS
Passport I, Lp — Global	12378	115	46	Aug 2000	Feb 2010	800,000	1.018	0.706	0.787	3.139	3.497	ELS
Tiger+	800	186	64	Jan 1986	Jun 2001		1.016	0.739	0.991	3.091	4.146	GM
Aggressive Appreciation 100 Strategy	470	171	66	Jan 1991	Mar 2005		1.02	0.616	0.719	3.047	3.556	SEC
Emerging Value Opportunities Fund — Class A Series 1–5	3547	151	61	Dec 1993	Jun 2006	750,000	1.02	0.668	0.78	3.04	3.553	EMM
Quantum Emerging Growth Fund	607	101	34	Feb 1992	Jun 2000	437,000,000	1.016	0.711	0.909	2.962	3.786	EMM
Cambrian Fund Ltd Class A	3175	209	73	Oct 1992	Feb 2010	250,000,000	1.015	0.697	0.844	2.851	3.453	ELO
Quota Fund Nv (A)	608	105	42	Jan 1992	Sep 2000		1.021	0.618	0.734	2.8	3.325	GM
Mcgarr Partners	767	180	61	Feb 1984	Jan 1999		1.02	0.515	0.654	2.742	3.484	ELS
Gulfstream Partners	1258	103	41	Jan 1992	Jul 2000		1.017	0.63	0.791	2.69	3.375	ELS

(Continued)

EXHIBIT 24: (Continued)

Fund name	Fund ID	Duration	Neg months	Inception date	Last report date	AUM	Av. Return	S	IR	DSSR	DISR	Strat.
Eastern European Fund (Usd)	3078	108	41	Oct 2000	Sep 2009	10,600,000	1.018	0.685	0.765	2.68	2.993	EMM
Fbr Ashton, Lp	3436	161	58	Mar 1992	Jul 2005	2,400,000	1.017	0.688	0.827	2.672	3.211	SEC
Quantum Endowment Fund Nv	2400	225	71	Mar 1985	Nov 2003		1.016	0.696	0.904	2.615	3.399	GM
Trophy Fund	11602	102	43	Sep 2001	Feb 2010	2,840,980	1.021	0.505	0.546	2.49	2.693	ELS
Polaris Prime Europe Limited (Usd)	2615	157	67	Feb 1997	Feb 2010	615,000	1.015	0.408	0.485	2.37	2.815	ELS
Challenger	3462	152	58	Jul 1997	Feb 2010	158,458	1.016	0.555	0.649	2.326	2.722	EMM
Russian Prosperity Fund Eur	13485	120	43	Mar 2000	Feb 2010		1.017	0.588	0.663	2.234	2.519	EMM
Access Turkey Ltd	9804	109	40	Apr 1999	Apr 2008		1.02	0.488	0.554	2.227	2.53	EMM
J.W. Partners, L.P.	7975	131	54	Feb 1999	Dec 2009	260,000	1.017	0.388	0.446	2.04	2.346	ELS
Senvest Partners	2666	155	64	Apr 1997	Feb 2010	5,840,000	1.016	0.451	0.528	1.927	2.256	ELS
Hermitage Fund (Lowest Bid)	2765	132	48	Apr 1996	Mar 2007	2,036,000	1.02	0.485	0.56	1.904	2.198	EMM
Firebird Fund Lp	3316	190	75	May 1994	Feb 2010	2,600,000	1.019	0.452	0.524	1.892	2.191	EMM
Russian Opportunities Fund Ltd	3497	158	70	Jan 1997	Feb 2010		1.017	0.412	0.478	1.864	2.162	EMM
Firebird New Russia Fund, Ltd.	3317	164	57	Jul 1996	Feb 2010	1,150,000	1.018	0.477	0.551	1.852	2.14	EMM

(Continued)

EXHIBIT 24: (*Continued*)

Fund name	Fund ID	Duration	Neg months	Inception date	Last report date	AUM	Av. Return	S	IR	DSSR	DISR	Strat.
Russian Prosperity Fund J	7744	115	42	Apr 2000	Feb 2010		1.016	0.493	0.56	1.837	2.084	EMM
Ashmore Russian Debt Portfolio	2876	108	25	Nov 1996	Oct 2005	79,681,000	1.017	0.446	0.529	1.636	1.938	EMM
Opportunity Fund Brazilian Equities	2440	147	58	Jan 1993	Mar 2005	48,000	1.016	0.414	0.506	1.61	1.969	EMM
Russian Prosperity Fund A	2025	162	63	Sep 1996	Feb 2010	21,884,000	1.018	0.419	0.485	1.61	1.861	EMM
Access Turkey Opportunities Fund, Llc	363	131	50	Apr 1999	Feb 2010	12,900,000	1.016	0.368	0.424	1.529	1.762	EMM
Russian Prosperity Fund B	7745	162	65	Sep 1996	Feb 2010		1.016	0.389	0.46	1.434	1.694	EMM
Tradewinds Russia Partners I, Lp	2453	138	60	Feb 1997	Jul 2008	7,748,000	1.017	0.334	0.394	1.355	1.599	EMM
Prospect Fund Lp	2021	156	62	Jan 1995	Dec 2007	643,000	1.016	0.339	0.414	1.327	1.624	ELO
Gam Money Markets Fund(Sfr)	1893	120	0	Jan 1987	Dec 1996		1.023	0.091	0.11	0	0	ELS
Gam Money Markets Fund (Bp)	1066	120	0	Jan 1987	Dec 1996		1.027	0.112	0.131	0	0	ELS

Note: SS: Single Strategy; MS: Multi Strategy; ELS: Equity Long/Short; SEC: Sector; ELO: Equity Long Only; EMM: Emerging Markets; GM: Global Macro; RVMS: Relative Value Multi Strategy; EDMS: Event Driven MS; DS: Distressed Securities; OA: Option Arbitrage; CA: Convertible Arbitrage; EMN: Equity Market Neutral.

Final Remarks

The new data since 2005 reaffirm and support the previous conclusion that the DSSR measure is useful to measure more accurately superior investors than the ordinary Sharpe measure which assumes normal not skewed return distributions. The DSSR measure becomes extremely high when there are very few losses and high mean returns which is a good measure of superior performance.

References

Conroy, T. (2011). Investment return of 21.9% brings Yale endowment value to $19.4 billion. *Yale News*, September 28.

Greenberg, M. (2010). Oklahoma court orders $26 million in penalties against Prestigue Ventures Corporation, Federated Management Group, Inc, Kenneth W. Lee and Simon Yangin in forex Ponzi scheme. Integral, December 10.

Insider Monkey (2010). Seeking Alpha: Best Hedge Funds Jim Simons Medallion Fund. December 31.

Lintner, J. (1983). The potential role of managed financial futures accounts (and/or funds) in portfolios of stocks and bonds. Presented at the Annual Conference of the Financial Analysts, Federation Toronto, May 16.

MacLean, L. C., E. O. Thorp, Y. Zhao, and W. T. Ziemba (2011). How does the Fortune's Formula-Kelly capital growth model perform? *Journal of Portfolio Management* (Summer).

MacLean, L. C., E. O. Thorp, and W. T. Ziemba (2010). The good and bad properties of the Kelly and fractional Kelly capital growth criterion. *Quantitative Finance* (August–September), 681–687.

Siegel, L. B., K. F. Kroner, and S. W. Clifford (2001). Greatest return stories ever told. *Journal of Investing* 10(2), 91–102.

Thorp, E. O. (2009). My encounters with the Madoff's scheme and other swindles. *Wilmott* (44, November), 60–64.

YER (2006–2010). Yale endowment reports.

Ziemba, R. E. S. and W. T. Ziemba (2007). *Scenarios for Risk Management and Global Investment Strategies.* New York, NY: Wiley.

Ziemba, W. T. (2003). *The Stochastic Programming Approach to Asset Liability and Wealth Management.* Charlottesville, VA: AIMR.

Ziemba, W. T. (2005). The symmetric downside risk sharpe ratio and the evaluation of great investors and speculators. *Journal of Portfolio Management*, Fall, 108–122.

Ziemba, W. T. and S. L. Schwartz (1991). *Invest Japan.* Chicago, IL: Probus.

Chapter 10

Is the 60-40 Stock-Bond Pension Fund Rule Wise?

William T. Ziemba

Alumni Professor of Financial Modeling and Stochastic Optimization (Emeritus),
University of British Columbia, Vancouver, BC,
ICMA Centre, University of Reading, UK

Pension funds typically suggest the 60-40 stock-bond rule to lower risk as during stock market declines bonds tend to rise. However, US investment returns have been presidential party dependent; and returns in the last two years of all administrations exceed those in the first two years. The strategies small cap stocks with Democrats and intermediate bonds or large cap stocks with Republicans yields final wealth about six times the large cap index, 50% more than small caps and more than twenty times the 60-40 mix since 1942.

This paper studies election cycles, the effect of presidential party affiliations in the White House and the wisdom of the 60-40 stock-bond and other long term investment rules from 1937 and 1942. I begin with the early literature.

Herbst and Slinkman [1984], using data from 1926–1977, found a 48-month political/economic cycle during which returns were higher than average; this cycle peaked in November of presidential election years. Riley and Luksetich [1980] and Hobbs and Riley [1984] showed that, from 1900–1980, positive short-term effects followed Republican victories and negative returns followed Democratic wins. Huang [1985], using data from 1832–1979 and for various subperiods, found higher stock returns in the last two years of political terms than in the first two. This finding is consistent

with the hypothesis that political reelection campaigns create policies that
stimulate the economy and are positive for stock returns. These studies
concerned large cap stocks.

Stovall [1992] and Hensel and Ziemba [1995, 2000] documented the
Presidential Election Cycle effect, which exhibited that stock markets
generally had low returns during the first two years after an US Presidential
election and high returns during the last two years. Other subsequent
studies have documented the economically and statistically significant
difference in equity returns during the first and second half of Presidential
terms for Republican and Democratic administrations. Some studies use
more detailed models. Wong and McAleer [2008] examine the cyclical effect
that Presidential elections have on equity markets using a spectral analysis
technique and an exponential GARCH Intervention model to correct for
time-dependence and heteroskedasticity. They consider the period from
January 1965 to December 2003 using weekly data with dummy variables
to designate the year of the term and the President's party.

Wong and McAleer find a cyclical trend that mirrors the four-year
election cycle with a modified cycle of between 40–53 months. They find
that stock prices generally fall until a low-point during the second-year
of a Presidency and then rise during the remainder, peaking in the third
or fourth year. During the current Obama Democratic administration,
the low was in March 2009 in his first year and the market has doubled
since then to the end of March 2011. Wong and McAleer also find this
Presidential Election Cycle effect to be notably more significant under
Republican administrations, leading them to posit that the Republican
Party may engage in policy manipulation in order to benefit during
elections relatively more than their Democratic counterparts. For instance,
the second-year and third-year effect estimates are not significant for
Democratic administrations.

Election Cycles

Wong and McAleer explain the Presidential Election Cycle as follows.
During the first year of a Presidency, voters are on average optimistic, and
Presidents are likely to put their most divergent and expensive new policies
in place, because they have the mandate of the voters and re-election time
is furthest away. These early measures are relatively disadvantageous to
business profits and stock prices because they usually involve higher taxes
and spending and possibly new regulations. Then, during the second year of

a term, Presidents begin to alter their policies to ones that are less drastic and more voter-friendly.

The Presidential Election Cycle effect persists when looked at by President and by party. For instance, the only two Presidents who did not exhibit the cycle effect were Ronald Reagan and Bill Clinton during their second terms, during which they would not have re-election incentives like first-term Presidents. Empirical results also find that Republicans who were subsequently re-elected had a positive effect during the second-year of their term instead of the negative effect expected by the Presidential Election Cycle hypothesis. This suggests these Republicans may have used government policies to their favor to win re-election and should be useful for incumbent Presidents to consider in their electoral strategy. This last conclusion, however, does not follow from the conflicting observation that bull markets have tended to coincide with sub-periods under Democratic administrations. Wong and McAleer conclude that this anomaly was present during most of the last forty years and is likely still present in the market.

Hensel and Ziemba [1995, 2000] investigated several questions concerning U.S. stock, bond and cash returns from 1928 to 1997. They asked: Do small and large capitalization stock returns differ between Democratic and Republican administrations? Do corporate bond, intermediate and long-term government bonds and Treasury bill returns differ between the two administrations? Do the returns of various assets in the second half of each four-year administration differ from those in the first half? Were Clinton's administrations analogous to past Democratic administrations? I also discuss here the terms of George W. Bush and Barack Obama to update to the end of 2010.

Their results indicate a significant small cap effect during Democratic presidencies. Small cap stocks (the bottom 20% by capitalization) had higher returns during Democratic than Republican administrations. There has also been a small cap minus large cap S&P advantage outside the month of January for the Democrats. The higher returns with Democrats for small cap stocks are the result of gains rather than losses in the April-December period. The turn-of-the-year small firm effect, in which small cap stock returns significantly exceed those for large cap stocks in January, under both Republican and Democratic administrations, occurred during these 70 years. This advantage was slightly higher for Democrats, but the difference is not significant. Large cap stocks had statistically identical returns under both administrations. For both Democratic and Republican administrations, small and large cap stock returns were significantly higher

216   *William T. Ziemba*

EXHIBIT 1:   Annual Average Equity Returns Minus Annualized Monthly Averages for Presidential Election Months and the Subsequent 13 Months, 1928–1997,
1998–2010 and 1928–2010*.

	1928–1997		1998–2010		1928–2010	
Return Period	Large	Small	Large	Small	Large	Small
Election + Next 13 Months	8.12	6.51	4.08	12.20	7.54	7.33
Annual Average	10.12	12.02	5.19	8.22	9.34	11.42
Annual Difference	−2.00	−5.51	−1.11	4.00	−1.79	−4.09

*Monthly means were annualized by multiplying by 12.
Source: Updated from Hensel and Ziemba [2000].

during the last two years of the presidential term than during the first two
years. Moreover, bond and cash returns were significantly higher during
Republican compared with Democratic administrations. The results also
confirm and extend previous findings that equity returns have been higher
in the second half compared with the first half of presidential terms.
This finding is documented for small and large cap stocks during both
Democratic and Republican administrations. Finally, two simple investment
strategies based on these findings yielded superior portfolio performance
compared with common alternatives during the sample period. The results
cast doubt on the long run wisdom of the common 60/40 stock-bond
strategy since all 100% equity strategies investigated had much higher
wealth at the end of the sample period. Indeed the 1942–1997 returns were
twenty-four times higher with the strategy small caps with Democrats and
large caps with Republicans than the 60/40 mix and the updated 1998–
2010 returns shown in Exhibit 9 show similar outperformance in an update
to the end of 2010.

Exhibit 1 shows that both small and large cap stocks had lower mean
returns in the 13 months following an election. Exhibit 7 shows the specific
months following the election for large (S&P500) and small cap (bottom
20%) stocks.

The 1928–97 period encompassed 18 presidential elections with an
update to 2010 with three more elections. The end of 1997 included the
first year of Clinton's second term. There were 33 years of Republican and
37 years of Democratic administrations during this period. The update to
the end of 2010 covers the last three years of Clinton's second term plus two
George W Bush terms plus the first two years of Barack Obama's administration, namely 1998 to 2010, a period where small cap stocks outperformed
large cap stocks. Exhibit 2 and 3 list and compare the first year, first two

EXHIBIT 2:   Average Annual Returns for the First and Second Years and the Four Years of Democratic and Republican Presidencies* to 1997.

	January 1937 to December 1997		January 1929 to December 1997	
	S&P 500 TR	U.S. Small Stk TR	S&P 500 TR	U.S. Small Stk TR
Democrat				
Avg 1st Yr	6.58	11.32	10.24	19.06
Avg 1st 2Yrs	6.14	11.85	8.09	15.90
Avg Last 2Yrs	16.13	24.11	17.40	24.65
Avg. Term	10.81	16.71	12.62	20.15
Std.Dev. Term	16.35	27.76	18.26	30.69
# Years	36.00	36.00	37.00	37.00
Republican				
Avg 1st Yr	1.87	−6.22	0.54	−14.45
Avg 1st 2Yrs	6.98	1.39	3.77	−6.29
Avg Last 2Yrs	15.03	16.95	9.06	10.18
Avg. Term	11.00	9.17	6.42	1.94
Std.Dev. Term	15.12	19.89	21.17	27.81
# Years	28.0	28.0	32.0	32.0
Diff 1st Yr	4.72	17.54	9.71	33.51
Diff 1st 2Yrs	−0.84	10.46	4.32	22.19
Diff Last 2Yrs	1.10	7.16	8.33	14.47
Diff Term	−0.19	7.55	6.20	18.21
1st year t-values (Ho:Diff = 0)	0.67	1.39	1.15	**2.58**
First 2-years t-values (Ho:Diff = 0)	−0.14	1.13	0.69	**2.39**
Last 2-years t-values (Ho:Diff = 0)	0.20	0.69	1.20	1.41
Term t-values (Ho:Diff = 0)	−0.05	1.04	1.29	**2.57**

*In this and subsequent tables, statistically significant differences at the 5% level (2-tail) are shown in bold.
Source: Hensel and Ziemba [2000].

year, last two year and whole term mean returns under Democratic and Republican administrations from January 1929 to December 1997 and for January 1937 to December 1997, a period that excludes one term for each party during the 1929 crash, subsequent depression and recovery period plus the update to 2010. Each term is considered separately, so two-term presidents have double entries. The t-values shown in Exhibit 2 test the

218   *William T. Ziemba*

EXHIBIT 3:   Average Annual Returns for the First Year and Four Years of Democratic
and Republican Presidencies* to 1997; Update to 2010.

	Jan 1937–Dec 2010		Jan 1929–Dec 2010		Jan 1998–Dec 2010	
	S&P500	Small Cap	S&P500	Small Cap	S&P500	Small Cap
Democrat						
Avg 1st yr	8.79	13.08	11.86	19.87	26.46	27.19
Avg 1st 2 yrs	8.74	12.65	10.19	16.07	23.49	17.16
Avg last 2 yrs	14.10	21.11	15.32	21.83	5.97	9.12
Avg Term	11.56	16.35	13.08	17.75	16.48	13.94
Std Dev Term	16.21	26.79	17.95	29.71	15.19	15.46
# years	38	38	42	42	5	5
Republican						
Avg 1st yr	0.68	−4.05	−0.19	−11.18	−3.49	3.52
Avg 1st 2 yrs	4.69	1.35	2.48	−4.92	−3.32	1.23
Avg last 2 yrs	12.14	14.86	7.78	9.70	2.02	7.56
Avg Term	8.41	8.11	5.01	2.43	−0.65	4.39
Std Dev Term	16.96	21.21	21.24	27.28	21.51	24.90
Avg 1st yr	36	36	40	40	8	8
# years	36	36	40	40	8	8

hypothesis that, during the 1928–97 period, returns did not differ between
Democratic and Republican administrations.

From 1929 to 1997, the mean returns for small stocks were statistically
higher during the Democratic presidential terms than during the Republican terms. The data confirm the advantage of small cap over large cap stocks
under Democratic administrations. Small cap stocks returned, on average,
20.15% a year under Democrats compared with 1.94% under Republicans
for the 1929–1997 period. This difference, 18.21%, was highly significant.
The first year return differences for this period were even higher, averaging
33.51%.

The right hand panel of Exhibit 2 presents the return results after
eliminating the 1929 crash, the Depression and the subsequent period of
stock price volatility. Removing these eight years (1929–1936) from the
study eliminates one Democratic and one Republican administration from
the data. The small stock advantage under Democrats was still large
(an average of 7.55% per four-year-term) but was no longer statistically
significant. The large cap (S&P500) returns during Democratic rule were
statistically indistinguishable from the returns under Republican administrations. Exhibit 3 has the update to 2010.

For Democratic and Republican administrations, the mean small and
large cap stock returns were much higher in the last two years compared

with the first two years of presidential terms for both of the time periods presented in Exhibit 2. For example, small cap stocks returned 24.65% during the last two years compared with 15.90% during the first two years for Democrats and 10.18% compared with −6.29% for Republicans from 1929 to 1992. Returns on large cap stocks increased to 17.40 from 8.09% for Democrats and to 9.06% from 3.77% for Republicans for the same period. This result is consistent with the hypothesis that incumbents embark on favorable economic policies in the last two years of their administrations to increase their reelection chances and that the financial markets view these policies favorably.

The advantage of small stocks over large stocks under Democratic administrations was not a manifestation of the January small stock effect. Instead Exhibit 5 and 6 and Exhibit 4 show the relative advantage of small over large cap stocks under Democrats compared with that under Republicans was attributable to having fewer small stock losses, as well as higher mean small stock returns, in the April-December period. Under Democrats, the mean returns were positive in each of these months, except October, and the small minus large differential was positive during 10 of the 12 months; under Republicans, the small minus large differential was negative during 9 of the 12 months.

The small cap advantage also occurred in the months following Democrat Clinton's first election. From November 1992 to December 1993 the small cap index rose 36.9% versus 14.9% for the S&P500. This domination continued until the second election. Small caps returned 1.58% per month versus 1.31% per month for the S&P500 from November 1992 to October 1996. However, large cap S&P500 returns began exceeding small cap returns in 1994 and this continued through 1997. The January 1994 to December 1996 returns were small cap 1.36% per month versus 1.50% per month for the S&P500. From November 1996 to December 1997 small caps returned 1.81% per month and the S&P500 2.44% per month. There was a phenomenal growth in S&P500 index funds and much foreign investment in large cap stocks during this period. While small caps had very large returns, those of the S&P500 were even higher.

How does inflation vary with political regimes? The results for the 1929–97 period, using the Ibbotson inflation index, indicate that inflation was significantly higher under Democrats, but this difference was contained in the 1929–36 period. Excluding this early period, inflation was slightly higher, on average, under Democrats but not statistically different from inflation under Republican. Inflation rates differed across the years of the

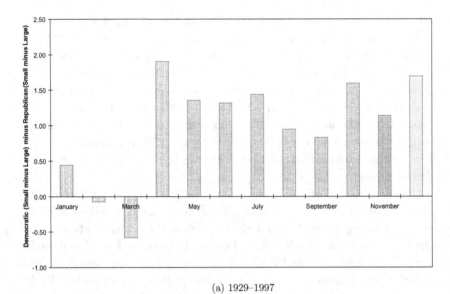

(a) 1929–1997

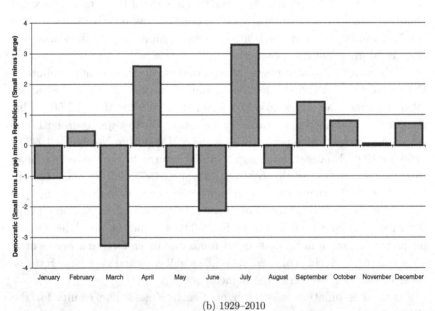

(b) 1929–2010

EXHIBIT 4:   Cap Size Effects and Presidential Party, Democratic (Small minus Large) minus Republican (Small minus Large).

EXHIBIT 5:   Average Monthly Small- and Large-Cap Stock Returns during Democratic and Republican Presidencies, January 1929–December 1997.

	Democratic Administrations			Republican Administrations		
	S&P 500 Total Return	US Small Cap Total Return	Small Cap minus Large Cap	S&P 500 Total Return	US Small Cap Total Return	Small Cap minus Large Cap
January	1.72	6.45	4.72	1.65	5.93	4.28
February	−0.38	0.74	1.11	1.59	2.78	1.19
March	−0.58	−0.91	−0.34	0.96	1.21	0.25
April	2.25	2.58	0.33	−0.24	−1.82	−1.57
May	1.07	1.40	0.33	−0.50	−1.52	−1.02
June	1.57	1.71	0.14	0.78	−0.40	−1.18
July	1.95	2.81	0.86	1.69	1.11	−0.58
August	1.17	1.65	0.47	1.73	1.25	−0.47
September	0.40	0.78	0.38	−2.87	−3.31	−0.45
October	0.42	−0.24	−0.67	−0.40	−2.66	−2.26
November	1.44	1.61	0.17	0.44	−0.53	−0.97
December	1.56	1.58	0.02	1.59	−0.09	−1.68

Source: Hensel and Ziemba [2000].

presidential terms. For example, for the 1937–97 period, in the first year of the presidential term, inflation under the Democrats was significantly lower than it was under the Republicans. An analysis of the first and second two years of administrations during this same period indicated that inflation was higher under Democrats but the difference was not statistically significant.

US Bond Returns after Presidential Elections

The bond data are also from Ibbotson Associates and consist of monthly, continuously compounded total returns for long term corporate bonds, long term (20-year) government bonds, intermediate (5-year) government bonds, and cash (90-day T-bills).

Exhibit 7(a) illustrates average return differences for bonds during election months and the subsequent 13 months (1929–97) minus each months 1928–1997 average return. Exhibit 7(b) updates this to 2010. Corporate, long term government, and intermediate government bond returns were all higher than the monthly average in the year following an election only in May, October, and November in the 1928–1997 period. Both government bonds also exceeded the average in some other months.

EXHIBIT 6: Average Monthly Small- and Large-Cap Stock Returns during Democratic and Republican Presidencies, January 1929–December 2010.

	Democratic			Republican		
	S&P500	Small Cap	Small - S&P	S&P500	Small Cap	Small - S&P
Jan 1929 to Dec 2010						
January	1.24	5.29	4.05	0.73	5.82	5.10
February	−0.46	0.85	1.31	−1.53	−0.68	0.85
March	0.29	−0.42	−0.71	0.18	2.74	2.56
April	2.29	2.86	0.56	3.23	1.21	−2.02
May	0.74	0.89	0.15	1.93	2.78	0.84
June	1.55	1.68	0.13	−2.61	−0.35	2.26
July	1.93	2.53	0.60	−0.63	−3.32	−2.68
August	0.80	0.98	0.18	1.62	2.52	0.90
September	0.62	1.24	0.62	−6.44	−7.23	−0.79
October	0.75	−0.28	−1.03	0.54	−1.30	−1.83
November	1.41	1.60	0.18	2.91	3.05	0.13
December	1.87	2.39	0.52	2.36	2.17	−0.20
Jan 1998 to Dec 2010						
January	−2.33	−3.33	−1.00	−2.97	5.39	8.36
February	−1.08	1.63	2.71	−13.99	−14.51	−0.52
March	6.75	3.23	−3.51	−2.95	8.85	11.80
April	2.62	4.92	2.30	17.12	13.35	−3.77
May	−1.71	−2.87	−1.16	11.66	19.96	8.30
June	1.42	1.43	0.02	−16.15	−0.15	16.00
July	1.78	0.49	−1.29	−9.93	−21.03	−11.10
August	−1.93	−4.00	−2.07	1.16	7.58	6.42
September	2.21	4.63	2.41	−20.71	−22.91	−2.20
October	3.21	−0.53	−3.75	4.28	4.16	−0.12
November	1.22	1.51	0.29	12.81	17.35	4.54
December	4.17	8.42	4.25	5.46	11.20	5.74

The update only has three elections and the monthly pattern is different than it was in the past.

As Exhibit 8 indicates, the performance of fixed income investments differed significantly between Democratic and Republican administrations. All fixed income and cash returns were significantly higher during Republican than during Democratic administrations during the two study periods. The high significance of the cash difference stems from the low standard deviation over terms. The performance of fixed income investments differed very little between the first two years and the last two years of presidential terms.

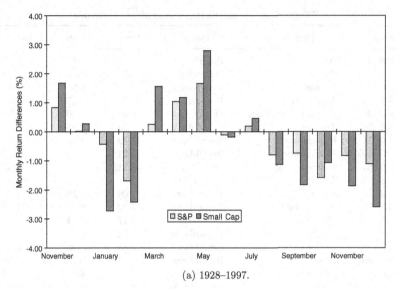

(a) 1928–1997.

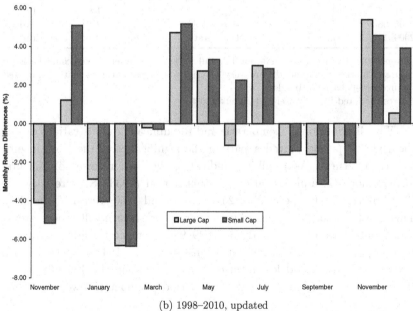

(b) 1998–2010, updated

EXHIBIT 7: Stock Monthly Return Differences: Presidential Election Months and the Subsequent 13 Months Minus Monthly Averages.

Source: Hensel and Ziemba [2000].

224   William T. Ziemba

EXHIBIT 8:   Annualized Average Monthly Return*.

Term	President	Party	Bonds	Cash	Bonds-Cash
1929–32	Hoover	Republican	4.61	2.26	2.35
1932–36	Roosevelt	Democratic	5.05	0.20	4.85
1937–40	Roosevelt	Democratic	3.73	0.08	3.65
1941–44	Roosevelt	Democratic	1.74	0.25	1.49
1945–48	Roosevelt/Truman	Democratic	1.48	0.50	0.98
1949–52	Truman	Democratic	1.24	1.35	−0.11
1953–56	Eisenhower	Republican	1.19	1.66	−0.47
1957–60	Eisenhower	Republican	4.24	2.54	1.70
1961–64	Kennedy/Johnson	Democratic	3.21	2.84	0.37
1965–68	Johnson	Democratic	2.76	4.43	−1.67
1969–72	Nixon	Republican	7.06	5.19	1.87
1973–76	Nixon/Ford	Republican	7.42	6.25	1.17
1977–80	Carter	Democratic	3.17	8.11	−4.94
1981–84	Reagan	Republican	13.71	10.39	3.32
1985–88	Reagan	Republican	10.35	6.22	4.13
1989–92	Bush	Republican	10.77	6.11	4.66
1993–96	Clinton	Democratic	5.74	4.30	1.44
1997–00	Clinton	Democratic	5.77	5.07	0.69
2001–04	Bush	Republican	3.69	1.84	1.85
2005–08	Bush	Republican	4.00	3.40	0.61
2009–10	Obama	Democratic	2.06	0.14	1.92

*From 1998–2010 we used the 3-month T-bill secondary market rate discount basis for cash and market yield and US Treasury securities at 5-year constant maturity, quoted on investment basis for bonds.
Source: updated from Hensel and Ziemba [2000].

The distribution of Democratic and Republican administrations during the 1929–97 period played a part in the significance of the fixed income and cash returns. As Exhibit 8 indicates, the cash returns for the first four Democratic administrations in this period (1933–48) were very low (0.20 percent, 0.08 percent, 0.25 percent and 0.50 percent annually). This result largely explains why the term cash-return differences are so significant (t-value = −12.31 for 1929–97). Democratic administrations were in power for three of the four terms during the 1941–56 period, when government bonds had low returns. Bond returns in the 1961–68 period (both Democratic terms) and 1977–80 period (Democratic) were also low.

Political Effects: When Congress is in Session

Ferguson and Witte [2006] find a strong correlation between Congressional activity and stock market returns such that returns are higher and volatility lower when Congress is in session. They use four data sets, including the

Dow Jones Industrial Average since 1897, the S&P500 index since 1957, and the CRSP value-weighted index and CRSP equal-weighted index since 1962. They compare mean daily stock returns and annualized returns when the U.S. Congress is in and out of session. Depending on the index tested, statistically significant differences in average daily returns range from 4–11 basis points per day. Annualized stock returns are 3.3–6.5% higher when Congress is out of session, and between 65–90% of capital gains have occurred when Congress is not in session (which is notably greater than the proportionate number of days Congress is not in session).

Ferguson and Witte also test these results in several ways. First, they analyze if the Congressional Effect is just a proxy for other known calendar effects, such as the Day-of-the-Week Effect, January Effect, and Pre-Holiday Effect. They conclude that, after controlling for these anomalies, there is still a Congressional Effect of 3–6 basis points per day, which means that no more than half of the Congressional Effect is captured by controlling for other known anomalies. The study also tests for robustness and finds there is a low probability that these results are the effect of a spurious statistical relationship.

Next they test if public opinion toward Congress accounts for the Congressional Effect by using public polling data as a proxy for general investors attitudes toward Congress. They use 162 polls from 1939 to 2004, though 112 of these were conducted after 1989. They find that an active Congress does not itself lead to poor stock returns but rather that the publics opinion of that active Congress accounts for the depressed returns. They also find that each index exhibits volatility that is significantly lower when Congress is not in session and that this is also driven by public opinion.

Then Ferguson and Witte test the implications of this predictive capability on optimal investor asset allocation using the models of Kandel and Stambaugh [1996] and Britten-Jones [1999]; they find that trading on the Congressional Effect would allow investors to better allocate between equities and cash and to achieve a higher Sharpe ratio.

Ferguson and Witte consider three alternatives as possible explanations of the Congressional Effect, concluding that their findings may be explained by viewing public opinion of Congress as a proxy for investors moods, regulatory uncertainty, or rent-seeking. The mood-based hypothesis follows other studies in behavioral finance that suggest depressed investors are relatively risk averse, which in this case would imply that negative public opinion of Congress was depressing investors and dampening returns. The regulatory uncertainty hypothesis follows from the implication that there is more uncertainty in the market when Congress is in session, such that risk and therefore returns are higher. The rent-seeking hypothesis is based on Rajan and Zingales [2003] and suggests that concentrated economic interests limit the efficiency of markets such that they are less efficient and biased toward powerful financial players when Congress is in session.

Some Simple Presidential Investment Strategies

Two presidential party based investment strategies suggest themselves. The first is equity only and invests in small caps with Democrats and large caps with Republicans; the second, a simple alternating stock-bond investment strategy, invests in small cap stocks during Democratic administrations and intermediate government bonds during Republican administrations. The test period was January 1937 through December 1997 with an update from 1998 to 2010.

The common 60/40 (large cap/bonds) portfolio investment strategy and provides a benchmark for comparison with the two strategies. Transaction costs were not included, but they would have a minor effect on the results because the higher return presidential strategies trade at most every four years. These investment strategies all lost money until the early 1940s, see Exhibit 9 which shows the cumulative wealth.

The two presidential investment strategies performed well over the sample period. The strategy of investing in small cap stocks during Democratic administrations and large cap stocks during Republican administrations produced greater cumulative wealth than other investment strategies. The alternating stock-bond strategy of investing in small cap stocks under Democrats and intermediate bonds under Republicans produced the second highest cumulative wealth. Both of these presidential party based strategies

EXHIBIT 9:   Value of $1 Initial Investment in 1997 and 2010.

Date	Large Cap (S&P)	Small Cap	Presidential (SC/Int)	Presidential (SC/LC)	60/40 Benchmark
Jan 1937–Dec 1997	346.1	453.2	527.9	963.2	140.5
Jan 1942–Dec 1997	639.0	2044.1	2380.9	4343.8	180.9
Jan 1937–Dec 2010	565.2	959.5	1310.6	1407.9	242.4
Jan 1942– Dec 2010	1043.5	4327.6	5910.8	6349.5	312.1

Source: Updated from Hensel and Ziemba [2000].

had higher standard deviations than large cap stocks alone during the 1937–97 period. Clinton's first administration had returns for small and large cap stocks, bonds, and cash consistent with the past. However, in the first fourteen months of his second administration large cap stocks produced higher returns than small cap stocks.

In the update in Exhibit 9 we see that, for the 1942–2010 period, small cap stocks (Russell2000 from 1998) produced about four times the gains of large cap S&P500 stocks (4327.6 versus 1043.5). But the small cap with Democrats and large cap with Republicans was even higher at 6349.5, a bit above the 5910.8 of small caps with Democrats and intermediate bonds with Republicans. Meanwhile, the 60/40 portfolio was at 312.1 less than $\frac{1}{20}^{th}$ as much!.

Exhibit 10 displays the mean returns and standard deviations for the various subperiods for the various strategies.

Final Remarks

An interesting finding of this study was the much higher small-stock returns during Democratic administrations as compared with Republican administrations. This finding is consistent with the hypothesis that Democrats devise economic policies that favor small companies and consequently, their stock prices. The 33.51 percentage point difference between small stock performance in Democratic and Republican administrations in the first year in office and the 18.21 percent difference for the full four-year term from 1929 to 2010 are very large. Also the update from 1998 to 2010 has similar results.

This political party effect is different from the well-known January small firm effect which has been present for Republicans as well as Democrats. There is also a substantial small stock/large stock differential outside of January during Democratic rule (see Exhibit 6). Large stock returns were statistically indistinguishable between Democrats and Republicans, but bond and cash returns were significantly higher during Republican than during Democratic administrations. This also confirms and updates Huang's finding that large cap stocks have had higher returns in the last two years of presidential terms; this finding applies regardless of political party and for both small and large cap stocks.

A study of the differences in economic policies that lead to the divergence of investment results according to which political party is in office would be interesting. Clearly, candidates seeking reelection are likely

EXHIBIT 10:   Average Returns and Standard Deviations for Different Investment Strategies for Different Investment Horizons.

| | | Large Cap | | Small Cap | | Strategies | | | | | |
| | | | | | | Pres (SC/Int) | | Pres (SC/LC) | | 60–40 | |
Dates	# years	Mean	StDev	Mean	StDev	Mean	StDev	Mean	StDev	Mean	StDev
Jan 1937–Dec 1997	61	10.9	15.8	13.3	24.5	12.6	20.7	14.1	22.8	8.6	10
Jan 1938–Dec 1997	60	11.8	15.5	14.9	23.7	14.3	19.8	15.8	22	9.2	9.8
Jan 1948–Dec 1997	50	12.3	14	13.9	19.2	13.1	12.7	14.9	16.5	9.7	9
Jan 1958–Dec 1997	40	11.6	14.2	14.7	20.2	14.6	13	15.6	17	9.7	9.3
Jan 1968–Dec 1997	30	11.4	15.1	12.7	21.5	14.3	12.4	14.3	17.5	10.1	9.9
Jan 1978–Dec 1997	20	15.4	14.7	16.3	19.5	15.9	13.8	17.2	17.9	12.9	9.9
Jan 1988–Dec 1997	10	16.6	11.9	15.2	14.9	13.7	9.9	16.2	13.2	13.2	8.2
Jan 1993–Dec 1997	5	18.4	10.6	17.7	13.3	17.7	13.3	17.7	13.3	13.5	7.4
Jan 1995–Dec 1997	3	27.1	11.2	22.1	15.1	22.1	15.1	22.1	15.1	19.7	7.6
Jan 1993–Dec 1993	1	9.5	6.1	19	9.4	19	9.4	19	9.4	10	4.3
Jan 1993–Dec 1994	2	5.4	8.5	11.1	9.8	11.1	9.8	11.1	9.8	4.3	6.5
Jan 1995–Dec 1996	2	26.3	8.4	22.9	14.2	22.9	14.2	22.9	14.2	19.3	5.9
Jan 1997–Dec 1997	1	28.8	15.8	20.5	17.6	20.5	17.6	20.5	17.6	20.5	10.5
Jan 1937–Dec 2010	74	8.9	16	12	23.5	11.9	20.1	12.5	22	7.9	11.7
Jan 1938–Dec 2010	73	9.6	15.7	13.3	22.8	13.2	19.3	13.9	21.2	8.4	11.6
Jan 1948–Dec 2010	63	9.7	14.6	12.3	18.7	12.1	13.7	12.8	16.5	8.7	11.5
Jan 1958–Dec 2010	43	10.7	14.9	15.5	19.5	16.1	14.1	16	16.9	10.4	12
Jan 1968–Dec 2010	33	10.2	15.6	14	20.3	16.3	14	14.9	17.3	11	12.7
Jan 1978–Dec 2010	23	13.2	15.5	17.7	18.5	18.5	15.1	17.7	17.4	13.9	13.4
Jan 1988–Dec 2010	13	12.4	15	17.8	16	18.9	14.5	17.3	15.4	14.9	14.3
Jan 2003–Dec 2010	8	7.7	15.2	12.4	20.5	9.7	13.3	9.3	17.4	5.9	9.1
Jan 2008–Dec 2010	3	-0.3	16.7	6.2	21.9	8.3	15.7	4.9	19.7	4.7	10

Source: Updated from Hensel and Ziemba [2000] to 2010.

to favor economic policies that are particularly attractive to the public; and those policies are consistent with higher stock prices. Cash returns did not differ significantly between the first and second two-year periods of Democratic and Republican presidential terms.

Endnote

Thanks go to the late Chris Hensel for joint work we did at the Frank Russell Company in the 1990s and Constantine S. Dzhabarov for help with the data calculations and recent joint work.

References

Britten-Jones, M. (1999). The sampling error in estimates of mean-variance efficient portfolio weights, *Journal of Finance*, 52(2).

Ferguson, M. F. and H. D. Witte (2006). Congress and the Stock Market, March 13. Available at SSRN: http://ssrn.com/abstract=687211 or http://dx.doi.org/10.2139/ssrn.687211.

Hensel, C. and W. T. Ziemba (1995). US investment returns during Democratic and Republican administrations, 1928–1993, *Financial Analysts Journal*, 51(2), 61–69.

———(2000). How does Clinton stand up to history? US investment returns and presidential party affiliations. In D. B. Keim and W. T. Ziemba, eds., *Security Market Imperfections in World Wide Equity Markets*, pp. 179–202. Cambridge, UK: Cambridge University Press.

Herbst, A. F. and C. W. Slinkman (1984). Political-economic cycles in the US stock market, *Financial Analysts Journal*, 40(2), 38–44.

Hobbs, G. R. and W. B. Riley (1984). Profiting from a presidential election. *Financial Analysts Journal*, 40(2), 46–52.

Huang, R. D. (1985). Common stock returns and presidential elections. *Financial Analysts Journal*, 41(2), 58–65.

Kandel, S. and R. F. Stambaugh (1996). On the predictability of stock returns: An asset allocation perspective. *Journal of Finance*, 51, 385–424.

Rajan, R. and R. L. Zingales (2003). The politics of financial development in the 20th century. *Journal of Financial Economics*, 69(1), 5–50.

Riley, Jr., W. B. and W. A. Luksetich (1980). The market prefers Republicans: myth or reality. *Journal of Financial and Quantitative Analysis*, 15(3), 541–59.

Stovall, R. (1992). Forecasting stock market performance via the presidential cycle. *Financial Analysts Journal*, 48(3), 5–8.

Wong, W. K. and M. McAleer (2008). Financial astrology: Mapping the presidential election cycle in US stock markets. Available at SSRN.

Chapter 11

When to Sell Apple and the NASDAQ? Trading Bubbles with a Stochastic Disorder Model

A. N. Shiryaev

Steklov Mathematical Institute, Moscow, Russia
albertsh@mi.ras.ru

M. V. Zhitlukhin

Steklov Mathematical Institute, Moscow, Russia and
University of Manchester, UK
mikhailzh@mi.ras.ru

W. T. Ziemba

Alumni Professor of Financial Modeling and
Stochastic Optimization (Emeritus),
University of British Columbia, Vancouver, BC, and
Visiting Professor University of Manchester,
and Sabanci University, Turkey, and
Distinguished Visiting Research Associate,
Systemic Risk Centre, London School of Economics
wtzimi@mac.com

In this paper, the authors apply a continuous time stochastic process model developed by Shiryaev and Zhutlukhin for optimal stopping of random price processes that appear to be bubbles. By a bubble we mean the rising price is largely based on the expectation of higher and higher future prices. Futures traders such as George Soros attempt to trade such markets. The idea is to exit near the peak from a starting long position. The model applies equally well on the short side, that is when to enter and exit a short position. In this paper we test the model in two technology markets. These include the price of

Apple computer stock AAPL from various times in 2009–2012 after the local low of March 6, 2009; plus a market where it is known that the generally very successful bubble trader George Soros lost money by shorting the NASDAQ-100 stock index too soon in 2000. The Shiryaev-Zhitlukhin model provides good exit points in both situations that would have been profitable to speculators following the model. who employed the model.

Trading bubbles is difficult and even the best traders like George Soros sometimes lose a lot of money by shorting too soon. The finance and economics literature has little on timing bubbles. There is however some interest by inefficient market types, see for example Stiglitz [1990] and Evanoff et al [2012)]. What we mean by a bubble is a price that is going up just because it is going up! In this paper we present a model developed by Shiryaev and Zhitlukhin [2012ab] that seems to work well timing when to exit a long position or when to exit a short position. To keep the exposition simple, we just apply the model here in two very interesting technology situations namely, Apple Computer stock (AAPL) in the past few years and the internet technology bubble around 2000 measured by the Nasdaq (NDX100) which has futures contracts sold on it. In both cases, the results are good. The mathematics of the model is sketched in the appendix and is an application of modern mathematical finance stochastic calculus. Shirayev has worked on such models for many years and Shiryaev and Zhitlukhin [2012b] present the model in a form that is useful to trade bubbles.

The basic idea is that there is a fast rate of growth in prices, then a peak and then a fast decline. The model tries to exit near the peak in prices or valley of its short position. Usually financial markets fall faster than they rise. But we have found that in these two markets and others that the rate of increase and decrease are very similar and different speeds add no value. The paper shows entries and exits. For readers interested in how the model works, the appendix should be helpful. But it is not important to read the appendix to understand the results of the model which are in tables and graphs in the exhibits.

AAPL Rises and Falls

AAPL had a spectacular run since the bottom of the 2007–2009 crash in March 2009, see Exhibit 1 which shows the price history from September

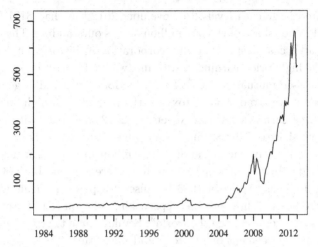

EXHIBIT 1:   The History of AAPL Stock Price from September 1984 to the End of 2012 (Adjusted for Dividends and Splits).

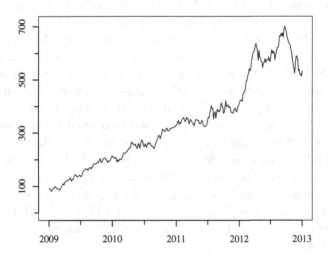

EXHIBIT 2:   AAPL Stock Price from the Beginning of 2009 to the End of 2012.

1984 to the end of 2012; Exhibit 2 shows the more recent period, from the beginning of 2009 to the end of 2012.

A sequence of valuable and easy to use products created huge interest and sales around the world. These include the iPod, the iPhone, and the iPad. All of these products had high margins for the company which accumulated large cash levels. In November 2012 they had $121 billion in cash or $128 per share of the 941 million shares outstanding. The company has generated cash faster than any corporation in history. The stock was never at a high price earnings ratio and was a favorite of hedge funds, open and closed mutual funds, ETFs and various small and large investors. And indeed it was traded as a proxy for the market with high liquidity. Its forward price earnings ratio in November 2012 was 10.17 with estimated earnings per share of $49.28. The company has a quarterly dividend of $2.65 per share and a buy back of about $10 million in stock. An increased or special dividend could also occur as well as increased buy back of stock.

Steve Jobs left Apple in 1985 because of a power struggle with John Sculley who he brought over from Pepsi asking "do you want to sell sugared water all your life or change the world". Sculley came to Apple but he and Jobs had a disagreement on strategy and marketing which stagnated the company. The board favored the marketer over the genius. Jobs sold all but one of his AAPL shares. The company languished while he continued developing ideas at NeXT and Pixar. When Jobs returned to Apple in 1996, he brought the new NeXT platform and ideas for user friendly products that had not yet been imagined by the market. He transformed the company into a winner. He held a lot of AAPL stock but more of Pixar which merged with Disney. After his death on October 5, 2011, many feared that the sequence of great products would cease and that the pace of innovation could not be maintained, that the market cap of about $500 billion, various lawsuits for patent infringement, competition and labour and supply chain issues might slow it down. Some thought it was a bubble and others thought it would continue rallying because it was not expensive not feeding on itself as in a typical bubble. Nonetheless, the stock peaked at 705.07 on September 21, 2012 and then fell dramatically to the local low of 505.75 on November 16, 2012. Later, in pre market trading on December 17, 2012, it fell to 499. On December 31, 2012, AAPL closed the year at 532.17; see Exhibit 3 for the price action in 2012.

The concentration of ownership by mutual funds (see Exhibit 4) creates conundrum for Apple as regulations prohibit ownership to exceed a percentage of a fund's assets, so as AAPL rises relative to other stocks, funds often must sell shares. Some of the selling was tax loss selling in 2012 before expected higher capital gains and dividend rates in 2013 since more gains are in AAPL than in any other stock. Despite the large decline in the latter part of 2012 the stock increased 30% in 2012.

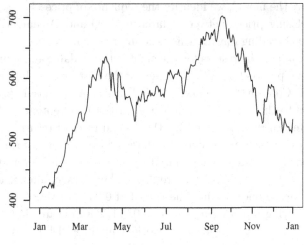

EXHIBIT 3: AAPL Stock Price in 2012.

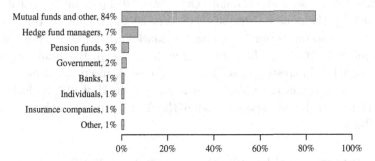

EXHIBIT 4: Holders of Apple, April 17, 2012.
Source: Bloomberg via Eric Jackson.

Application of the Model to the AAPL Bubble

We apply the model to the Apple price bubble starting at the local low of 82.33 on March 6, 2009 and considering eight different entering dates for opening a long position: June 30, 2009; December 31, 2009; June 30, 2010; December 31, 2010; June 30, 2011; December 30, 2011; June 29, 2012; and July 31, 2012. It is assumed that the trend reversal will happen before the end of 2012. Higher tax rates on dividends and capital gains are expected in 2013, thus a sale in 2012 is suggested.

To apply the model, we identify the sequence of prices $P_0, \ldots, P_N$ with the daily closing prices between March 6, 2009 and December 31, 2012. There are 962 trading days in this time interval, so $N = 961$.

Exhibit 5 lists the results for the eight entering dates and four different choices of the parameter μ_2. The names of the first seven columns are self-explanatory. Column "% of max." gives the ratio of the closing price on the exiting date to the highest closing price ($702.10 on September 19, 2012). Column "Return rate, %" contains the annual rates of return, if one buys Apple shares on each of the entering dates and sells on the date suggested by the model. The rate is computed by the compound interest formula $r = \log(S_\tau/S_0) \cdot (\tau/0.252)^{-1}$, where 252 is the average number of trading days in a year, so one year has the length of 0.252 in t-time.

Tests varying $\mu_2 = -\alpha\mu_1$ for $\alpha = 0.5, 1, 2, 3$ indicate that the choice $\mu_2 = -\mu_1$ is the optimal one, and works equally well both for early and late entering dates giving nearly 90% of the maximum price.

Exhibit 6 presents the graph of AAPL prices with entering dates marked by the dots, and the date October 8, 2012 (one of the exit dates) marked by the square. Exhibits 7–8 present the graphs of the exiting process ψ_t and the optimal stopping boundaries $a(t)$ for the entering dates December 30, 2011 and June 29, 2012 with $\mu_2 = -\mu_1$. By comparing with Exhibit 3, it is interesting to see how the process ψ_t reacts on changes in the price process S_t: for example, the increase of ψ_t in May 2012 on Exhibit 7 was caused by the corresponding fall of the AAPL price as can be seen from Exhibit 3.

The Internet Bubble Crash During 2000–2002

Alan Greenspan, the chairman of the US Federal Reserve System (Fed), began in 1994 a low interest rate policy that dropped short term rates continuously over a multiyear period. This led to an increase in the S&P500 stock index from 470.42 in January 1995 to 1469.25 at the end of 1999, as shown in Exhibits 9 and 10. The price earnings ratios were high and Shiller used these to predict the crash starting in 1996, see Campbell and Shiller [1998] and Shiller [1996, 2000, 2009]. It is known that stock price rises usually start with low price earnings ratios and end with high price earnings ratios, see Exhibit 11. But predicting when the market will crash using just price earnings ratios is problematic.

EXHIBIT 5: Results of Applying the Model to AAPL Stock with Various Entry Dates and Values of μ_2.

Entering Date	Entering Price	μ_1	σ	T	Exit Date	Exit Price	% of Max.	Return Rate, %
				$\mu_2 = -\mu_1$				
2009-06-30	142.43	0.666	0.224	8.81	2012-10-11	628.10	89.46	45.11
2009-12-31	210.73	0.452	0.186	7.53	2012-10-11	628.10	89.46	39.26
2010-06-30	251.53	0.344	0.192	6.29	2012-10-09	635.85	90.56	40.64
2010-12-31	322.56	0.305	0.177	5.01	2012-10-08	638.17	90.89	38.55
2011-06-30	335.67	0.249	0.169	3.76	2012-10-08	638.17	90.89	50.44
2011-12-30	405.00	0.234	0.173	2.49	2012-10-08	638.17	90.89	59.07
2012-06-29	584.00	0.245	0.175	1.24	2012-10-09	635.85	90.56	30.62
2012-07-31	610.76	0.245	0.174	1.03	2012-10-11	628.10	89.46	13.83
				$\mu_2 = -0.5\mu_1$				
2009-06-30	142.43	0.666	0.224	8.81	2011-11-18	374.94	53.40	40.38
2009-12-31	210.73	0.452	0.186	7.53	2012-10-08	638.17	90.89	40.00
2010-06-30	251.53	0.344	0.192	6.29	2012-10-09	635.85	90.56	40.64
2010-12-31	322.56	0.305	0.177	5.01	2012-10-09	635.85	90.56	38.26
2011-06-30	335.67	0.249	0.169	3.76	2012-10-11	628.10	89.46	48.73
2011-12-30	405.00	0.234	0.173	2.49	2012-10-11	628.10	89.46	56.13
2012-06-29	584.00	0.245	0.175	1.24	2012-10-19	609.84	86.86	13.99
2012-07-31	610.76	0.245	0.174	1.03	2012-10-19	609.84	86.86	−0.67
				$\mu_2 = -2\mu_1$				
2009-06-30	142.43	0.666	0.224	8.81	2012-10-31	595.32	84.79	42.86
2009-12-31	210.73	0.452	0.186	7.53	2012-10-11	628.10	89.46	39.26
2010-06-30	251.53	0.344	0.192	6.29	2012-10-09	635.85	90.56	40.64
2010-12-31	322.56	0.305	0.177	5.01	2012-10-08	638.17	90.89	38.55
2011-06-30	335.67	0.249	0.169	3.76	2012-05-17	530.12	75.50	51.87
2011-12-30	405.00	0.234	0.173	2.49	2012-05-17	530.12	75.50	71.41
2012-06-29	584.00	0.245	0.175	1.24	2012-10-08	638.17	90.89	32.40
2012-07-31	610.76	0.245	0.174	1.03	2012-10-08	638.17	90.89	23.05
				$\mu_2 = -3\mu_1$				
2009-06-30	142.43	0.666	0.224	8.81	2012-11-07	558.00	79.48	40.67
2009-12-31	210.73	0.452	0.186	7.53	2012-10-19	609.84	86.86	37.88
2010-06-30	251.53	0.344	0.192	6.29	2012-10-11	628.10	89.46	39.97
2010-12-31	322.56	0.305	0.177	5.01	2012-10-09	635.85	90.56	38.26
2011-06-30	335.67	0.249	0.169	3.76	2012-10-08	638.17	90.89	50.44
2011-12-30	405.00	0.234	0.173	2.49	2012-10-08	638.17	90.89	59.07
2012-06-29	584.00	0.245	0.175	1.24	2012-10-08	638.17	90.89	32.40
2012-07-31	610.76	0.245	0.174	1.03	2012-10-08	638.17	90.89	23.05

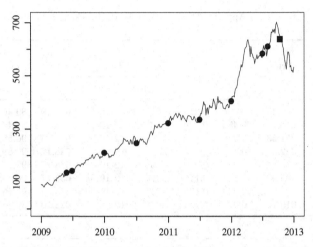

EXHIBIT 6: Buying and Selling Dates for AAPL When $\mu_2 = -\mu_1$. The Dots Indicate the Eight Entering Dates, and the Square Indicates the Exit Date on October 8, 2012.

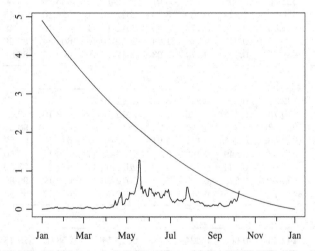

EXHIBIT 7: The Process ψ_t and the Function $a(t)$ for AAPL When Buying Long on December 30, 2011; $\mu_2 = -\mu_1$.

However, Ziemba has found in many markets over many years that the *bond-stock earnings yield differential (BSEYD) model*[1] predicts crashes

---

[1]The BSEYD model relates the yield on stocks, measured by the ratio of earnings to stock prices, to the yield on nominal Treasury bonds. When the bond yield is too high, there is a shift out of stocks into bonds. If the adjustment is large, it causes an equity market correction (a decline of 10% within one year). See e.g. (Ziemba, 2003) for details.

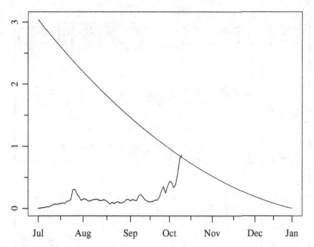

EXHIBIT 8: The Process ψ_t and the Function $a(t)$ for AAPL When Buying Long on June 29, 2012; $\mu_2 = -\mu_1$.

EXHIBIT 9: S&P500 index, 1994–2012.

better than just high price-earnings ratios, see Ziemba and Schwartz [1991], Ziemba [2003] and Lleo and Ziemba [2012]. The model signaled a crash in the S&P500 in April 1999. It was in the danger zone all of 1999 starting in April and it got deeper in the danger zone as the year progressed, see Exhibit 10. The S&P500 rose from 1229.23 at the end of December 1998 to 1469.25 at the end of December 1999. The PE ratio was flat, increasing

EXHIBIT 10:　BSEYD Model for the S&P500, 1995–1999.

Month	S&P500	(a) P/E	(b) 30 yr. Bond	(c = 1/a) Stocks Return	(b − c) Crash Signal	Month	S&P500	(a) P/E	(b) 30 yr. Bond	(c = 1/a) Stocks Return	(b − c) Crash Signal
95 Jan	470.42	17.10	8.02	5.85	2.17	98 Jan	980.28	24.05	6.01	4.16	1.85
Mar	500.71	16.42	7.68	6.09	1.59	Mar	1101.75	27.71	6.11	3.61	2.50
May	533.40	16.39	7.29	6.10	1.19	May	1090.82	27.62	6.10	3.62	2.48
Jul	562.06	17.23	6.90	5.80	1.10	Jul	1120.67	28.46	5.83	3.51	2.32
Sep	584.41	16.88	6.74	5.92	0.82	Sep	1017.01	26.10	5.47	3.83	1.64
Nov	605.37	17.29	6.36	5.78	0.58	Nov	1163.63	31.15	5.54	3.21	2.33
96 Jan	636.02	18.09	6.18	5.53	0.65	99 Jan	1279.64	32.64	5.49	3.06	2.43
Mar	645.50	19.09	6.82	5.24	1.58	Feb	1238.33	32.91	5.66	3.04	2.62
May	669.12	19.62	7.21	5.10	2.11	Mar	1286.37	34.11	5.87	2.93	2.94
Jul	639.96	18.80	7.23	5.32	1.91	Apr	1335.18	35.82	5.82	2.79	3.03
Sep	687.31	19.65	7.26	5.09	2.17	May	1301.84	34.60	6.08	2.89	3.19
Nov	757.02	20.92	6.79	4.78	2.01	Jun	1372.71	35.77	6.36	2.80	3.56
97 Jan	786.16	21.46	6.95	4.66	2.29	Jul	1328.72	35.58	6.34	2.81	3.53
Mar	757.12	20.45	7.11	4.89	2.22	Aug	1320.41	36.00	6.35	2.78	3.57
May	848.28	21.25	7.08	4.71	2.37	Sep	1282.70	30.92	6.50	3.23	3.27
Jul	954.29	23.67	6.78	4.22	2.56	Oct	1362.92	31.61	6.66	3.16	3.50
Sep	947.28	23.29	6.70	4.29	2.41	Nov	1388.91	32.24	6.48	3.10	3.38
Nov	955.40	23.45	6.27	4.26	2.01	Dec	1469.25	33.29	6.69	3.00	3.69

Source: Ziemba [2003].

EXHIBIT 11:   Nine 20-year Periods of Gains Beginning Low PE and Ending High PE.

Begin Year	End Year	Geometric Mean, %	Beg PE	End PE	Begin Year	End Year	Geometric Mean, %	Beg PE	End PE
1975	1994	9.6	10.9	20.5	1981	2000	12.8	8.8	41.7
1977	1996	9.7	11.5	25.9	1979	1998	12.9	9.4	36.0
1942	1961	9.9	12.2	20.5	1982	2001	13.0	8.5	32.1
1983	2002	10.9	7.3	25.9	1980	1999	14.0	8.9	42.1
1978	1997	11.9	10.4	31.0					

Source: Bertocchi, Schwartz and Ziemba [2010].

only from 32.34 to 33.29 while long bond yield rose from 5.47% to 6.69%. The lowest value of S&P500 in April 1999 was 1282.56 on April 1, and the highest value was 1371.56 on April 27. The signal did work but the real decline was not until September 2000 with a temporary fall from the March 24, 2000 high of 1552.87 and a recovery into the September 1, 2000 peak of 1530.09. By October 10, 2002 S&P500 fell to 768.63 having two temporary recoveries from the local lows of 1091.99 on April 4, 2001 and 944.75 on September 21, 2001. There were other signals:

> History shows that a period of shrinking breadth is usually followed by a sharp decline in stock values of the small group of leaders. Then broader market takes a more modest tumble. Paul Bagnell in late November 1999 in the *Globe and Mail*.

Ziemba [2003, Chapter 2] describes this episode in stock market history. There was considerable mean-reversion in the eventual crash in 2000 the September 11, 2001 attack and in the subsequent 2002 decline of 22%. This decline was similar to previous crashes.

The concentration of stock market gains into very few stocks with momentum and size being the key variables predicting performance was increasing before 1997 in Europe and North America. Table 2.6 in Ziemba [2003] shows that in 1998, the largest cap stocks had the highest return in North America and Europe but small cap stocks outperformed in Asia and Japan. The situation was similar from 1995 to 1999 with 1998 and 1999 the most exaggerated.

Fully 41% of the stocks in the S&P500 did not fall or actually rose during this period and an additional 19% declined by 10% or less annualized. These were small cap stocks with market values of $10 billion of less. The fall in the S&P500 was mainly in three areas: information technology, telecommunications and large cap stocks. Information technology stocks in the S&P500 fell 64% and telecom stocks fell 60% from January 1 to October 31, 2002. The largest cap stocks (with market caps of $50 billion plus) lost 37%. But most other stocks either lost only a little or actually gained. Materials fell 10% but consumer discretionary gained 4.5%, consumer staples gained 21%, energy gained 12%, financial services gained 19%, health care gained 29%, industrials gained 7% and utilities gained 2%. Equally weighted, the S&P500 index lost only 3%. So there was a strong small cap effect. The stocks that gained were the very small cap stocks with market caps below $10 billion. Some 138 companies with market caps between $5–10 billion gained 4% on average and 157 companies with market caps below $5 billion gained on average 23%.

While the BSEYD model has been shown to be useful in predicting S&P500 declines, it is silent on the NASDAQ technology index of the largest 100 stocks by market capitalization, the NDX100, see Exhibit 12. This index with a major Internet component had a spectacular increase during a period where many thought the Internet companies would prosper despite price earnings ratios of 100 plus and many with no earnings at all. Valuation attempts were made to justify these high prices; see Schwartz and Moon [2000] for one such example. Predicting the top of this bubble was not easy as the Internet index (not shown) fell 17% one day and then proceeded to reach new highs. For example, the noted investor George Soros lost some $5 billion of the $12 billion in the Quantum hedge fund during this crash.

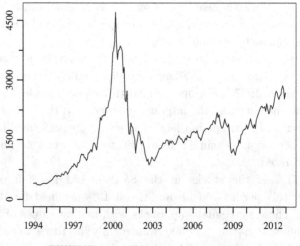

EXHIBIT 12:   NDX100 index, 1994–2012.

EXHIBIT 13:   Results of Applying the Model to a Long Position on NDX-100 Index.

Entering Date	Entering Price	μ_1	σ	T	Exit Date	Exit Price	% of Max.	Growth Rate, %
				$\mu_2 = -\mu_1$				
1994-12-30	404.27	0.014	0.105	15.15	2000-04-12	3633.63	77.23	41.48
1995-12-29	576.23	0.082	0.124	12.63	2000-04-12	3633.63	77.23	42.89
1996-12-31	821.36	0.105	0.130	10.09	2000-04-12	3633.63	77.23	45.26
1997-06-30	957.30	0.109	0.134	8.84	2000-04-12	3633.63	77.23	47.81
1997-12-31	990.83	0.101	0.141	7.56	2000-04-13	3553.81	75.54	55.88
1998-06-30	1337.34	0.117	0.142	6.32	2000-04-12	3633.63	77.23	55.85
1998-12-31	1836.01	0.134	0.156	5.04	2000-04-13	3553.81	75.54	51.37
1999-06-30	2296.77	0.140	0.164	3.80	2000-04-13	3553.81	75.54	55.00
				$\mu_2 = -2\mu_1$				
1996-12-31	821.36	0.105	0.130	10.09	2000-04-11	3909.21	83.09	47.54
1997-06-30	957.30	0.109	0.134	8.84	2000-04-11	3909.21	83.09	50.51
1997-12-31	990.83	0.101	0.141	7.56	2000-04-12	3633.63	77.23	56.95
1998-06-30	1337.34	0.117	0.142	6.32	2000-04-12	3633.63	77.23	55.85
1998-12-31	1836.01	0.134	0.156	5.04	2000-04-12	3633.63	77.23	53.26
1999-06-30	2296.77	0.140	0.164	3.80	2000-04-12	3633.63	77.23	58.09
				$\mu_2 = -3\mu_1$				
1996-12-31	821.36	0.105	0.130	10.09	1998-08-31	1140.34	24.24	19.69
1997-06-30	957.30	0.109	0.134	8.84	1998-08-31	1140.34	24.24	14.95
1997-12-31	990.83	0.101	0.141	7.56	2000-04-10	3998.26	84.98	61.35
1998-06-30	1337.34	0.117	0.142	6.32	2000-04-10	3998.26	84.98	61.47
1998-12-31	1836.01	0.134	0.156	5.04	2000-04-11	3909.21	83.09	59.14
1999-06-30	2296.77	0.140	0.164	3.80	2000-04-11	3909.21	83.09	67.69

The NDX100 peaked at 4816.35 on March 24, 2000 starting from 398.26 in 1994. In the decline it fell to 795.25 on October 8, 2002. Below we apply the Shiryaev and Zhitlukhin model to both the questions when to close a long and a short positions on NDX100 for various entering dates. The results appear in Exhibits 13–16. For a long position we assume that the bubble bursts by the end of 2000, and for a short position we assume that the market recovery starts by the end of 2003.

Depending upon the long position entry, the exit yielded about 75% of the maximum price with investor gains of about 40–60% a year. Again, like with AAPL, the speed of decrease $\mu_2 = -\mu_1$ provides optimal results. The shorting analysis was also successful for the model with the exits gaining about 25–45% a year (for $\mu_2 = -\mu_1$) and getting close to the minimum over the time period considered.

EXHIBIT 14: Entering and Exit Dates for a Long Position on the NDX100 When $\mu_2 = -\mu_1$. The Dots Indicate the Eight Entering Dates, and the Square Indicates the Exit Date on April 12, 2000.

EXHIBIT 15: Results of Applying the Model to a Short Position on NDX-100 Index.

Entering Date	Entering Price	μ_1	σ	T	Exit Date	Exit Price	% of Min.	Growth Rate, %
				$\mu_2 = -\mu_1$				
2001-01-31	2593.00	−0.309	0.412	7.31	2002-11-27	1125.67	139.90	46.01
2001-06-29	1830.19	−0.287	0.395	6.27	2003-01-09	1076.05	133.73	35.13
2002-02-28	1359.22	−0.226	0.345	4.64	2003-03-13	1029.79	127.98	26.80
				$\mu_2 = -0.25\mu_1$				
2001-01-31	2593.00	−0.309	0.412	7.31	2003-03-17	1077.01	133.85	41.78
2001-06-29	1830.19	−0.287	0.395	6.27	2003-04-22	1102.44	137.01	28.32
2002-02-28	1359.22	−0.226	0.345	4.64	2003-06-03	1198.57	148.96	10.00
				$\mu_2 = -0.5\mu_1$				
2001-01-31	2593.00	−0.309	0.412	7.31	2003-01-09	1076.05	133.73	45.70
2001-06-29	1830.19	−0.287	0.395	6.27	2003-03-13	1029.79	127.98	34.18
2002-02-28	1359.22	−0.226	0.345	4.64	2003-04-17	1083.56	134.66	19.97
				$\mu_2 = -2\mu_1$				
2001-01-31	2593.00	−0.309	0.412	7.31	2003-03-17	1077.01	133.85	41.78
2001-06-29	1830.19	−0.287	0.395	6.27	2003-03-17	1077.01	133.85	31.37
2002-02-28	1359.22	−0.226	0.345	4.64	2003-01-14	1094.87	136.07	24.66

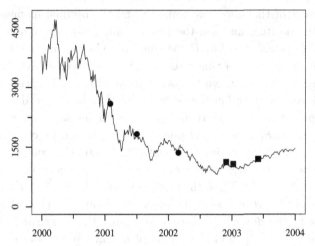

EXHIBIT 16: Entering and Exit Dates for a Short Position on the NDX100 When $\mu_2 = -\mu_1$. The Dots Indicate the Three Entering Dates, and the Squares Indicate the Three Exit Dates.

Appendix

The model of Shiryaev and Zhitlukhin [2012b][2] assumes that the prices are modeled by *geometric Brownian motion with a disorder* $(S_t)_{t\geq 0}$, which is a stochastic process defined by the differential:

$$dS_t = [\mu_1 \mathbb{I}(t < \theta) + \mu_2 \mathbb{I}(t \geq \theta)]S_t dt + \sigma dB_t,$$

where $\mu_1 > 0 > \mu_2$ or $\mu_1 < 0 < \mu_2$, $\sigma > 0$ are constant parameters, $B = (B_t)_{t\geq 0}$ is a standard Brownian motion, and θ is an unknown moment of trend reversal,[3] when the drift coefficient of the process S changes from value μ_1 to value μ_2.

We observe a sequence of asset prices $P_0, P_1, \ldots, P_N$, which initially has a positive trend and at some unknown moment of time the trend reverses. It is assumed that the trend will definitely reverse before the final time, N. Choosing an entering time $n < N$ for opening a long position (i.e. buying

---

[2]The model extends the previous result by Novikov and Shiryaev [2009]. Other papers that consider similar models related to detecting changes in price processes include Beibel and Lerche [1997], Gapeev and Peskir [2006], and Ekström and Lindberg [2013].

[3]The moment θ of trend reversal in the model is commonly called the *moment of disorder*. This terminology comes from the theory of quality control, where similar models were first applied.

some amount of the asset), we want to find the optimal moment of time
to close the position and sell the assets while sequentially observing the
prices $P_n, P_{n+1}, \ldots, P_N$. Let P_k be the *daily* closing values (of AAPL or
NDX100), although other time scales can be considered as well. The model
also applies to the case when the prices have initially a negative trend and
one opens a short position (i.e. sells assets that he or she does not hold
with the objective to return them later after buying for a lower price).

The process S_t runs in continuous time $t \geq 0$, and we choose the time
scale where each trading day has length $\Delta t = 0.01$ (for convenience), and
$t = 0$ represents the entering date n, while $t = T$ represents the final date N,
where $T = (N - n)\Delta t$. Thus, the observed sequence of prices P_k represents
the values of the process S_t at the moments of time $t = (k - n)\Delta t$.

Adopting the *Bayesian approach*, we assume that θ is a random variable
taking values in $[0, T]$ and independent of B. Since in practice it is difficult
to determine the actual structure of the distribution of θ, we consider "the
worst" case — when θ is *uniformly distributed* on $[0, T]$ (as the uniform
distribution has the maximum entropy on a finite interval).

Mathematically, the moment when one closes the position is represented
by a *stopping time*[4] τ of the observable process S. If a long position
is opened on date n, the problem consists in finding the stopping time
$\tau^*_{\text{long}} \leq T$ that maximizes the mean price at τ^*_{long}; if a short position is
open, we seek for the $\tau^*_{\text{short}} \leq T$ which minimizes the mean closing price.
In other words

$$\mathsf{E} S_{\tau^*_{\text{long}}} = \sup_{\tau \leq T} \mathsf{E} S_\tau, \qquad \mathsf{E} S_{\tau^*_{\text{short}}} = \inf_{\tau \leq T} \mathsf{E} S_\tau,$$

where E denotes mathematical expectation, and $\sup_{t \leq T}$, and $\inf_{t \leq T}$ denote
the supremum and the infimum over all stopping times $\tau \leq T$.

The Shiryaev and Zhitlukhin model for finding the optimal τ^* is based
on the observation of the process $\psi = (\psi_t)_{t \geq 0}$, called the *Shiryaev–Roberts
statistic* (see e. g. Poor and Hadjiliadis, 2009), on the time interval $[0, T]$,
specified by

$$\psi_t = \frac{1}{T} \exp(-\mu X_t - \mu^2 t/2) \int_0^t \exp(\mu X_s + \mu^2 s/2) ds,$$

---

[4]A *stopping time* τ of a process X defined on some probability space $(\Omega, \mathcal{F}, \mathsf{P})$ is a
mapping $\tau \colon \Omega \to [0, \infty)$ such that the set $\{\omega : \tau(\omega) \leq t\}$ belongs to the σ-algebra
$\sigma(X_s; s \leq t)$ for any $t \geq 0$, see e. g. (Liptser and Shiryaev, 2000). It represents
the idea that a decision to stop at a time t should be based only on the information obtained
from the paths of the process X up to time t.

where $X_t = \sigma^{-1}(\log(S_t/S_0) - (\mu_1 - \sigma^2/2)t)$, and $\mu = (\mu_1 - \mu_2)/\sigma$. The method closes a position (a long position as well as a short one) at the first time τ^* when the process ψ_t crosses some time-dependent level $a(t)$:

$$\tau^* = \inf\{t \geq 0 : \psi_t \geq a(t)\}.$$

The function $a(t)$ depends on the parameters μ_1, μ_2, σ, T and can be found from a certain integral equation, see (Shiryaev and Zhitlukhin, 2012b) for details. This function is decreasing and $a(T) = 0$, so ψ_t always crosses it by time T.

To apply the method, we must estimate the parameters μ_1, μ_2, and σ. The values of μ_1 and σ are found using the data $P_0, \ldots, P_n$. Under the assumption of geometric Brownian motion, the sequence $\{\xi_k\}_{k=1}^n$, $\xi_k = \log(P_k/P_{k-1})$, consists of independent normal random variables with mean $(\mu_1 - \sigma^2/2)\Delta t$ and standard deviation $\sigma\Delta t$. So we apply the standard formulae

$$\sigma = \sqrt{\frac{1}{(n-1)\Delta t}\sum_{k=1}^n (\xi_k - \overline{\xi})^2}, \quad \mu_1 = \overline{\xi}/\Delta t + \sigma^2/2, \quad \text{where } \overline{\xi} = \frac{1}{n}\sum_{k=1}^n \xi_k.$$

The choice of μ_2 is subjective. In our applications we mainly use $\mu_2 = -\mu_1$, so that, in the model, the decrease of the price has the same "speed" as the increase. We know that prices of financial assets generally fall faster than they rise but in a bubble both the increase and decrease can be similar as the calculations below show. We also consider $\mu_2 = -0.5\mu_1$, $\mu_2 = -2\mu_1$, and $\mu_2 = -3\mu_1$, which however do not give any significant improvement of $\mu_2 = -\mu_1$.

Acknowledgment

The work is partially supported by Laboratory for Structural Methods of Data Analysis in Predictive Modeling, MIPT, RF government grant, ag. 11.G34.31.0073. The work of M. V. Zhitlukhin is also partially supported by The Russian Foundation for Basic Research, grant 12-01-31449-mol_a. The work of Ziemba was partially supported by the University of Manchester and its Hallsworth Lecture series fund.

References

Bagnell, P. (1999). Shrinking breadth in a stock market danger. *Globe and Mail*, November 26.

248   A. N. Shiryaev, M. V. Zhitlukhin and W. T. Ziemba

Beibel, M. and H. R. Lerche (1997). A new look at optimal stopping problems related to mathematical finance. *Statistica Sinica*, pp. 93–108.

Bertocchi, M., S. Schwartz, and W. Ziemba (2015). *Optimizing the Aging, Retirement, and Pensions Dilemma*, 2nd ed. New York, NY:.

Campbell, J. Y. and R. J. Shiller (1998). Valuation ratios and the long run stock market. *Journal of Portfolio Management*, 24(2), 11–26.

——— (1998). Valuation ratios and the long run stock market. *Journal of Portfolio Management*, 24(2), 11–26.

Ekström, E. and C. Lindberg (2013). Optimal closing of a momentum trade. To appear in *Journal of Applied Probability*.

Evanoff, D. D., G. Kaufman and A. G. Malliaris (2012). *New Perspectives On Asset Price Bubbles*. Oxford, UK: Oxford University Press.

French, K. R. and J. Poterba (1991). Were Japanese stock prices too high? *Journal of Financial Economics*, 29(2), 337–363.

Gapeev, P. V. and G. Peskir (2006). The Wiener disorder problem with finite horizon. *Stochastic Processes and Their Applications*, 116(12), 1770–1791.

Lipster, R. S. and A. N. Shiryaev. *Statistics of Random Processes, 2nd ed.* Springer 2000.

Lleo, S. and W. T. Ziemba (2012). Stock market crashes in 2007–2009: Were we able to predict them? *Quantitative Finance*, 12(8), 1161–1187.

Poor, H. V. and O. Hadjiliadis (2009). *Quickest Detection*. Cambridge, UK: Cambridge University Press.

Schwartz, E. S. and M. Moon (2000). Pricing of Internet Companies, *Financial Analysts Journal*, 62–73.

Shiller, R. J. (1996). Price-earnings ratios as forecasters of returns: The stock market outlook in 1996, Department of Economics, Yale University, July 21.

——— (2009). *Irrational Exuberance*, 2nd ed. Princeton, NJ: Princeton University Press.

——— (2000). *Irrational Exuberance*. Princeton, NJ: Princeton University Press.

Shiryaev, A. N. and A. A. Novikov (2009). On a stochastic version of the trading rule buy and hold. *Statistics & Decisions*, 26(4), 289–302.

Shiryaev, A. N. and M. V. Zhitlukhin (2012). Bayesian disorder detection problems on filtered probability spaces. *Theory of Probability and Its Applications*, 57(3), 453–470.

——— (2012). Optimal stopping problems for a Brownian motion with a disorder on a finite interval, *arXiv*, No. 1212.3709.

Soros, G. (2008). *The Crash Of 2008 And What It Means*. Public Affairs.

Stiglitz, J. E. (1990). Symposium on bubbles. *Journal of Economic Perspectives*, 4(2), 13–18.

Ziemba, W. T. (2003). *The Stochastic Programming Approach To Asset Liability And Wealth Management*. Charlottesville, VA: AIMR.

Ziemba, W. T., S. L. Schwartz, S. L. (1991). *Invest Japan*. Chicago, IL: Probus.

Chapter 12

A Response to Professor
Paul A. Samuelson's Objections
to Kelly Capital Growth Investing

William T. Ziemba

*Alumni Professor of Financial Modeling
and Stochastic Optimization (Emeritus),
University of British Columbia, Vancouver, BC
Distinguished Visiting Research Associate,
Systemic Risk Centre
London School of Economics, UK*

The Kelly Capital Growth Investment Strategy maximizes the expected utility of final wealth with a Bernoulli logarithmic utility function. In 1956 Kelly showed that static expected log maximization yields the maximum asymptotic long run growth. Good properties include minimizing the time to large asymptotic goals, maximizing the median, and being ahead on average after the first period. Bad properties include extremely large bets for short term favorable investment situations because the Arrow-Pratt risk aversion index is essentially zero. Paul Samuelson was a critic of this approach. His various points sent in letters to Ziemba are responded to. Samuelson's criticism is partially responsible for the current situation that most finance academics and investment professionals, except superior investors, do not recommend Kelly strategies. Samuelson's points are theoretically correct and sharpen the theory. They caution users of this approach to be careful and understand the true characteristics of these investments including ways to lower the investment exposure. His objections help us understand the theory better, but they do not detract from numerous valuable applications, some of which are briefly surveyed.

The Kelly capital growth criterion which maximizes the expected log of final wealth, provides the strategy that maximizes long run wealth growth asymptotically for repeated investments over time. A shortcoming

is its very risky short-term behavior because of log's essentially zero
Arrow-Pratt absolute risk aversion and consequently the large concentrated
non-diversified investment bets that it suggests. The criterion is used by
many investors, hedge funds, bank trading departments, sports bettors and
its seminal application is to a long sequence of favorable investment situations. Some of these applications are briefly surveyed later in this paper.

Since I have a long history with Professor Paul A. Samuelson starting
with his papers in my 1975 book Ziemba and Vickson, he wrote me from
time to time on various topics. Paul was a critic of the Kelly theory
concerned with the Kelly criterion and how that impacted its use in
practice. Because of Paul's status, arguably the most important economist
of the last century, people took note of the fact that he was objecting
even though they did not actually know what these objections were. As a
consequence of this and other reasons, the most important being the non-
diversification and large investment wagers suggested, the Kelly strategy
is not used much in the investment industry except for investors looking
for superior long run performance. Also it is not a standard topic in MBA
finance courses.

My motivation for this paper comes from two sources. First, Paul wrote
me three letters on this topic and his papers objecting to the Kelly criterion
are reprinted in my 2011 book with Thorp and MacLean. So I wanted
to respond to these letters and his papers. The second reason for this
paper was a request from Fidelity Investments in August 2011 in Boston, a
multi trillion dollar investment firm, to explain exactly what Samuelson's
objections to Kelly. Should they be using Kelly strategies and, if so, when
and with what caution. After a five hour session on this and other topics,
I think they were convinced to consider Kelly strategies and did understand
the advantages and disadvantages of the strategy.

The first letter was the correspondence of November 16, 2005 to Professor Elwyn Berlekamp[1] and forwarded to me by Samuelson on December 13,
2006. Samuelson sent additional letters to me on 17 May 2007 and 12 May
2008. Sadly he died before I was able to finish this paper.The letters are
downloadable from the web at http://www.williamtziemba.com/support-
materials.html.

My colleague Edward Thorp was the first one to employ this *Fortune's
Formula* as he called it to the game of blackjack in his 1960 book *Beat*

---

[1]Berlekamp was a main intellectual force in the Renaissance Medallion hedge fund,
arguably the world's most successful hedge fund, see Gergaud and Ziemba (2012). Later
he was a professor of mathematics at the University of California, Berkeley.

the Dealer that changed the way this game was played once he showed that there was a winning strategy. There are other notable investors who use such strategies in various forms. These include Jim Simons of the Renaissance Mediallion, arguably the world's most successful hedge fund manager, who I taught this approach to in 1992 and Bill Gross, the world's top bond trader. Others who behave as if they were full or close to full Kelly investors include George Soros, Warren Buffett and John Maynard Keynes because the portfolios they hold are very concentrated in very few assets with huge positions in each asset, monthly performances with many losses but more gains and their very high long run growth of wealth.

The plan of this paper is as follows: I first describe Samuelson's objections one by one in general terms and my response to them aided by some research of Ed Thorp, David Luenberger and Harry Markowitz all of whom agree with me in this debate with the deceased giant thinker. Then I describe three investors Samuelson posed to me in letters with the addition of two tail investors that allows us to study risk aversion effects on portfolio choice. Various applications and endorsements and information relevant to the actual use of Kelly and fractional Kelly strategies in practice by me and others are then briefly discussed. In the conclusion, I argue that Samuelson's points are basically valid and sharpen our understanding of these strategies but the Kelly approach, if properly used, is extremely valuable in many applications.

The Objections of Professor Paul A. Samuelson to Kelly Capital Growth Investing

The great economist Paul A. Samuelson was a long time critic of the Kelly strategy which maximizes the expected logarithm of final wealth, see, for example, Samuelson (1963, 1969, 1979, 1991) and Merton and Samuelson (1974). His four basic objections to Elog investing were:

Objection 1. It does not maximize expected utility for utility functions other than log.

That is correct and there is no controversy here, Elog maximizes only log utility. Indeed no utility function can maximize expected utility for other utility functions. Thorp and Whitley (1972) show that different concave utility functions do indeed produce different optimal decisions.

Samuelson seemed to imply that Kelly proponents thought that the Kelly strategy maximizes for other utility functions but this was neither argued nor implied. It is true that the expected value of wealth is higher with the Kelly strategy but bad outcomes with low final wealth are possible.

Mike Stutzer pointed out to me referring to Latané (1959), see also Latané (1978):

> "I think Samuelson was referring to a claim or conjecture (likely a footnote) in the Latané article. So the real problem is that some of Samuelson's critiques were misused by later readers to falsely tar other non-problematic growth optimal results in that and other papers."

In his letters to me (private correspondence, 2006, 2007, 2008), Samuelson implied that half Kelly, namely a 50-50 of the Kelly strategy wager and cash, explains the data better. I agree that in practice, half Kelly is a toned down version of full Kelly that provides more security to compensate for its loss in long term growth.

Objection 2. Despite the fact that in the long run, E log investors asymptotically dominate all essentially different utility functions it does not follow that an Elog investor will have good performance. Indeed, no matter how long the investment sequence is and how favorable the investment situations are, it is possible to lose a lot of money.

In his letters to me, he formulated this as

Theorem (Samuelson): In no run, however long, does Kelly's Rule effectuate a *dominating* retirement next egg.

I agree completely and illustrate this with a simple simulated example in which with a 14% advantage in each period and many independent wagers over 700 periods it is possible with no leveraging to lose 98% of one's initial wealth.

Consider the example described in Exhibit 1. There are five possible investments each with a 14% advantage. The difference between them is that some have a higher chance of winning and, for some, this chance is smaller. For the latter, we receive higher odds if we win than for the former. But we always receive 1.14 for each 1 bet on average. Hence we have a favorable game. The optimal expected log utility bet with one asset (here we either win or lose the bet) equals the edge divided by the odds.[2] So for the 1-1 odds bet, the wager is 14% of ones fortune and at 5-1 its only

---

[2] For one or two assets with fixed odds, take derivatives and solve for the optimal wagers; for multi-asset bets under constraints; and when portfolio choices affect returns (odds), one must solve a stochastic nonlinear program which, possibly, is non-concave.

EXHIBIT 1: The Investments.

Probability of Winning	Odds	Probability of Being Chosen in the Simulation at at Each Decision Point	Optimal Kelly Bets Fraction of Current Wealth
0.57	1-1	0.1	0.14
0.38	2-1	0.3	0.07
0.285	3-1	0.3	0.047
0.228	4-1	0.2	0.035
0.19	5-1	0.1	0.028

Source: Ziemba and Hausch (1986).

EXHIBIT 2: Statistics of the Simulation.

Final Wealth Strategy	Min	Max	Mean	Median	Number of Times the Final Wealth Out of 1000 Trials was				
					>500	>1000	>10,000	>50,000	>100,000
Kelly	18	483,883	48,135	17,269	916	870	598	302	166
Half Kelly	145	111,770	13,069	8,043	990	954	480	30	1

Source: Ziemba and Hausch (1986).

2.8%. We bet more when the chance that we will lose our bet is smaller, and we bet more when the edge is higher. The bet is linear in the edge so doubling the edge doubles the optimal bet. However, the bet is non-linear in the chance of losing our money, which is reinvested so the size of the wager depends more on the chance of losing and less on the edge.

Simulations were run assuming that investor's initial wealth is 1000 and that there are 700 investment decision points. The simulation was repeated 1000 times. The results in Exhibit 2 show the number of times out of the possible 1000 that each particular goal was reached. The first line is with log or full Kelly betting, The second line is half Kelly betting. For lognormal investments α-fractional Kelly wagers are equivalent to the optimal bet obtained from using the concave risk averse, negative power utility function, $-w^{-\beta}$, where $\alpha = \frac{1}{1-\beta}$. For non lognormal assets this is an approximation (see MacLean, Ziemba and Li, 2005 and Thorp, 2010, 2011). For half Kelly ($\alpha = 1/2$), $\beta = -1$ and the utility function is $w^{-1} = \frac{1}{w}$. Here the marginal increase in wealth drops off as w^2, which is more conservative than log's w. Log utility is the case $\beta \to -\infty$, $\alpha = 1$ and cash is $\beta \to -\infty$, $\alpha = 0$.

A major advantage of full Kelly log utility betting is the 166 in the last column. In fully 16.6% of the 1000 cases in the simulation, the final wealth is more than 100 times as much as the initial wealth. Also in 302 cases, the final wealth is more than 50 times the initial wealth. This huge growth in final wealth for log is not shared by the half Kelly strategies, which have only 1 and 30, respectively, for their 50 and 100 times growth levels. Indeed, log provides an enormous growth rate but at a price, namely a very high volatility of wealth levels. That is, the final wealth is very likely to be higher than with other strategies, but the wealth path will likely be very very bumpy. The maximum, mean, and median statistics in Exhibit 2 illustrate the enormous gains that log utility strategies usually provide.

Let us now focus on bad outcomes. The first column provides the following remarkable fact that answers Samuelson's Objection 2: one can make 700 independent bets of which the chance of winning each one is at least 19% and usually is much more, having a 14% advantage on each bet and still turn 1000 into 18, a loss of more than 98%.

Even with half Kelly, the minimum return over the 1000 simulations of the 700 bets each with a 14% advantage was 145, a loss of 85.5%. Half Kelly has a 99% chance of not losing more than half the wealth versus only 91.6% for Kelly. The chance of not being ahead is almost three times as large for full versus half Kelly. Hence to protect ourselves from bad scenario outcomes, we need to lower our bets and diversify across many independent investments.

Exhibit 3a,b shows the highest and lowest final wealth trajectories for full, $\frac{3}{4}$, $\frac{1}{2}$, $\frac{1}{4}$ and $\frac{1}{8}$ Kelly strategies for this example. Most of the gain is in the final 100 of the 700 decision points. Even with these maximum graphs, there is much volatility in the final wealth with the amount of volatility generally higher with higher Kelly fractions. Indeed with $\frac{3}{4}$ Kelly, there were losses from about decision points 610 to 670.

The final wealth levels are much higher on average, the higher the Kelly fraction. As you approach full Kelly, the typical final wealth escalates dramatically. This is shown also in the maximum wealth levels in Exhibit 4. There is a chance of loss (final wealth is less than the initial $1000) in all cases, even with 700 independent bets each with an edge of 14%. The size of the losses can be large as shown in the >50, >100, and >500 and columns of Exhibit 4.

If capital is infinitely divisible and there is no leveraging then the Kelly bettor cannot go bankrupt since one never bets everything (unless the probability of losing anything at all is zero and the probability of winning is positive). If capital is discrete, then presumably Kelly bets are rounded down to avoid overbetting, in which case, at least one unit is never bet.

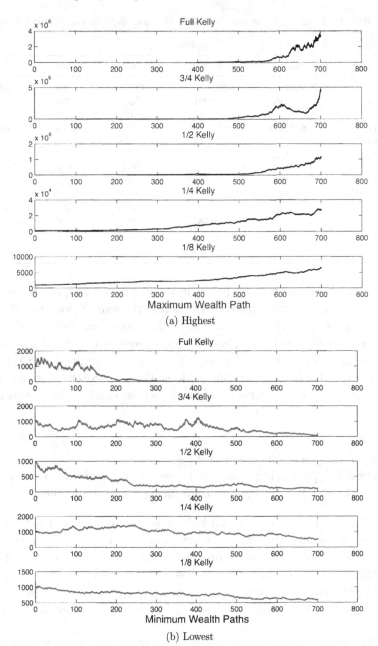

EXHIBIT 3: Final Wealth Trajectories: Ziemba-Hausch (1986) Model.

Source: MacLean, Thorp, Zhao and Ziemba (2011).

EXHIBIT 4:   Final Wealth Statistics by Kelly Fraction: Ziemba-Hausch (1986) Model.

| | Kelly Fraction | | | | |
Statistic	1.0k	0.75k	0.50k	0.25k	0.125k
Max	318854673	4370619	1117424	27067	6330
Mean	524195	70991	19005	4339	2072
Min	4	56	111	513	587
St. Dev.	8033178	242313	41289	2951	650
Skewness	35	11	13	2	1
Kurtosis	1299	155	278	9	2
$>5 \times 10$	1981	2000	2000	2000	2000
10^2	1965	1996	2000	2000	2000
$>5 \times 10^2$	1854	1936	1985	2000	2000
$>10^3$	1752	1855	1930	1957	1978
$>10^4$	1175	1185	912	104	0
$>10^5$	479	284	50	0	0
$>10^6$	111	17	1	0	0

Hence, the worst case with Kelly is to be reduced to one unit, at which point betting stops. Since fractional Kelly bets less, the result follows for all such strategies. For levered wagers, that is, betting more than one's wealth with borrowed money, the investor can lose much more than their initial wealth and become bankrupt. See MacLean, Thorp, Zhao and Ziemba (2011).

Further discussion: there are at least three approaches for dynamic investment that one could consider as stated, for example, by Luenberger (1993):

1. $E \log w$
2. $\max Eu(w)$ for u concave for $u \neq \log$
3. $\max E \sum_{t=1}^{T} \beta^t u(c_t)$, where c_t is consumption drawn out of wealth in period t and $0 < \beta < 1$ is a discount factor (Samuelson, 1969)

Many great investors use full Kelly $E \log w$ and fractional Kelly αw^α, $\alpha < 0$ successfully. But this does not mean that they will have optimal policies for the 2nd and 3rd approaches or will always have positive gains in finite time. $E \log$ betting can yield substantial losses even without leveraging and with leveraging the losses can be many times the initial wealth and lead to bankruptcy, see MacLean, Thorp, Zhao and Ziemba (2011).

The Kelly strategy maximizes the asymptotic long run growth of the investor's wealth, and I agree with Samuelson that this is a Breiman (1961) property.

Objection 3. The Kelly strategy always leads to more wealth than any essentially different strategy.

I know from the simulations that this is not true since it is possible to have a large number of very good investments and still lose most of one's fortune even without leveraging. So this could not be claimed by anyone and Samuelson's theorem above demonstrates this.

Luenberger (1993) investigated investors who are only interested in tail returns in the iid case. In response to Samuelson regarding the long run Kelly behavior, Luenberger shows when $E \log W_t$ is optimal (simple utility functions) and when a $(E \log W_t)$, $var \log w_t$) tradeoff is optimal (compound utility functions).

Samuelson (1970) showed that there was an accurate log mean-log variance approximation to concave terminal utility if uncertainty is small and the distributions are compact; see also Ohlson (1975) on this power expansion approximation. This is because a two term power expansion to E log will be accurate with compact distributions.

Objection 4. A long run technical criticism of Samuelson articulated in Merton and Samuelson (1974) while pointing out math errors in Hakansson (1971a) is that $\lim_{t \to \infty} E(u(w_t))$ is not an expected utility. So log mean criteria and log mean-log variance criteria are not consistent with expected utility.

To respond, I refer to Luenberger (1993).who uses compound utility functions that subtract $m = E \log x_1$ and deal with the $m = 0$ case, and $m < 0, m > 0$ are dealt with using simple utility functions.

$$u(w) = \overline{\lim_{t \to \infty}} \psi(\log w_t - tm, m, t)$$

a.s. $m = 0$

An investor with $m = 0$ prefers increased variance. The compound utility function is equivalent to a function of the expected logarithm and variance of the logarithm of wealth, analogous to mean-variance tradeoff. A tail utility function involving the limits of total return must be equivalent to a log mean-variance criterion. Thus there is an efficient frontier just like mean-variance analysis, and the investor chooses a point on this frontier

Luenberger uses a different approach that establishes preferences on infinite sequences of wealth rather than wealth at a fixed (but later taken to the limit) terminal time.

Simple $\rightarrow$ tail utility function: $u(w) = u(\overline{w})$ if w, and $\overline{w}$ differ in at most a finite number of elements.

$$u(w) = \overline{\lim_{t \to \infty}} \, \overline{\rho}(w_t, t)$$

$$\overline{\rho}(w_t, t) = \rho(\log w_t, t)$$

$$u(w) = \overline{\lim_{t \to \infty}} \, \rho(\log w_t, t)$$

where $\overline{\rho}$ is continuous and increasing in w_t for each t.

Tail events have probability of either zero or one. The criterion is not expected value $E \log w_1$ but is actually an "almost sure criterion". I accept this and conclude that we have the three approaches for dynamic investment.

This theoretical discussion of the long run properties of Elog investing which while interesting has little to do with most of the various Kelly applications in long but finite time.

Markowitz (1976, 2006) adds to this in the simple utility function case. Assuming iid investments in discrete time, as Luenberger did, he shows that

"with probability one, there comes a time such that forever after the wealth of the investor who rebalances to portfolio P exceeds that of the investor who rebalances to portfolio Q, surely one can say P does better than Q in *the long run*"

where P maximizes $E \log(1 + r_t^p)$, r_t^p is the return on the portfolio during time $t - 1$ and t, and Q is another iid portfolio, possibly correlated with P, where $\mu_p = E \log(1 + r_t^P) > E \log(1 + r_t^Q)$. This

"does not necessarily imply that any particular investor with a finite life and imminent consumption needs, should invest in P rather than Q. But it seems an unobjectionable use of language to summarize relationship 17.10 by saying that portfolio P does better than portfolio Q in the long run (Markowitz (2006, p. 256)"

where 17.10 says that with probability 1, there is a time T_0 such that w_T^P exceeds w_T^Q ever after, that is

$$\exists T_0 \forall T > T_0, \quad w_P^T > w_Q^T.$$

Markowitz (1976) relaxes the iid assumption. See also Algoet and Cover (1988) and Thorp (2011).

So what do we conclude on this Samuelson objection number 4? We can just dismiss it based on the Luenberger and Markowitz results as its maximizing the wrong quantity? Or we can say, yes, he is right but does that matter as we have other limiting results supporting the E log case?

The essence of Samuelson's objection #4, as articulated by Markowitz (2006), is that: if the investor seeks to maximize the expected value of a certain type of function of final wealth, for a long game of fixed length, then maximizing E log is not the optimal strategy.

What Samuelson had in mind here is $u(w) = \alpha w^\alpha$, namely,the negative and power utility functions of which log, namely $\alpha \to 0$ is the limiting member. Of course, $\alpha > 0$, positive power is definitely over betting so we assume that $\alpha < 0$, namely the utility function not dominated by having less growth and more risk.

This argument rests on the Samuelson (1969) and Mossin (1968) results for power utility that show myopic behavior assuming independent period by period assets where the investor rebalances to the same fixed mix portfolio in each period. So the optimal strategy is this fixed mix portfolio which is not the E log portfolio. When $u(w) = \log u$, the $\alpha \to 0$ case, then there is a myopic policy even for dependent assets, see Hakansson (1971b).

"the wealth of the investor who rebalances to portfolio P exceeds that of the investor who rebalances to portfolio Q, surely one can say that P does better than Q in the *long run*."

Then, as Markowitz (2006, p 260) concludes:

"Indeed, if we let the length of the game increase, the utility supplied by the max E log strategy does not even approach that supplied by the optimal strategy. This assumes that utility of final wealth remains the same as game length varies. On the other hand, if we assume that it is the utility of rate-of-growth-achieved, rather than utility of final wealth, that remains the same as length of game varies, then the E log rule is asymptotically optimal."

And Markowitz reminds us that betting more than full Kelly is dominated.

"Perhaps this is a sufficient caveat to attach to the observation that the cautious investor should not select a mean-variance efficient portfolio higher on the frontier than the point which approximately maximizes expected log(1+return): for a point higher on the frontier subjects the investor to greater volatility in the short run and, almost surely, no greater rate-of-growth in the long run."

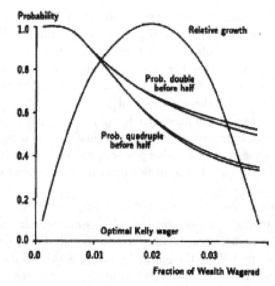

EXHIBIT 5: Probability of Doubling and Quadrupling Before Halving and Relative Growth Rates versus Fraction of Wealth Wagered for Blackjack (2% Advantage, p = 0.51 and q = 0.49).

Source: McLean, Ziemba and Blazenko (1992).

Exhibit 5 shows the relative growth rate versus the fraction of the investor's wealth wagered. The security curves show the bounds on the true probability of doubling or quadrupling before halving. This is maximized by the Kelly log bet. The growth rate is lower for smaller and for larger bets than the Kelly bet. Superimposed on this graph is also the probability that the investor doubles or quadruples the initial wealth before losing half of this initial wealth. Since the growth rate and the security are both decreasing for higher than than the optimal Kelly wager, it follows that it is never advisable to wager more than the optimal Kelly wager.

The growth rate of a bet that is exactly twice the Kelly bet is zero plus the risk-free rate of interest.[3] Hence log betting is the most aggressive investing that one should ever consider. The root of hedge fund disasters is almost always caused by bets above the full Kelly meaning they are highly

---

[3]See Harry Markowitz's proof in Ziemba (2003) and the more general proof of Thorp (2011) and the graphs in MacLean, Ziemba and Blazenko (1992).

levered. See Ziemba and Ziemba (2013) for discussions of several hedge fund disaster including Long Term Capital Management, Amarath, Niederhoffer and Societié Generale.

The Samuelson Investors

To understand risk aversion and investment behavior, Samuelson postulated three investors with concave risk averse utility functions:

- Tom with $u(w) = w^{1/2}$, a positive power maximizer.
- Dick with $\log w$, a geometric mean Kelly criterion optimizer and
- Harriet with $u(w) = -1/w$, who is a half Kelly optimizer (exactly if assets are lognormal and approximately otherwise).

Harriet has a limited degree of risk aversion and according to Samuelson fits well with lots of empirical Wall Street equity premium data. Tom, who is betting double Kelly, is over betting, and will eventually go bankrupt. I add two more investors to complete the spectrum, namely, one very conservative investor and one very risky investor.

- Ida who is approaching infinitely risk averse has $u(w) = -\frac{1}{Nw}$, with $N \to \infty$
- Victor is on the other extreme, infinitely risky with linear utility

Ida represents the famous Ida May Fuller of Ludlow, Vermont who was the first US social security recipient receiving check number 00-000-001 on January 31, 1940. Ida paid $24.75 into the social security fund, then lived to be 100 and collected nearly 1000 times her investment, namely $22,889, before she died at age 100.

On the other extreme is Victor, who is inspired by hedge fund trader Victor Niederhoffer. who historically has alternated between huge returns and disasters with a much greater than full Kelly betting strategy. This is over betting and dominated in a mean risk sense where risk is the probability of not achieving a high goal before falling to a low wealth level, see Exhibit 5. An account of some of his trading up to mid 2007 is in Ziemba and Ziemba (2013). In the ensuing years, more ups and downs have occurred. Our Victor is at the absolute limit of 0 absolute and relative risk aversion. Exhibit 6 describes the absolute and relative risk aversion

EXHIBIT 6:   The Five Investors in the Samuelson Experiment.

	Victor	Tom	Dick	Harriet	Ida
			The Investors		
	w linear	$w^{\frac{1}{2}}$ positive power	$\log w$ geometric mean optimizer	$-\dfrac{1}{w}$ half Kelly	$-\dfrac{1}{NW}$, $N \to \infty$ infinitely risk averse
Absolute $R_A - \dfrac{u'}{u'(w)}$	0	$\dfrac{1}{2w}$	$\dfrac{1}{2}$	$\dfrac{2}{w}$	∞
Relative $R_A - \dfrac{wu''(w)}{u'(w)}$	0	$\dfrac{1}{2}$	1	2	∞

properties of these five investors, all of which had constant relative risk aversion (CRRA).

Consider the investment where cash returns zero and stock returns with equal $1/2$ probability either \$4 or \$0.25 for each \$1 bet in each period.

Test 1: If you must put 100% of your nest egg in only one option, which do you pick?

$$\max_{x=0,1} \left[\frac{1}{2}xu(4) + (1-x)u\left(\frac{1}{4}\right) \right]$$

Tom and Victor choose all stock, $x^* = 1$
Dick is indifferent
Harriet and Ida choose all cash $x^*=0$ stock

Given a horizon of $n > 1$ periods until the final date of your retirement. All three say *no change*.

Test 2: The blending portfolio optimization case. Using

$$\max_x \left[\frac{1}{2}u(4x + 1 - x) + \frac{1}{2}u\left(\frac{1}{4}\right)x + 1 - x \right]$$

gives

Harriet $x^* = \frac{2}{9}$ stock, $1 - x^* = \frac{7}{9}$ cash

Tom $x^* = 1$ stock,   cash $= 0$

Dick $x^* = \frac{1}{2}$ stock, $1 - x^* = \frac{1}{2}$ cash

With certainty equivalents

$$u(CE) = \frac{1}{2}u(4) + \frac{1}{2}u\left(\frac{1}{4}\right)$$

$$CE = u^{-1}\left[\frac{1}{2}u(4) + \frac{1}{2}u\left(\frac{1}{4}\right)\right] \equiv E(4,1)$$

Tom $CE = KM = \left[\frac{1}{2}\sqrt{4} + \frac{1}{2}\sqrt{1/4}\right]^2 = 1 + \frac{9}{16}$

Dick $CE = GM = \sqrt{4 * \frac{1}{4}} = 1$

Harriet $CE = HM = \left[\frac{1}{2}\left(\frac{1}{4}\right) + \frac{1}{2}(4)\right]^{-1} = 1 - \frac{9}{17}$

Victor   bets 2 by borrowing 1 at zero interest so $CE = AM = 2 + \frac{1}{8}$.

Ida   bets zero so $CE = IM = 0$.

Here, IM, HM, GM, KM and AM are infinitely risk averse mean, harmonic mean, geometric mean, root-squared mean, and the arithmetic mean, respectively.

$$0 = IM < HM < GM < KM \leq AM = \frac{1}{2}(4) + \frac{1}{2}\left(\frac{1}{4}\right) = 2\frac{1}{8}$$

For the double full Kelly betting case, the growth rate is zero plus the risk free rate which is assumed to be zero (see Thorp, 2011). Dick who bet $x^* = \frac{1}{2}$ stock maximizing Elog now bets $x^* = 1$, all stock.

- The 4th investor **Victor**, with a linear utility w, bets $x^* = 1$ all stock, the same as **Tom** but in more complex multi-asset cases, **Victor** will bet even more than **Tom** and have a negative growth rate and go bankrupt faster than **Tom**

- The 5th investor, who is infinitely risk averse, **Harriet**'s sister **Ida**, bets nothing and lives off her cash until she dies

What if Dick persuades Harriet to replace her $x^* = \frac{2}{9}$ with his $x^* = \frac{1}{2}$? The loss in her CE dollars below her best CE* dollars is equivalent to her having agreed to throw away a definable percentage of her initial wealth. What is left,invested her *proper* way, will fall short of what she could have received by measurable deadweight loss. Dick could also do harm to Tom if Tom gives up $x^* = 1$ and goes along with Dick's $x^* = \frac{1}{2}$

Can these one-period harms erode away after Tom and Harriet come to shoot themselves in their respective feet two times, three times ... N = 100^{10} times? No. No such Limit Theorem is valid. For N large, N $\gg$ 1, $x^* = \frac{2}{9}$ and $x^* = \frac{1}{2}$ and $x^* = 1$ each produce *on retirement date* three different wide-spread Log Normal limit distributions. Tom's Log Normal has the largest absolute arithmetic mean dollars. Harriet's has the least absolute arithmetic mean dollars. However, at Harriet's request we calculate the three H.M's. Hers is the largest!

In a duel between any two neighbors, where we maximize **A**'s probability of being ahead of **B** when they both retire at the same time and start to invest at the same time, Dick types will beat out both Harriet and Tom. Dick's probability edge will go to 1 (*almost*) as N $\to$ ∞ These are then the Breiman (1961) Theorems in the limit.

In Samuelson's words

"the MacLean and Ziemba (see MacLean, Ziemba and Blazenko, 1992) probability, $t_{w_{large}} < t_{w_{small}}$ versus the growth rate do this, but in finite, calculable time, as shown in Exhibit 5."

For two outcome stocks, we can solve for x^* as the root of the equation

$$\frac{d}{dx}\left[\frac{1}{2}U(3x+1) + \frac{1}{2}U\left(1 - \frac{3}{4}x\right)\right] = 0.$$

x^* can be found for these three neighbors by solving a *linear* equation because all three utilities have Constant *Relative* Risk Aversion,

Selected Applications and Endorsements

In general, to obtain the max E log portfolio and the large and risky investment bets, one must solve a constrained non-linear one-period

EXHIBIT 7:   Summary of Kelly Applications.

Application or Trade	Comment	References
Blackjack bet sizing: Bet more when the card counting edge is more favorable	The original Kelly application	Thorp (1960)
January turn-of-the-year: Small cap minus large cap advantage in futures markets now in December	Very successful over many years	Clark and Ziemba (1988) Ziemba (2012a)
Unpopular number in lotto games: Unpopular numbers are chosen less than other numbers so have an edge	Very small bets because most of the edge is in the very low chance of winning the biggest prizes	MacLean, Ziemba and Blazenko (1992) While there is a substantial edge, the chance of winning a substantial amount is small and to have a high probability of a large gain requires a very long time, in the millions of years
Horse race betting: Positive expectation bets exist because simple market probabilities can be used successfully in more complex markets. Racing is viewed as a stock market where all bets are priced	Kentucky Derby place and show bets show the effect of full and half Kelly with a winning system versus betting on the non-winning system of betting on the favorite. A breeding filter eliminates horses whose pedigree suggests they lack the stamina to win the $1^1/_4$ mile Derby which is run on the first Saturday of their 3-year-old year (Exhibit 8).	Hausch, Ziemba and Rubinstein (1981) derived the weak market inefficiency anomaly. Hausch and Ziemba (1985) and their trade books Ziemba and Hausch (1984, 1985, 1987) extended it. Professional betting is discussed in Ziemba (2012, 2015)

stochastic programming model to calculate the optimal portfolio weights like the following the racetrack portfolio model where the effect of our bets on the odds (prices) is in the model. The model considers exact transaction costs.

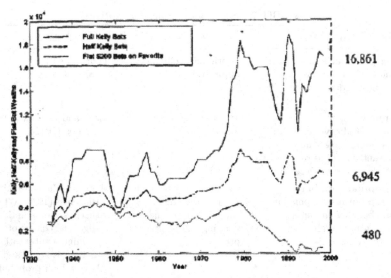

EXHIBIT 8:   Wealth History of Some Place and Show Kentucky Derby Bets, 1934–2005,
Kelly, Half Kelly and Betting on the Favorite, Using a Dosage Filter.
Source: Hausch, Ziemba and Bain (2006).

The model to maximize the expected utility capital growth model for
racetrack place and show bets is

$$\max_{p_i,s_i}\sum_{i=1}^{n}\sum_{\substack{j=i\\j\neq i}}^{n}\sum_{\substack{k=i\\k\neq i,j}}^{n}\frac{q_iq_jq_k}{(1-q_i)(1-q_i-q_j)}\log\left[\begin{array}{c}\frac{Q\left(P+\sum_{l=1}^{n}p_l\right)-(p_i+p_j+P_{ij})}{2}\\ \times\left[\frac{p_i}{p_i+P_i}+\frac{p_j}{p_j+P_j}\right]\\ +\frac{Q\left(S+\sum_{l=1}^{n}s_l\right)-(s_i+s_j+s_k+S_{ijk})}{3}\\ \times\left[\frac{s_i}{s_i+S_i}+\frac{s_j}{s_j+S_j}+\frac{s_k}{s_k+S_k}\right]\\ +w_0-\sum_{\substack{l=i\\l\neq i,j,k}}^{n}s_l-\sum_{\substack{l=i\\l\neq i,j}}^{n}p_l\end{array}\right]$$

$$\text{s.t.}\sum_{l=1}^{n}(p_l+s_l)\leq w_0,\quad p_l\geq 0,\quad s_l\geq 0,\quad l=1,\ldots,n,$$

Plus constraints on the size of the p_l and s_l.

If rebate is available it is added to final wealth inside the large brackets
by adding the rebate rate times all the bets, winners and losers, namely

$$r\sum_{l=1}^{n}(p_l+s_l)$$

where

- The effect of transactions costs (slippage in commodity trading) is illustrated with place/show horseracing optimization formulation; see Hausch, Ziemba and Rubinstein (1981).

- q_i is the probability that i wins. The Harville probability of an ij finish is $\frac{q_i q_j}{1 - q_i}$, so $q_j/1 - q_j$ is the probability that j wins a race that does not contain i, that is, comes second to i. In practice, the q_{ij} are adjusted for the bias that horses that are favored and do not win have lower probabilities of being second and third, see Ziemba (2015).

- Q, the track payback, is about 0.83 (and about 0.88 with professional rebates).

- The players' bets are to place p_j and show s_k for each of the about ten horses in the race out of the players' wealth w_0. The bets by the crowd are P_i with $\sum_{i=1}^{n} P_i = P$ and S_k with $\sum_{k=1}^{n} S_k = S$.

- The place and show payoffs are computed so that for place, the first two finishers, say i and j, in either order share the net pool profits once each P_i and p_i bets cost of \$1 is returned.

In practice, given limited time to make the bets, one uses regression approximations to the expected value and optimal wager that are functions of only four numbers, namely, the totals to win and place for the horse in question and the bet totals. These approximations are used in a hand held calculator. An application of real money bet with this system in 2004 is shown in Exhibit 9 with initial wealth w_0=US\$5,000. At each wagering

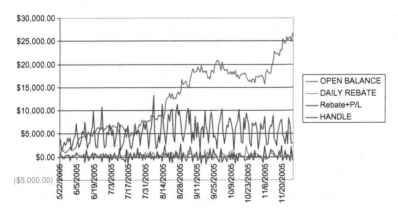

EXHIBIT 9: Racetrack Betting Record of the Place and Show System.

opportunity there is either no bet or a full Kelly bet using the model with rebate collected on winning and losing bets. Then $w(t)$ became $w(t+1)$ after each wager winning or losing. The system was programmed by John Swetye to search for bets at 80 racetracks in North America. The system lost about 7% largely because the racetrack market now combines bets made at many other racetracks and betting sites into one pool at the last minute. So such betting is not recorded into the pools until after the race is running. About half the money is entered then and that alters the odds used at the end of betting. The calculations take into account the bets by other people and the effect of our bets on the odds. The rebate averaged 9% so we had a net gain of about 2% or $26,500.

   The seminal application of the Kelly strategy is to a large sequence of similar investments. A good example of this is the Renaissance Medallion hedge fund which has thousands of 3-8 second trades. They were the original high frequency trading operation. I taught Jim Simons, head of the Medallion Fund, about the advantages of Kelly betting in 1992. The Kelly strategy provides good wagers where the size of the bets depend upon the characteristics of the situation. Despite very high fees of 5% for management plus 44% of the net new profits, the gains have been outstanding as shown in Exhibit 10. There are very few monthly losses and a smooth wealth graph. The data available was monthly from January 1993 to April 2005, see Gergaud and Ziemba (2012). Subsequent monthly results are not available but the yearly net returns up to the end of 2009 according to Insider

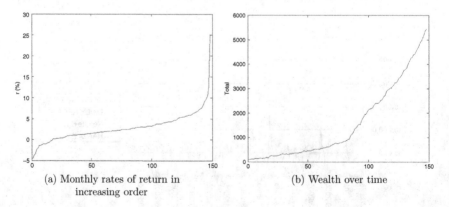

(a) Monthly rates of return in   (b) Wealth over time
        increasing order

EXHIBIT 10:   Renaissance Medallion Fund, January 1993 to April 2005.

Monkey (2010) were 44.3% (2008), 73.0% (2007), 80.0% (2008), and 39.0% (2009).

George Soros and Warren Buffett, two of the world's most successful investors, bet as if they were fully Kelly investors. There is no direct proof of this but there is a lot of circumstantial evidence. Each of them has many investments but these portfolios are very concentrated in very few investments and have other characteristics of full Kelly portfolios. For example, on September 30, 2008, Soros had 50.53% of his portfolio in Petroleo Brasileiro SA, 11.58% in Potash Corp Sask Inc, and 5.95% in Wal Mart Stores Inc. Buffett had 8.17% in Conoco Phillips, 8.00% in Procter & Gamble Co and 5.02% in Kraft Foods Inc.

Both Soros and Buffett go for long term growth with many monthly losses but large final wealth, another characteristic of full Kelly betting.

Berkshire, with the highest final wealth, had the most large monthly gains and the most large monthly losses for the funds in the sample that Ziemba (2005) received from Larry Siegel of the Ford Foundation. Both the Sharpe ratio and my downside symmetric Sharpe ratio (DSSR) are not high compared to other great traders such as Thorp or Simons. But as shown by Frazzani, Kabiller and Petersen (2012), Berkshire had a higher Sharpe ratio than any US stock or mutual fund with a history of more than 30 years. The secret to Buffett's success seems to be leveraging, about 1.6 to 1, using low cost and stable sources of financing much from his insurance businesses which is essentially selling overpriced puts plus a focus on cheap, safe, quality, low beta stocks.

Other famed investors such as John Maynard Keynes, running the King's College Cambridge endowment from 1927-1945; Bill Benter, the famed Hong Kong racing guru; and Ed Thorp, running the Princeton Newport hedge fund from 1968-88, all had excellent records and used Kelly and fractional Kelly strategies. Harry McPike, a Nassau trend follower, made extra millions using a Kelly model that Andrew Mart and I built.

How much should you bet?

A real example of this by Mohnish Pabrai (2007), who won the bidding for the 2008 lunch with Warren Buffett paying more than $600,000, had the following investment in Stewart Enterprises as discussed by Thorp (2010). Over a 24-month period, with probability 0.80 the investment at least doubles, with 0.19 probability the investment breaks even and with 0.01 probability all the investment is lost.

The optimal Kelly bet is 97.5% of wealth and half Kelly is 38.75%. Pabrai invested 10%. While this seems rather low, other investment opportunities, miscalculation of probabilities, risk tolerance, possible short run losses, bad scenario *Black Swan* events, price pressures, buying in and exiting suggest that a bet a lot lower than 97.5% is appropriate.

Bill Gross, the world's largest bond trader uses Kelly betting at PIMCO. During an interview in the Wall Street Journal (March 22-23, 2008), he and Ed Thorp discussed turbulence in the markets, hedge funds and risk management. Bill considered the question of risk management after he read Ed Thorp's *Beat the Dealer* in 1966. That summer he was off to Las Vegas to beat blackjack. Just as Ed did some years earlier, he sized his bets in proportion to his advantage, following the Kelly Criterion as described in Beat the Dealer, and ran his $200 bankroll up to $10,000 over the summer. Bill went from managing risk for his tiny bankroll to managing risk for Pacific Investment Management Companys (PIMCO) investment pool of almost $1 trillion. He still applies lessons he learned from the Kelly Criterion. As Bill said, "Here at PIMCO it doesn't matter how much you have, whether its $200 or $1 trillion Professional blackjack is being played in this trading room from the standpoint of risk management and thats a big part of our success". [Note: Gross left PIMCO for Janus.]

In a cover quote for the book MacLean, Thorp and Ziemba (2011), Gross added that

"Ed Thorp and the Kelly criterion have been a lighthouse for risk management for me and PIMCO for over 45 years. First at the blackjack tables and then in portfolio management, the Kelly system has helped to minimize risk and maximize return for thousands of PIMCO clients"

Most applications choose Kelly fractions in an ad hoc way. One approach to determining discrete time *optimal* Kelly fractions was proposed by MacLean, Sanegre, Zhao and Ziemba (2004). Their model has a pre-determined ex ante wealth path through time. Then the fractional Kelly wagers that maximize the growth rate are determined subject to the constraint that the portfolio stays above the path a high percentage of the time. In MacLean, Zhao and Ziemba (2015), they extend the analysis to have the additional feature that if the path is violated, then the violations are penalized with a convex penalty function. So the larger the violation, the larger the penalty. This model then tends to force the decisions to be such that the path is not violated. One cannot have too aggressive wealth paths. But for example, if the wealth path is constant at $w(0)$ you have a form of portfolio insurance aiming for close to zero losses but with reasonably high growth.

Conclusions

The Kelly capital growth strategy has been used successfully by many investors and speculators during the past fifty years. Rubinstein (1976) makes the case for it to be the premier model of financial markets. Poundstone (2005) popularized this in *Fortune's Formula*. Its main advantage is its superiority in producing long run maximum wealth from a sequence of favorable investments. The seminal application is to an investment situation that has many repeated similar bets over a long time horizon. In all cases one must have a winning system that is one with a positive expectation. Then the Kelly and fractional Kelly strategies (those with less long run growth but more security) provide a superior bet sizing strategy. The mathematical properties prove maximum asymptotic long run growth. But short term usually is high volatility. One makes the investment bets using static stochastic non-linear programming that takes the effect of our wagers on the prices into account. This paper responds to the critique of Professor Paul A Samuelson in letters to me and papers reprinted in the Kelly book by MacLean, Thorp and Ziemba (2011). The basic criticisms are largely concerned with over betting, the major culprit of hedge fund disasters and theoretical long run properties of the strategy that do not affect the applications.

If properly used the Kelly strategy provides a superior long term wealth maximizing technique and the examples in the paper show its use in practice. The main conclusions are:

1. the great superiority of full Kelly and close to full Kelly strategies to other strategies over longer horizons with very large gains a large fraction of the time;
2. that the short term performance of Kelly and high fractional Kelly strategies is very risky;
3. that there is a consistent tradeoff of growth versus security as a function of the bet size determined by the various strategies; and
4. that no matter how favorable the investment opportunities are or how long the finite horizon is, a sequence of bad scenarios can lead to very poor final wealth outcomes, with a loss of most of the investor's initial capital.

272 William T. Ziemba

Acknowledgements

Without implicating them, thanks go to Harry M. Markowitz and Edward
O. Thorp for helpful discussions and comments. Thanks also to seminar
participants at the FMA meetings in Chicago, the University of Manchester
Hallsworth lectures, Stanford University, London School of Economics,
University of Zurich, University of Bonn and the Reims Management
School.

References

Algoet, P. H. and T. M. Cover (1988). Asymptotic optimality and asymptotic equipartition properties of log-optimum investment. *Annals of Probability*, 16(2), 876–898.

Bernoulli, D. (1954). Exposition of a new theory on the measurement of risk (translated from the latin by Louise Sommer). *Econometrica*, 16, 23–36.

Breiman, L. (1960). Investment policies for expanding businesses optimal in a long run sense. *Naval Research Logistics Querterly*, 16(4), 647–651.

Breiman, L. (1961). Optimal gambling system for favorable games. *Proceedings of the 4th Berkeley Symposium on Mathematical Statistics and Probability*, 16, 63–8.

Clark, R. and W. T. Ziemba (1988). Playing the turn-of-the-year effect with index futures. *Operations Research*, 35, 799–813.

Frazzini, A., D. Kabiller, and L. H. Peterson (2012). Buffett's alpha. NYU technical report, August 30.

Gergaud, O. and W. T. Ziemba (2012). Great investors: Their methods, results and evaluation. *Journal of Portfolio Management*, 16(4), 128–147.

Hakansson, N. H. (1971a). Capital growth and the mean-variance approach to portfolio selection. *Journal of Financial Quantitative Analysis*, 16, 517–557.

Hakansson, N. H. (1971b). On optimal myopic portfolio policies with and without serial correlation. *Journal of Business*, 16, 324–334.

Hausch, D., R. Bain, and W. Ziemba (2006). An application of expert information to win betting on the Kentucky Derby, 1934–2005. *European Journal of Finance*, 16, 283–301.

Hausch, D. B., W. T. Ziemba, and M. E. Rubinstein (1981). Efficiency of the market for racetrack betting. *Management Science*, 27, 1435–1452.

Insider Monkey (2010). Seeking alpha: Best hedge funds, Jim Simons Medallion Fund. December 31.

Kelly, Jr., J. R. (1956). A new interpretation of the information rate. *Bell System Technical Journal*, 16, 917–926.

Latané, H. (1959). Criteria for choice among risky ventures. *Journal of Political Economy*, 16, 144–155.

Latané, H. (1978). The geometric-mean principle revisited — a reply. *Journal of Banking and Finance*, 16(4), 395–398.

Luenberger, D. G. (1993). A preference foundation for log mean-variance criteria in portfolio choice problems. *Journal of Economic Dynamics and Control*, 16, 887–906.

MacLean, L., E. O. Thorp, and W. T. Ziemba (Eds.) (2011). *The Kelly Capital Growth Investment Criterion*. Singapore: World Scientific.

MacLean, L., W. T. Ziemba, and G. Blazenko (1992). Growth versus security in dynamic investment analysis. *Management Science*, 16, 1562–85.

MacLean, L. C., R. Sanegre, Y. Zhao, and W. T. Ziemba (2004). Capital growth with security. *Journal of Economic Dynamics and Control*, 16(4), 937–954.

MacLean, L. C., E. O. Thorp, Y. Zhao, and W. T. Ziemba (2011). How does the Fortune's Formula-Kelly capital growth model perform? *Journal of Portfolio Management*, 16(4), 96–11.

MacLean, L. C., Y. Zhao, and W. T. Ziemba (2015). Optimal capital growth with convex shortfall penalties. *Quantitative Finance (in progress)*.

MacLean, L. C., W. T. Ziemba, and Y. Li (2005). Time to wealth goals in capital accumulation and the optimal trade-off of growth versus security. *Quantitative Finance*, 16(4), 343–357.

Markowitz, H. M. (1976). Investment for the long run: New evidence for an old rule. *Journal of Finance*, 16(5), 1273–1286.

Markowitz, H. M. (2006). Samuelson and investment for the long run. *Samuelsonian Economics and the Twenty-first Century*, pp. 252–261. New York, NY: Oxford University Press.

Merton, R. C. and P. A. Samuelson (1974). Fallacy of the log-normal approximation to optimal portfolio decision-making over many periods. *Journal of Financial Economics*, 16, 67–94.

Mossin, J. (1968). Optimal multi period portfolio policies. *Journal of Business*, 16(2), 215–229.

Ohlson, J. (1975). The asymptotic validity of quadratic utility with trading interval approaches zero. In W. T. Ziemba and R. G. Vickson (Eds.), *Stochastic Optimization Models in Finance*, pp. 221–234. New York, NY: Academic Press.

Pabrai, M. (2007). *The Dhandho Investor: The Low-risk Value Method to High Returns*. New York, NY: Wiley.

Poundstone, W. (2005). *Fortune" Formula: The Untold Story of the Scientific System that Beat the Casinos and Wall Street*. New York, NY: Hill and Wang.

Roll, R. (1973). Evidence on the growth optimum model. *The Journal of Finance*, 16(3), 551–566.

Rubinstein, M. (1976). The strong case for the generalized logarithmic utility model as the premier model of financial markets. *Journal of Finance*, 16(2), 551–571.

Samuelson, P. A. (1963). Risk and uncertainty: a fallacy of large numbers. *Scientia* (6th Series, 57th year, April-May), 153–158.

Samuelson, P. A. (1969). Lifetime portfolio selection by dynamic stochastic programming. *Review of Economics and Statistics*, 16, 239–246.

Samuelson, P. A. (1970). The fundamental approximation theorem of portfolio analysis in terms of means, variances and higher moments. *Review of Economic Studies*, 16(4), 537–542.

Samuelson, P. A. (1977). St. Petersburg paradoxes: Defanged, dissected and historically described. *Journal of Economic Literature*, 16(1), 24–55.

Samuelson, P. A. (1979). Why we should not make mean log of wealth big though years to act are long. *Journal of Banking and Finance*, 16, 305–307.

Samuelson, P. A. (1991). Long-run risk tolerance when equity returns are mean regressing: Pseudoparadoxes and vindication of businessmen's risk. In W. C. Brainard, W. D. Nordhaus, and H. W. Watts (Eds.), *Money, Macroeconomics and Economic Policy*, pp. 181–200. Cambridge, MA: MIT Press.

Samuelson, P. A. (various). Letters to W. T. Ziemba, December 13, 2006, May 17, 2007, and May 12, 2008.

Siegel, L. B., K. F. Kroner, and S. W. Clifford (2001). Greatest return stories ever told. *Journal of Investing*, 16(2), 91–102.

Sommer, L. (1975). Translation of an exposition of a new theory on the measurement of risk by D. Bernoulli (1738). *Econometrica*, 16, 23–36.

Thorp, E. O. (1960). *Beat the Dealer*. New York, NY: Random House.

Thorp, E. O. (2010). Understanding the Kelly criterion. *Wilmott*.

Thorp, E. O. (2011). The Kelly criterion in blackjack, sports betting and the stock market. In L. C. MacLean, E. O. Thorp, and W. T. Ziemba (Eds.), *The Kelly Capital Growth Investment Criterion*, pp. 789–832. Singapore: World Scientific.

Thorp, E. O. and Whitley (1972). Concave utilities are distinguished by their optimal strategies. Colloquia Mathematica Societatis Janos Bolyai. pp. 813-830.

Ziemba, R. E. S. and W. T. Ziemba (2013). *Investing in the Modern Age*. Singapore: World Scientific.

Ziemba, W. T. (2005). The symmetric downside risk sharpe ratio and the evaluation of great investors and speculators. *Journal of Portfolio Management Fall*, 108–122.

Ziemba, W. T. (2012a). *Calendar Anomalies and Arbitrage*. Singapore: World Scientific.

Ziemba, W. T. (2012b). Stochastic programming and optimization in horserace betting. In H. I. Gassman and W. T. Ziemba (Eds.), *Stochastic Programming Applications in Finance, Energy and Production*, pp. 221–256. Singapore: World Scientific.

Ziemba, W. T. (2016). *Exotic Betting at the Racetrack*. Singapore: World Scientific.

Ziemba, W. T. and D. B. Hausch (1984). *Beat the Racetrack*. San Diego, CA: Harcourt.

Ziemba, W. T. and D. B. Hausch (1986). *Betting at the Racetrack*. Dr Z Investments, Inc.

Ziemba, W. T. and D. B. Hausch (1987). *Dr Z's Beat the Racetrack*. William Morrow.

Index